Operating Systems Concepts

NOS 110

Authors

Silberschatz, Galvin and Gagne • Microsoft Official Academic Course • Smith

Printed in the United States of America 10 9 8 7 6 5 4 3 2

List of Titles

Table of Contents

MODULE 1: Introduction to Operating Systems Concepts

CHAPTER 1

Introduction

An operating system is a program that manages the computer hardware. It also provides a basis for application programs and acts as an intermediary between the computer user and the computer hardware. An amazing aspect of operating systems is how varied they are in accomplishing these tasks. Mainframe operating systems are designed primarily to optimize utilization of hardware. Personal computer (PC) operating systems support complex games, business applications, and everything in between. Operating systems for handheld computers are designed to provide an environment in which a user can easily interface with the computer to execute programs. Thus, some operating systems are designed to be *convenient*, others to be *efficient*, and others some combination of the two.

Before we can explore the details of computer system operation, we need to know something about system structure. We begin by discussing the basic functions of system startup, I/O, and storage. We also describe the basic computer architecture that makes it possible to write a functional operating system.

Because an operating system is large and complex, it must be created piece by piece. Each of these pieces should be a well-delineated portion of the system, with carefully defined inputs, outputs, and functions. In this chapter, we provide a general overview of the major components of an operating system.

CHAPTER OBJECTIVES

- To provide a grand tour of the major components of operating systems.
- To describe the basic organization of computer systems.

1.1 What Operating Systems Do

We begin our discussion by looking at the operating system's role in the overall computer system. A computer system can be divided roughly into

3

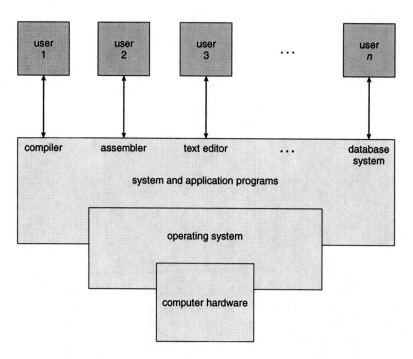

Figure 1.1 Abstract view of the components of a computer system.

four components: the *hardware,* the *operating system,* the *application programs,* and the *users* (Figure 1.1).

The hardware—the central processing unit (CPU), the memory, and the input/output (I/O) devices—provides the basic computing resources for the system. The application programs—such as word processors, spreadsheets, compilers, and Web browsers—define the ways in which these resources are used to solve users' computing problems. The operating system controls the hardware and coordinates its use among the various application programs for the various users.

We can also view a computer system as consisting of hardware, software, and data. The operating system provides the means for proper use of these resources in the operation of the computer system. An operating system is similar to a *government.* Like a government, it performs no useful function by itself. It simply provides an *environment* within which other programs can do useful work.

To understand more fully the operating system's role, we next explore operating systems from two viewpoints: that of the user and that of the system.

1.1.1 User View

The user's view of the computer varies according to the interface being used. Most computer users sit in front of a PC, consisting of a monitor, keyboard, mouse, and system unit. Such a system is designed for one user to monopolize its resources. The goal is to maximize the work (or play) that the user is performing. In this case, the operating system is designed mostly for ease of use, with some attention paid to performance and none paid to resource utilization—how various hardware and software resources are shared. Performance is, of course, important to the user; but such systems are optimized for the single-user experience rather than the requirements of multiple users.

In other cases, a user sits at a terminal connected to a mainframe or a minicomputer. Other users are accessing the same computer through other terminals. These users share resources and may exchange information. The operating system in such cases is designed to maximize resource utilization—to assure that all available CPU time, memory, and I/O are used efficiently and that no individual user takes more than her fair share.

In still other cases, users sit at workstations connected to networks of other workstations and servers. These users have dedicated resources at their disposal, but they also share resources such as networking and servers—file, compute, and print servers. Therefore, their operating system is designed to compromise between individual usability and resource utilization.

Recently, many varieties of handheld computers have come into fashion. Most of these devices are standalone units for individual users. Some are connected to networks, either directly by wire or (more often) through wireless modems and networking. Because of power, speed, and interface limitations, they perform relatively few remote operations. Their operating systems are designed mostly for individual usability, but performance per unit of battery life is important as well.

Some computers have little or no user view. For example, embedded computers in home devices and automobiles may have numeric keypads and may turn indicator lights on or off to show status, but they and their operating systems are designed primarily to run without user intervention.

1.1.2 System View

From the computer's point of view, the operating system is the program most intimately involved with the hardware. In this context, we can view an operating system as a resource allocator. A computer system has many resources that may be required to solve a problem: CPU time, memory space, file-storage space, I/O devices, and so on. The operating system acts as the manager of these resources. Facing numerous and possibly conflicting requests for resources, the operating system must decide how to allocate them to specific programs and users so that it can operate the computer system efficiently and fairly. As we have seen, resource allocation is especially important where many users access the same mainframe or minicomputer.

A slightly different view of an operating system emphasizes the need to control the various I/O devices and user programs. An operating system is a control program. A control program manages the execution of user programs to prevent errors and improper use of the computer. It is especially concerned with the operation and control of I/O devices.

1.1.3 Defining Operating Systems

We have looked at the operating system's role from the views of the user and of the system. How, though, can we define what an operating system is? In general, we have no completely adequate definition of an operating system. Operating systems exist because they offer a reasonable way to solve the problem of creating a usable computing system. The fundamental goal of computer systems is to execute user programs and to make solving user

> **STORAGE DEFINITIONS AND NOTATION**
>
> A bit is the basic unit of computer storage. It can contain one of two values, zero and one. All other storage in a computer is based on collections of bits. Given enough bits, it is amazing how many things a computer can represent: numbers, letters, images, movies, sounds, documents, and programs, to name a few. A byte is 8 bits, and on most computers it is the smallest convenient chunk of storage. For example, most computers don't have an instruction to move a bit but do have one to move a byte. A less common term is word, which is a given computer architecture's native storage unit. A word is generally made up of one or more bytes. For example, a computer may have instructions to move 64-bit (8-byte) words.
>
> A kilobyte, or KB, is 1,024 bytes; a megabyte, or MB, is $1,024^2$ bytes; and a gigabyte, or GB, is $1,024^3$ bytes. Computer manufacturers often round off these numbers and say that a megabyte is 1 million bytes and a gigabyte is 1 billion bytes.

problems easier. Toward this goal, computer hardware is constructed. Since bare hardware alone is not particularly easy to use, application programs are developed. These programs require certain common operations, such as those controlling the I/O devices. The common functions of controlling and allocating resources are then brought together into one piece of software: the operating system.

In addition, we have no universally accepted definition of what is part of the operating system. A simple viewpoint is that it includes everything a vendor ships when you order "the operating system." The features included, however, vary greatly across systems. Some systems take up less than 1 megabyte of space and lack even a full-screen editor, whereas others require gigabytes of space and are entirely based on graphical windowing systems. A more common definition, and the one that we usually follow, is that the operating system is the one program running at all times on the computer—usually called the kernel. (Along with the kernel, there are two other types of programs: systems programs, which are associated with the operating system but are not part of the kernel, and application programs, which include all programs not associated with the operation of the system.)

The matter of what constitutes an operating system has become increasingly important. In 1998, the United States Department of Justice filed suit against Microsoft, in essence claiming that Microsoft included too much functionality in its operating systems and thus prevented application vendors from competing. For example, a Web browser was an integral part of the operating systems. As a result, Microsoft was found guilty of using its operating-system monopoly to limit competition.

1.2 Computer-System Organization

Before we can explore the details of how computer systems operate, we need general knowledge of the structure of a computer system. In this section, we look at several parts of this structure. The section is mostly concerned

THE STUDY OF OPERATING SYSTEMS

There has never been a more interesting time to study operating systems, and it has never been easier to do so. The open-source movement has overtaken operating systems, causing many of them to be made available in both source and binary (executable) format. This list includes Linux, BSD UNIX, Solaris, and part of Mac OS X. The availability of source code allows us to study operating systems from the inside out. Questions that previously could be answered only by looking at documentation or the behavior of an operating system can now be answered by examining the code itself.

In addition, the rise of virtualization as a mainstream (and frequently free) computer function makes it possible to run many operating systems on top of one core system. For example, VMware (`http://www.vmware.com`) provides a free "player" on which hundreds of free "virtual appliances" can run. Using this method, students can try out hundreds of operating systems within their existing operating systems at no cost.

Operating systems that are no longer commercially viable have been open-sourced as well, enabling us to study how systems operated in a time of fewer CPU, memory, and storage resources. An extensive but not complete list of open-source operating-system projects is available from `http://dmoz.org/Computers/Software/Operating_Systems/Open_Source/`. Simulators of specific hardware are also available in some cases, allowing the operating system to run on "native" hardware, all within the confines of a modern computer and modern operating system. For example, a DECSYSTEM-20 simulator running on Mac OS X can boot TOPS-20, load the source tapes, and modify and compile a new TOPS-20 kernel. An interested student can search the Internet to find the original papers that describe the operating system and the original manuals.

The advent of open-source operating systems also makes it easy to make the move from student to operating-system developer. With some knowledge, some effort, and an Internet connection, a student can even create a new operating-system distribution! Just a few years, ago it was difficult or impossible to get access to source code. Now that access is limited only by how much time and disk space a student has.

with computer-system organization, so you can skim or skip it if you already understand the concepts.

1.2.1 Computer-System Operation

A modern general-purpose computer system consists of one or more CPUs and a number of device controllers connected through a common bus that provides access to shared memory (Figure 1.2). Each device controller is in charge of a specific type of device (for example, disk drives, audio devices, and video displays). The CPU and the device controllers can execute concurrently, competing for memory cycles. To ensure orderly access to the shared memory, a memory controller is provided whose function is to synchronize access to the memory.

For a computer to start running—for instance, when it is powered up or rebooted—it needs to have an initial program to run. This initial

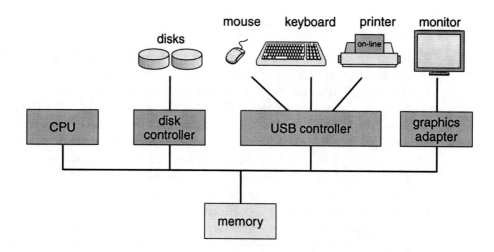

Figure 1.2   A modern computer system.

program, or bootstrap program, tends to be simple. Typically, it is stored in read-only memory (ROM) or electrically erasable programmable read-only memory (EEPROM), known by the general term firmware, within the computer hardware. It initializes all aspects of the system, from CPU registers to device controllers to memory contents. The bootstrap program must know how to load the operating system and how to start executing that system. To accomplish this goal, the bootstrap program must locate and load into memory the operating-system kernel. The operating system then starts executing the first process, such as "init," and waits for some event to occur.

The occurrence of an event is usually signaled by an interrupt from either the hardware or the software. Hardware may trigger an interrupt at any time by sending a signal to the CPU, usually by way of the system bus. Software may trigger an interrupt by executing a special operation called a system call (also called a monitor call).

When the CPU is interrupted, it stops what it is doing and immediately transfers execution to a fixed location. The fixed location usually contains the starting address where the service routine for the interrupt is located. The interrupt service routine executes; on completion, the CPU resumes the interrupted computation. A time line of this operation is shown in Figure 1.3.

Interrupts are an important part of a computer architecture. Each computer design has its own interrupt mechanism, but several functions are common. The interrupt must transfer control to the appropriate interrupt service routine. The straightforward method for handling this transfer would be to invoke a generic routine to examine the interrupt information; the routine, in turn, would call the interrupt-specific handler. However, interrupts must be handled quickly. Since only a predefined number of interrupts is possible, a table of pointers to interrupt routines can be used instead to provide the necessary speed. The interrupt routine is called indirectly through the table, with no intermediate routine needed. Generally, the table of pointers is stored in low memory (the first hundred or so locations). These locations hold the addresses of the interrupt service routines for the various devices. This array, or interrupt vector, of addresses is then indexed by a unique device number, given with the interrupt request, to provide the address of the interrupt service routine for

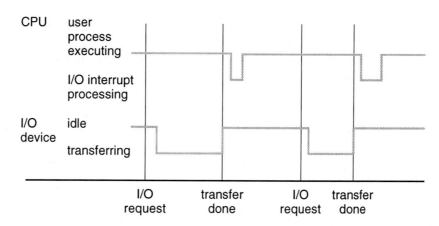

Figure 1.3 Interrupt time line for a single process doing output.

the interrupting device. Operating systems as different as Windows and UNIX dispatch interrupts in this manner.

The interrupt architecture must also save the address of the interrupted instruction. Many old designs simply stored the interrupt address in a fixed location or in a location indexed by the device number. More recent architectures store the return address on the system stack. If the interrupt routine needs to modify the processor state—for instance, by modifying register values—it must explicitly save the current state and then restore that state before returning. After the interrupt is serviced, the saved return address is loaded into the program counter, and the interrupted computation resumes as though the interrupt had not occurred.

1.2.2 Storage Structure

The CPU can load instructions only from memory, so any programs to run must be stored there. General-purpose computers run most of their programs from rewriteable memory, called main memory (also called random-access memory or **RAM**). Main memory commonly is implemented in a semiconductor technology called dynamic random-access memory (DRAM). Computers use other forms of memory as well. Because the read-only memory (ROM) cannot be changed, only static programs are stored there. The immutability of ROM is of use in game cartridges. EEPROM cannot be changed frequently and so contains mostly static programs. For example, smartphones have EEPROM to store their factory-installed programs.

All forms of memory provide an array of words. Each word has its own address. Interaction is achieved through a sequence of load or store instructions to specific memory addresses. The load instruction moves a word from main memory to an internal register within the CPU, whereas the store instruction moves the content of a register to main memory. Aside from explicit loads and stores, the CPU automatically loads instructions from main memory for execution.

A typical instruction–execution cycle, as executed on a system with a von Neumann architecture, first fetches an instruction from memory and stores that instruction in the instruction register. The instruction is then decoded and may cause operands to be fetched from memory and stored in some internal register. After the instruction on the operands has been executed, the result may be stored back in memory. Notice that the memory unit sees only a stream of memory addresses; it does not know how they are generated (by the instruction counter, indexing, indirection, literal addresses, or some other means) or what they are for (instructions or data). Accordingly, we can ignore *how* a memory address is generated by a program. We are interested only in the sequence of memory addresses generated by the running program.

Ideally, we want the programs and data to reside in main memory permanently. This arrangement usually is not possible for the following two reasons:

1. Main memory is usually too small to store all needed programs and data permanently.

2. Main memory is a *volatile* storage device that loses its contents when power is turned off or otherwise lost.

Thus, most computer systems provide secondary storage as an extension of main memory. The main requirement for secondary storage is that it be able to hold large quantities of data permanently.

The most common secondary-storage device is a magnetic disk, which provides storage for both programs and data. Most programs (system and application) are stored on a disk until they are loaded into memory. Many programs then use the disk as both the source and the destination of their processing. Hence, the proper management of disk storage is of central importance to a computer system, as we discuss in Chapter 11.

In a larger sense, however, the storage structure that we have described—consisting of registers, main memory, and magnetic disks—is only one of many possible storage systems. Others include cache memory, CD-ROM, magnetic tapes, and so on. Each storage system provides the basic functions of storing a datum and holding that datum until it is retrieved at a later time. The main differences among the various storage systems lie in speed, cost, size, and volatility.

The wide variety of storage systems in a computer system can be organized in a hierarchy (Figure 1.4) according to speed and cost. The higher levels are expensive, but they are fast. As we move down the hierarchy, the cost per bit generally decreases, whereas the access time generally increases. This trade-off is reasonable; if a given storage system were both faster and less expensive than another—other properties being the same—then there would be no reason to use the slower, more expensive memory. In fact, many early storage devices, including paper tape and core memories, are relegated to museums now that magnetic tape and semiconductor memory have become faster and cheaper. The top four levels of memory in Figure 1.4 may be constructed using semiconductor memory.

In addition to differing in speed and cost, the various storage systems are either volatile or nonvolatile. As mentioned earlier, volatile storage loses its contents when the power to the device is removed. In the absence of expensive battery and generator backup systems, data must be written to nonvolatile storage for safekeeping. In the hierarchy shown in Figure 1.4, the storage systems above the electronic disk are volatile, whereas those below

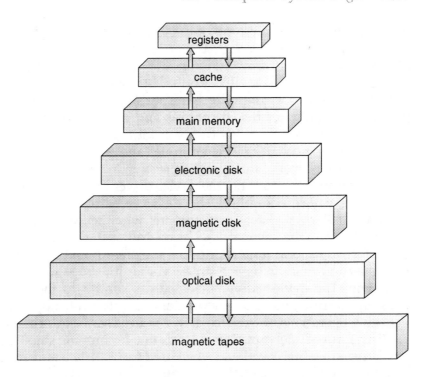

Figure 1.4 Storage-device hierarchy.

are nonvolatile. An electronic disk can be designed to be either volatile or nonvolatile. During normal operation, the electronic disk stores data in a large DRAM array, which is volatile. But many electronic-disk devices contain a hidden magnetic hard disk and a battery for backup power. If external power is interrupted, the electronic-disk controller copies the data from RAM to the magnetic disk. When external power is restored, the controller copies the data back into RAM. Another form of electronic disk is flash memory, which is popular in cameras and personal digital assistants (PDAs), in robots, and increasingly as removable storage on general-purpose computers. Flash memory is slower than DRAM but needs no power to retain its contents. Another form of nonvolatile storage is NVRAM, which is DRAM with battery backup power. This memory can be as fast as DRAM and (as long as the battery lasts) is nonvolatile.

The design of a complete memory system must balance all the factors just discussed: it must use only as much expensive memory as necessary while providing as much inexpensive, nonvolatile memory as possible. Caches can be installed to improve performance where a large access-time or transfer-rate disparity exists between two components.

1.2.3 I/O Structure

Storage is only one of many types of I/O devices within a computer. A large portion of operating-system code is dedicated to managing I/O, both because of its importance to the reliability and performance of a system and because of the varying nature of the devices. Next, we provide an overview of I/O.

A general-purpose computer system consists of CPUs and multiple device controllers that are connected through a common bus. Each device controller is in charge of a specific type of device. Depending on the controller, more than one device may be attached. For instance, seven or more devices can be attached to the small computer-systems interface (SCSI) controller. A device controller maintains some local buffer storage and a set of special-purpose registers. The device controller is responsible for moving the data between the peripheral devices that it controls and its local buffer storage. Typically, operating systems have a device driver for each device controller. This device driver understands the device controller and presents a uniform interface to the device to the rest of the operating system.

To start an I/O operation, the device driver loads the appropriate registers within the device controller. The device controller, in turn, examines the contents of these registers to determine what action to take (such as "read a character from the keyboard"). The controller starts the transfer of data from the device to its local buffer. Once the transfer of data is complete, the device controller informs the device driver via an interrupt that it has finished its operation. The device driver then returns control to the operating system, possibly returning the data or a pointer to the data if the operation was a read. For other operations, the device driver returns status information.

This form of interrupt-driven I/O is fine for moving small amounts of data but can produce high overhead when used for bulk data movement such as disk I/O. To solve this problem, direct memory access (DMA) is used. After setting up buffers, pointers, and counters for the I/O device, the device controller transfers an entire block of data directly to or from its own buffer storage to memory, with no intervention by the CPU. Only one interrupt is generated per block, to tell the device driver that the operation has completed, rather than the one interrupt per byte generated for low-speed devices. While the device controller is performing these operations, the CPU is available to accomplish other work.

Some high-end systems use switch rather than bus architecture. On these systems, multiple components can talk to other components concurrently, rather than competing for cycles on a shared bus. In this case, DMA is even more effective. Figure 1.5 shows the interplay of all components of a computer system.

1.3   Computer-System Architecture

In Section 1.2, we introduced the general structure of a typical computer system. A computer system may be organized in a number of different ways, which we can categorize roughly according to the number of general-purpose processors used.

1.3.1   Single-Processor Systems

Most systems use a single processor. The variety of single-processor systems may be surprising, however, since these systems range from PDAs through mainframes. On a single-processor system, there is one main CPU capable of executing a general-purpose instruction set, including instructions from user processes. Almost all systems have other special-purpose processors as well. They may come in the form of device-specific processors, such as disk,

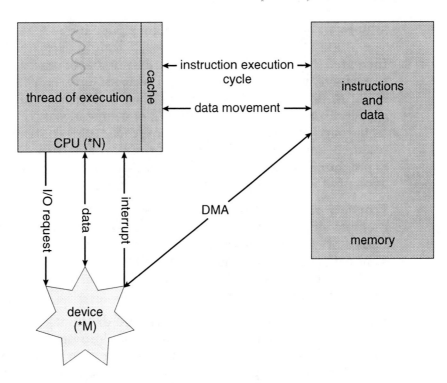

Figure 1.5 How a modern computer system works.

keyboard, and graphics controllers; or, on mainframes, they may take in the form of more general-purpose processors, such as I/O processors that move data rapidly among the components of the system.

All of these special-purpose processors run a limited instruction set and do not run user processes. Sometimes they are managed by the operating system, in that the operating system sends them information about their next task and monitors their status. For example, a disk-controller microprocessor receives a sequence of requests from the main CPU and implements its own disk queue and scheduling algorithm. This arrangement relieves the main CPU of the overhead of disk scheduling. PCs contain a microprocessor in the keyboard to convert the keystrokes into codes to be sent to the CPU. In other systems or circumstances, special-purpose processors are low-level components built into the hardware. The operating system cannot communicate with these processors; they do their jobs autonomously. The use of special-purpose microprocessors is common and does not turn a single-processor system into a multiprocessor. If there is only one general-purpose CPU, then the system is a single-processor system.

1.3.2 Multiprocessor Systems

Although single-processor systems are most common, multiprocessor systems (also known as parallel systems or tightly coupled systems) are growing in importance. Such systems have two or more processors in close communication, sharing the computer bus and sometimes the clock, memory, and peripheral devices.

Multiprocessor systems have three main advantages:

1. **Increased throughput.** By increasing the number of processors, we expect to get more work done in less time. The speed-up ratio with N processors is not N, however; rather, it is less than N. When multiple processors cooperate on a task, a certain amount of overhead is incurred in keeping all the parts working correctly. This overhead, plus contention for shared resources, lowers the expected gain from additional processors. Similarly, N programmers working closely together do not produce N times the amount of work a single programmer would produce.

2. **Economy of scale.** Multiprocessor systems can cost less than equivalent multiple single-processor systems, because they can share peripherals, mass storage, and power supplies. If several programs operate on the same set of data, it is cheaper to store those data on one disk and to have all the processors share them than to have many computers with local disks and many copies of the data.

3. **Increased reliability.** If functions can be distributed properly among several processors, then the failure of one processor will not halt the system, only slow it down. If we have ten processors and one fails, then each of the remaining nine processors can pick up a share of the work of the failed processor. Thus, the entire system runs only 10 percent slower, rather than failing altogether.

Increased reliability of a computer system is crucial in many applications. The ability to continue providing service proportional to the level of surviving hardware is called graceful degradation. Some systems go beyond graceful degradation and are called fault tolerant, because they can suffer a failure of any single component and still continue operation. Note that fault tolerance requires a mechanism to allow the failure to be detected, diagnosed, and, if possible, corrected. The HP NonStop (formerly Tandem) system uses both hardware and software duplication to ensure continued operation despite faults. The system consists of multiple pairs of CPUs, working in lockstep. Both processors in the pair execute each instruction and compare the results. If the results differ, then one CPU of the pair is at fault, and both are halted. The process that was being executed is then moved to another pair of CPUs, and the instruction that failed is restarted. This solution is expensive, since it involves special hardware and considerable hardware duplication.

The multiple-processor systems in use today are of two types. Some systems use asymmetric multiprocessing, in which each processor is assigned a specific task. A master processor controls the system; the other processors either look to the master for instruction or have predefined tasks. This scheme defines a master–slave relationship. The master processor schedules and allocates work to the slave processors.

The most common systems use symmetric multiprocessing (SMP), in which each processor performs all tasks within the operating system. SMP means that all processors are peers; no master–slave relationship exists between processors. Figure 1.6 illustrates a typical SMP architecture. Notice that each processor has its own set of registers, as well as a private—or local— cache; however, all processors share physical memory. An example of the SMP

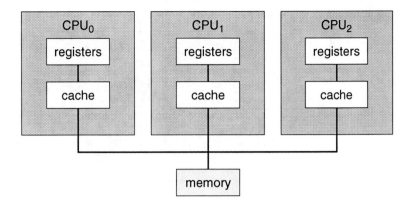

Figure 1.6 Symmetric multiprocessing architecture.

system is Solaris, a commercial version of UNIX designed by Sun Microsystems. A Solaris system can be configured to employ dozens of processors, all running Solaris. The benefit of this model is that many processes can run simultaneously —*N* processes can run if there are *N* CPUs—without causing a significant deterioration of performance. However, we must carefully control I/O to ensure that the data reach the appropriate processor. Also, since the CPUs are separate, one may be sitting idle while another is overloaded, resulting in inefficiencies. These inefficiencies can be avoided if the processors share certain data structures. A multiprocessor system of this form will allow processes and resources—such as memory—to be shared dynamically among the various processors and can lower the variance among the processors. Such a system must be written carefully, as we shall see in Chapter 6. Virtually all modern operating systems—including Windows, Mac OS X, and Linux—now provide support for SMP.

The difference between symmetric and asymmetric multiprocessing may result from either hardware or software. Special hardware can differentiate the multiple processors, or the software can be written to allow only one master and multiple slaves. For instance, Sun's operating system SunOS Version 4 provided asymmetric multiprocessing, whereas Version 5 (Solaris) is symmetric on the same hardware.

Multiprocessing adds CPUs to increase computing power. If the CPU has an integrated memory controller, then adding CPUs can also increase the amount of memory addressable in the system. Either way, multiprocessing can cause a system to change its memory-access model from uniform memory access (UMA) to non-uniform memory access (NUMA). UMA is defined as the situation in which access to any RAM from any CPU takes the same amount of time. With NUMA, some parts of memory may take longer to access than other parts, creating a performance penalty. Operating systems can minimize the NUMA penalty through resource management, as discussed in Section 8.5.4.

A recent trend in CPU design is to include multiple computing cores on a single chip. In essence, these are multiprocessor chips. They can be more efficient than multiple chips with single cores because on-chip communication is faster than between-chip communication. In addition, one chip with multiple cores uses significantly less power than multiple single-core chips. As a result,

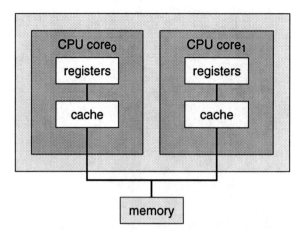

Figure 1.7 A dual-core design with two cores placed on the same chip.

multicore systems are especially well suited for server systems such as database and Web servers.

In Figure 1.7, we show a dual-core design with two cores on the same chip. In this design, each core has its own register set as well as its own local cache; other designs might use a shared cache or a combination of local and shared caches. Aside from architectural considerations, such as cache, memory, and bus contention, these multicore CPUs appear to the operating system as *N* standard processors. This tendency puts pressure on operating system designers—and application programmers—to make use of those CPUs.

Finally, blade servers are a recent development in which multiple processor boards, I/O boards, and networking boards are placed in the same chassis. The difference between these and traditional multiprocessor systems is that each blade-processor board boots independently and runs its own operating system. Some blade-server boards are multiprocessor as well, which blurs the lines between types of computers. In essence, these servers consist of multiple independent multiprocessor systems.

1.3.3 Clustered Systems

Another type of multiple-CPU system is the clustered system. Like multiprocessor systems, clustered systems gather together multiple CPUs to accomplish computational work. Clustered systems differ from multiprocessor systems, however, in that they are composed of two or more individual systems—or nodes—joined together. The definition of the term *clustered* is not concrete; many commercial packages wrestle with what a clustered system is and why one form is better than another. The generally accepted definition is that clustered computers share storage and are closely linked via a local-area network (LAN) (as described in Section 1.10) or a faster interconnect, such as InfiniBand.

Clustering is usually used to provide high-availability service; that is, service will continue even if one or more systems in the cluster fail. High availability is generally obtained by adding a level of redundancy in the system. A layer of cluster software runs on the cluster nodes. Each node can monitor one or more of the others (over the LAN). If the monitored machine fails, the monitoring machine can take ownership of its storage and restart the

BEOWULF CLUSTERS

Beowulf clusters are designed for solving high-performance computing tasks. These clusters are built using commodity hardware—such as personal computers—that are connected via a simple local area network. Interestingly, a Beowulf cluster uses no one specific software package but rather consists of a set of open-source software libraries that allow the computing nodes in the cluster to communicate with one another. Thus, there are a variety of approaches for constructing a Beowulf cluster, although Beowulf computing nodes typically run the Linux operating system. Since Beowulf clusters require no special hardware and operate using open-source software that is freely available, they offer a low-cost strategy for building a high-performance computing cluster. In fact, some Beowulf clusters built from collections of discarded personal computers are using hundreds of computing nodes to solve computationally expensive problems in scientific computing.

applications that were running on the failed machine. The users and clients of the applications see only a brief interruption of service.

Clustering can be structured asymmetrically or symmetrically. In asymmetric clustering, one machine is in hot-standby mode while the other is running the applications. The hot-standby host machine does nothing but monitor the active server. If that server fails, the hot-standby host becomes the active server. In symmetric mode, two or more hosts are running applications and are monitoring each other. This mode is obviously more efficient, as it uses all of the available hardware. It does require that more than one application be available to run.

As a cluster consists of several computer systems connected via a network, clusters may also be used to provide high-performance computing environments. Such systems can supply significantly greater computational power than single-processor or even SMP systems because they are capable of running an application concurrently on all computers in the cluster. However, applications must be written specifically to take advantage of the cluster by using a technique known as parallelization, which consists of dividing a program into separate components that run in parallel on individual computers in the cluster. Typically, these applications are designed so that once each computing node in the cluster has solved its portion of the problem, the results from all the nodes are combined into a final solution.

Other forms of clusters include parallel clusters and clustering over a wide-area network (WAN) (as described in Section 1.10). Parallel clusters allow multiple hosts to access the same data on the shared storage. Because most operating systems lack support for simultaneous data access by multiple hosts, parallel clusters are usually accomplished by use of special versions of software and special releases of applications. For example, Oracle Real Application Cluster is a version of Oracle's database that has been designed to run on a parallel cluster. Each machine runs Oracle, and a layer of software tracks access to the shared disk. Each machine has full access to all data in the database. To provide this shared access to data, the system must also supply access control and locking to ensure that no conflicting operations occur. This

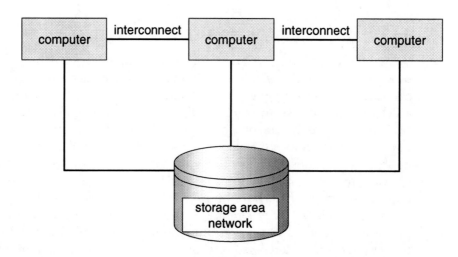

Figure 1.8   General structure of a clustered system.

function, commonly known as a distributed lock manager (DLM), is included in some cluster technology.

Cluster technology is changing rapidly. Some cluster products support dozens of systems in a cluster, as well as clustered nodes that are separated by miles. Many of these improvements are made possible by storage-area networks (SANs), as described in Section 11.3.3, which allow many systems to attach to a pool of storage. If the applications and their data are stored on the SAN, then the cluster software can assign the application to run on any host that is attached to the SAN. If the host fails, then any other host can take over. In a database cluster, dozens of hosts can share the same database, greatly increasing performance and reliability. Figure 1.8 depicts the general structure of a clustered system.

1.4   Operating-System Structure

Now that we have discussed basic information about computer-system organization and architecture, we are ready to talk about operating systems. An operating system provides the environment within which programs are executed. Internally, operating systems vary greatly in their makeup, since they are organized along many different lines. There are, however, many commonalities, which we consider in this section.

One of the most important aspects of operating systems is the ability to multiprogram. A single program cannot, in general, keep either the CPU or the I/O devices busy at all times. Single users frequently have multiple programs running. Multiprogramming increases CPU utilization by organizing jobs (code and data) so that the CPU always has one to execute.

The idea is as follows: The operating system keeps several jobs in memory simultaneously (Figure 1.9). Since, in general, main memory is too small to accommodate all jobs, the jobs are kept initially on the disk in the job pool. This pool consists of all processes residing on disk awaiting allocation of main memory.

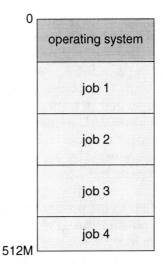

Figure 1.9 Memory layout for a multiprogramming system.

The set of jobs in memory can be a subset of the jobs kept in the job pool. The operating system picks and begins to execute one of the jobs in memory. Eventually, the job may have to wait for some task, such as an I/O operation, to complete. In a non-multiprogrammed system, the CPU would sit idle. In a multiprogrammed system, the operating system simply switches to, and executes, another job. When *that* job needs to wait, the CPU is switched to *another* job, and so on. Eventually, the first job finishes waiting and gets the CPU back. As long as at least one job needs to execute, the CPU is never idle.

This idea is common in other life situations. A lawyer does not work for only one client at a time, for example. While one case is waiting to go to trial or have papers typed, the lawyer can work on another case. If he has enough clients, the lawyer will never be idle for lack of work. (Idle lawyers tend to become politicians, so there is a certain social value in keeping lawyers busy.)

Multiprogrammed systems provide an environment in which the various system resources (for example, CPU, memory, and peripheral devices) are utilized effectively, but they do not provide for user interaction with the computer system. Time sharing (or multitasking) is a logical extension of multiprogramming. In time-sharing systems, the CPU executes multiple jobs by switching among them, but the switches occur so frequently that the users can interact with each program while it is running.

Time sharing requires an interactive (or hands-on) computer system, which provides direct communication between the user and the system. The user gives instructions to the operating system or to a program directly, using a input device such as a keyboard or a mouse, and waits for immediate results on an output device. Accordingly, the response time should be short—typically less than one second.

A time-shared operating system allows many users to share the computer simultaneously. Since each action or command in a time-shared system tends to be short, only a little CPU time is needed for each user. As the system switches rapidly from one user to the next, each user is given the impression that the entire computer system is dedicated to his use, even though it is being shared among many users.

A time-shared operating system uses CPU scheduling and multiprogramming to provide each user with a small portion of a time-shared computer. Each user has at least one separate program in memory. A program loaded into memory and executing is called a process. When a process executes, it typically executes for only a short time before it either finishes or needs to perform I/O. I/O may be interactive; that is, output goes to a display for the user, and input comes from a user keyboard, mouse, or other device. Since interactive I/O typically runs at "people speeds," it may take a long time to complete. Input, for example, may be bounded by the user's typing speed; seven characters per second is fast for people but incredibly slow for computers. Rather than let the CPU sit idle as this interactive input takes place, the operating system will rapidly switch the CPU to the program of some other user.

Time sharing and multiprogramming require that several jobs be kept simultaneously in memory. If several jobs are ready to be brought into memory, and if there is not enough room for all of them, then the system must choose among them. Making this decision is job scheduling, which is discussed in Chapter 5. When the operating system selects a job from the job pool, it loads that job into memory for execution. Having several programs in memory at the same time requires some form of memory management, which is covered in Chapters 7 and 8. In addition, if several jobs are ready to run at the same time, the system must choose among them. Making this decision is CPU scheduling, which is discussed in Chapter 5. Finally, running multiple jobs concurrently requires that their ability to affect one another be limited in all phases of the operating system, including process scheduling, disk storage, and memory management. These considerations are discussed throughout the text.

In a time-sharing system, the operating system must ensure reasonable response time, which is sometimes accomplished through swapping, where processes are swapped in and out of main memory to the disk. A more common method for achieving this goal is virtual memory, a technique that allows the execution of a process that is not completely in memory (Chapter 8). The main advantage of the virtual-memory scheme is that it enables users to run programs that are larger than actual physical memory. Further, it abstracts main memory into a large, uniform array of storage, separating logical memory as viewed by the user from physical memory. This arrangement frees programmers from concern over memory-storage limitations.

Time-sharing systems must also provide a file system (Chapters 9 and 10). The file system resides on a collection of disks; hence, disk management must be provided (Chapter 11). Also, time-sharing systems provide a mechanism for protecting resources from inappropriate use (Chapter 13). To ensure orderly execution, the system must provide mechanisms for job synchronization and communication (Chapter 6), and it may ensure that jobs do not get stuck in a deadlock, forever waiting for one another (Section 6.9).

1.5   Operating-System Operations

As mentioned earlier, modern operating systems are interrupt driven. If there are no processes to execute, no I/O devices to service, and no users to whom to respond, an operating system will sit quietly, waiting for something to happen. Events are almost always signaled by the occurrence of an interrupt or a trap. A trap (or an exception) is a software-generated interrupt caused either by an error (for example, division by zero or invalid memory access) or by a specific request from a user program that an operating-system service be performed. The interrupt-driven nature of an operating system defines that system's general structure. For each type of interrupt, separate segments of code in the operating system determine what action should be taken. An interrupt service routine is provided that is responsible for dealing with the interrupt.

Since the operating system and the users share the hardware and software resources of the computer system, we need to make sure that an error in a user program could cause problems only for the one program running. With sharing, many processes could be adversely affected by a bug in one program. For example, if a process gets stuck in an infinite loop, this loop could prevent the correct operation of many other processes. More subtle errors can occur in a multiprogramming system, where one erroneous program might modify another program, the data of another program, or even the operating system itself.

Without protection against these sorts of errors, either the computer must execute only one process at a time or all output must be suspect. A properly designed operating system must ensure that an incorrect (or malicious) program cannot cause other programs to execute incorrectly.

1.5.1 Dual-Mode Operation

In order to ensure the proper execution of the operating system, we must be able to distinguish between the execution of operating-system code and user-defined code. The approach taken by most computer systems is to provide hardware support that allows us to differentiate among various modes of execution.

At the very least, we need two separate modes of operation: user mode and kernel mode (also called supervisor mode, system mode, or privileged mode). A bit, called the mode bit, is added to the hardware of the computer to indicate the current mode: kernel (0) or user (1). With the mode bit, we are able to distinguish between a task that is executed on behalf of the operating system and one that is executed on behalf of the user. When the computer system is executing on behalf of a user application, the system is in user mode. However, when a user application requests a service from the operating system (via a system call), it must transition from user to kernel mode to fulfill the request. This is shown in Figure 1.10. As we shall see, this architectural enhancement is useful for many other aspects of system operation as well.

At system boot time, the hardware starts in kernel mode. The operating system is then loaded and starts user applications in user mode. Whenever a trap or interrupt occurs, the hardware switches from user mode to kernel mode (that is, changes the state of the mode bit to 0). Thus, whenever the operating system gains control of the computer, it is in kernel mode. The system always switches to user mode (by setting the mode bit to 1) before passing control to a user program.

The dual mode of operation provides us with the means for protecting the operating system from errant users—and errant users from one another. We accomplish this protection by designating some of the machine instructions that

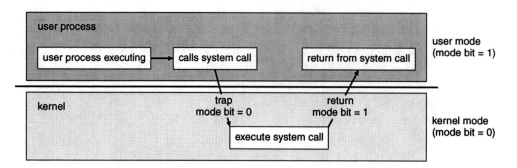

Figure 1.10   Transition from user to kernel mode.

may cause harm as privileged instructions. The hardware allows privileged instructions to be executed only in kernel mode. If an attempt is made to execute a privileged instruction in user mode, the hardware does not execute the instruction but rather treats it as illegal and traps it to the operating system.

The instruction to switch to kernel mode is an example of a privileged instruction. Some other examples include I/O control, timer management, and interrupt management. As we shall see throughout the text, there are many additional privileged instructions.

We can now see the life cycle of instruction execution in a computer system. Initial control resides in the operating system, where instructions are executed in kernel mode. When control is given to a user application, the mode is set to user mode. Eventually, control is switched back to the operating system via an interrupt, a trap, or a system call.

System calls provide the means for a user program to ask the operating system to perform tasks reserved for the operating system on the user program's behalf. A system call is invoked in a variety of ways, depending on the functionality provided by the underlying processor. In all forms, it is the method used by a process to request action by the operating system. A system call usually takes the form of a trap to a specific location in the interrupt vector. This trap can be executed by a generic `trap` instruction, although some systems (such as the MIPS R2000 family) have a specific `syscall` instruction.

When a system call is executed, it is treated by the hardware as a software interrupt. Control passes through the interrupt vector to a service routine in the operating system, and the mode bit is set to kernel mode. The system-call service routine is a part of the operating system. The kernel examines the interrupting instruction to determine what system call has occurred; a parameter indicates what type of service the user program is requesting. Additional information needed for the request may be passed in registers, on the stack, or in memory (with pointers to the memory locations passed in registers). The kernel verifies that the parameters are correct and legal, executes the request, and returns control to the instruction following the system call. We describe system calls more fully in Section 2.3.

The lack of a hardware-supported dual mode can cause serious shortcomings in an operating system. For instance, MS-DOS was written for the Intel 8088 architecture, which has no mode bit and therefore no dual mode. A user program running awry can wipe out the operating system by writing over it with data; also, multiple programs are able to write to a device at the same time, with potentially disastrous results. Recent versions of the Intel CPU do provide dual-mode operation. Accordingly, most contemporary operating systems— such as Windows, as well as Unix, Linux, and Solaris—take advantage of this dual-mode feature and provide greater protection for the operating system.

Once hardware protection is in place, it detects errors that violate modes. These errors are normally handled by the operating system. If a user program fails in some way—such as by making an attempt either to execute an illegal instruction or to access memory that is not in the user's address space—then the hardware traps to the operating system. The trap transfers control through the interrupt vector to the operating system, just as an interrupt does. When a program error occurs, the operating system must terminate the program abnormally. This situation is handled by the same code as a user-requested abnormal termination. An appropriate error message is given, and the memory of the program may be dumped. The memory dump is usually written to a file so that the user or programmer can examine it and perhaps correct and restart the program.

1.5.2 Timer

We must ensure that the operating system maintains control over the CPU. We cannot allow a user program to get stuck in an infinite loop or to fail to call system services and never return control to the operating system. To accomplish this goal, we can use a timer. A timer can be set to interrupt the computer after a specified period. The period may be fixed (for example, 1/60 second) or variable (for example, from 1 millisecond to 1 second). A variable timer is generally implemented by a fixed-rate clock and a counter. The operating system sets the counter. Every time the clock ticks, the counter is decremented. When the counter reaches 0, an interrupt occurs. For instance, a 10-bit counter with a 1-millisecond clock allows interrupts at intervals from 1 millisecond to 1,024 milliseconds, in steps of 1 millisecond.

Before turning over control to the user, the operating system ensures that the timer is set to interrupt. If the timer interrupts, control transfers automatically to the operating system, which may treat the interrupt as a fatal error or may give the program more time. Clearly, instructions that modify the content of the timer are privileged.

Thus, we can use the timer to prevent a user program from running too long. A simple technique is to initialize a counter with the amount of time that a program is allowed to run. A program with a 7-minute time limit, for example, would have its counter initialized to 420. Every second, the timer interrupts and the counter is decremented by 1. As long as the counter is positive, control is returned to the user program. When the counter becomes negative, the operating system terminates the program for exceeding the assigned time limit.

1.6 Process Management

A program does nothing unless its instructions are executed by a CPU. A program in execution, as mentioned, is a process. A time-shared user program such as a compiler is a process. A word-processing program being run by an individual user on a PC is a process. A system task, such as sending output to a printer, can also be a process (or at least part of one). For now, you can consider a process to be a job or a time-shared program, but later you will learn that the concept is more general. As we shall see in Chapter 3, it is possible to provide system calls that allow processes to create subprocesses to execute concurrently.

A process needs certain resources—including CPU time, memory, files, and I/O devices—to accomplish its task. These resources are either given to the process when it is created or allocated to it while it is running. In addition to the various physical and logical resources that a process obtains when it is created, various initialization data (input) may be passed along. For example, consider a process whose function is to display the status of a file on the screen of a terminal. The process will be given as an input the name of the file and will execute the appropriate instructions and system calls to obtain and display on the terminal the desired information. When the process terminates, the operating system will reclaim any reusable resources.

We emphasize that a program by itself is not a process; a program is a *passive* entity, like the contents of a file stored on disk, whereas a process is an *active* entity. A single-threaded process has one **program counter** specifying the next instruction to execute. (Threads are covered in Chapter 4.) The execution of such a process must be sequential. The CPU executes one instruction of the process after another, until the process completes. Further, at any time, one instruction at most is executed on behalf of the process. Thus, although two processes may be associated with the same program, they are nevertheless considered two separate execution sequences. A multithreaded process has multiple program counters, each pointing to the next instruction to execute for a given thread.

A process is the unit of work in a system. Such a system consists of a collection of processes, some of which are operating-system processes (those that execute system code) and the rest of which are user processes (those that execute user code). All these processes can potentially execute concurrently—by multiplexing on a single CPU, for example.

The operating system is responsible for the following activities in connection with process management:

* Scheduling processes and threads on the CPUs
* Creating and deleting both user and system processes
* Suspending and resuming processes
* Providing mechanisms for process synchronization
* Providing mechanisms for process communication

We discuss process-management techniques in Chapters 3 through 6.

1.7   Memory Management

As we discussed in Section 1.2.2, the main memory is central to the operation of a modern computer system. Main memory is a large array of words or bytes, ranging in size from hundreds of thousands to billions. Each word or byte has its own address. Main memory is a repository of quickly accessible data shared by the CPU and I/O devices. The central processor reads instructions from main memory during the instruction-fetch cycle and both reads and writes data from main memory during the data-fetch cycle (on a von Neumann architecture). As noted earlier, the main memory is generally the only large storage device that the CPU is able to address and access directly. For example, for the CPU to process data from disk, those data must first be transferred to main memory by CPU-generated I/O calls. In the same way, instructions must be in memory for the CPU to execute them.

For a program to be executed, it must be mapped to absolute addresses and loaded into memory. As the program executes, it accesses program instructions and data from memory by generating these absolute addresses. Eventually, the program terminates, its memory space is declared available, and the next program can be loaded and executed.

To improve both the utilization of the CPU and the speed of the computer's response to its users, general-purpose computers must keep several programs in memory, creating a need for memory management. Many different memory-management schemes are used. These schemes reflect various approaches, and the effectiveness of any given algorithm depends on the situation. In selecting a memory-management scheme for a specific system, we must take into account many factors—especially the *hardware* design of the system. Each algorithm requires its own hardware support.

The operating system is responsible for the following activities in connection with memory management:

* Keeping track of which parts of memory are currently being used and by whom

* Deciding which processes (or parts thereof) and data to move into and out of memory

* Allocating and deallocating memory space as needed

Memory-management techniques are discussed in Chapters 7 and 8.

1.8 Storage Management

To make the computer system convenient for users, the operating system provides a uniform, logical view of information storage. The operating system abstracts from the physical properties of its storage devices to define a logical storage unit, the file. The operating system maps files onto physical media and accesses these files via the storage devices.

1.8.1 File-System Management

File management is one of the most visible components of an operating system. Computers can store information on several different types of physical media. Magnetic disk, optical disk, and magnetic tape are the most common. Each of these media has its own characteristics and physical organization. Each medium is controlled by a device, such as a disk drive or tape drive, that also has its own unique characteristics. These properties include access speed, capacity, data-transfer rate, and access method (sequential or random).

A file is a collection of related information defined by its creator. Commonly, files represent programs (both source and object forms) and data. Data files may be numeric, alphabetic, alphanumeric, or binary. Files may be free-form (for example, text files) or they may be formatted rigidly (for example, fixed fields). Clearly, the concept of a file is an extremely general one.

The operating system implements the abstract concept of a file by managing mass-storage media, such as tapes and disks, and the devices that control them. Also, files are normally organized into directories to make them easier to use. Finally, when multiple users have access to files, it may be desirable to control by whom and in what ways (for example, read, write, append) files may be accessed.

The operating system is responsible for the following activities in connection with file management:

* Creating and deleting files

* Creating and deleting directories to organize files

* Supporting primitives for manipulating files and directories

* Mapping files onto secondary storage

* Backing up files on stable (nonvolatile) storage media

File-management techniques are discussed in Chapters 9 and 10.

1.8.2   Mass-Storage Management

As we have already seen, because main memory is too small to accommodate all data and programs, and because the data that it holds are lost when power is lost, the computer system must provide secondary storage to back up main memory. Most modern computer systems use disks as the principal on-line storage medium for both programs and data. Most programs—including compilers, assemblers, word processors, editors, and formatters—are stored on a disk until loaded into memory and then use the disk as both the source and destination of their processing. Hence, the proper management of disk storage is of central importance to a computer system. The operating system is responsible for the following activities in connection with disk management:

* Free-space management

* Storage allocation

* Disk scheduling

Because secondary storage is used frequently, it must be used efficiently. The entire speed of operation of a computer may hinge on the speeds of the disk subsystem and the algorithms that manipulate that subsystem.

There are, however, many uses for storage that is slower and lower in cost (and sometimes of higher capacity) than secondary storage. Backups of disk data, seldom-used data, and long-term archival storage are some examples. Magnetic tape drives and their tapes and CD and DVD drives and platters are typical tertiary storage devices. The media (tapes and optical platters) vary between WORM (write-once, read-many-times) and RW (read–write) formats.

Tertiary storage is not crucial to system performance, but it still must be managed. Some operating systems take on this task, while others leave tertiary-storage management to application programs. Some of the functions that operating systems can provide include mounting and unmounting media in devices, allocating and freeing the devices for exclusive use by processes, and migrating data from secondary to tertiary storage.

Techniques for secondary and tertiary storage management are discussed in Chapter 11.

1.8.3 Caching

Caching is an important principle of computer systems. Information is normally kept in some storage system (such as main memory). As it is used, it is copied into a faster storage system—the cache—on a temporary basis. When we need a particular piece of information, we first check whether it is in the cache. If it is, we use the information directly from the cache; if it is not, we use the information from the source, putting a copy in the cache under the assumption that we will need it again soon.

In addition, internal programmable registers, such as index registers, provide a high-speed cache for main memory. The programmer (or compiler) implements the register-allocation and register-replacement algorithms to decide which information to keep in registers and which to keep in main memory. There are also caches that are implemented totally in hardware. For instance, most systems have an instruction cache to hold the instructions expected to be executed next. Without this cache, the CPU would have to wait several cycles while an instruction was fetched from main memory. For similar reasons, most systems have one or more high-speed data caches in the memory hierarchy. We are not concerned with these hardware-only caches in this text, since they are outside the control of the operating system.

Because caches have limited size, cache management is an important design problem. Careful selection of the cache size and of a replacement policy can result in greatly increased performance. Figure 1.11 compares storage performance in large workstations and small servers. Various replacement algorithms for software-controlled caches are discussed in Chapter 8.

Main memory can be viewed as a fast cache for secondary storage, since data in secondary storage must be copied into main memory for use, and data must be in main memory before being moved to secondary storage for safekeeping. The file-system data, which resides permanently on secondary storage, may appear on several levels in the storage hierarchy. At the highest level, the operating system may maintain a cache of file-system data in main memory. In addition, electronic RAM disks (also known as solid-state disks) may be used for high-speed storage that is accessed through the file-system interface. The bulk of secondary storage is on magnetic disks. The magnetic-disk storage, in turn, is often backed up onto magnetic tapes or removable disks to protect against data loss in case of a hard-disk failure. Some systems automatically archive old file data from secondary storage to tertiary storage, such as tape jukeboxes, to lower the storage cost (see Chapter 11).

Level	1	2	3	4
Name	registers	cache	main memory	disk storage
Typical size	< 1 KB	< 16 MB	< 64 GB	> 100 GB
Implementation technology	custom memory with multiple ports, CMOS	on-chip or off-chip CMOS SRAM	CMOS DRAM	magnetic disk
Access time (ns)	0.25 – 0.5	0.5 – 25	80 – 250	5,000.000
Bandwidth (MB/sec)	20,000 – 100,000	5000 – 10,000	1000 – 5000	20 – 150
Managed by	compiler	hardware	operating system	operating system
Backed by	cache	main memory	disk	CD or tape

Figure 1.11   Performance of various levels of storage.

The movement of information between levels of a storage hierarchy may be either explicit or implicit, depending on the hardware design and the controlling operating-system software. For instance, data transfer from cache to CPU and registers is usually a hardware function, with no operating-system intervention. In contrast, transfer of data from disk to memory is usually controlled by the operating system.

In a hierarchical storage structure, the same data may appear in different levels of the storage system. For example, suppose that an integer A that is to be incremented by 1 is located in file B, and file B resides on magnetic disk. The increment operation proceeds by first issuing an I/O operation to copy the disk block on which A resides to main memory. This operation is followed by copying A to the cache and to an internal register. Thus, the copy of A appears in several places: on the magnetic disk, in main memory, in the cache, and in an internal register (see Figure 1.12). Once the increment takes place in the internal register, the value of A differs in the various storage systems. The value of A becomes the same only after the new value of A is written from the internal register back to the magnetic disk.

In a computing environment where only one process executes at a time, this arrangement poses no difficulties, since an access to integer A will always be to the copy at the highest level of the hierarchy. However, in a multitasking environment, where the CPU is switched back and forth among various processes, extreme care must be taken to ensure that, if several processes wish to access A, then each of these processes will obtain the most recently updated value of A.

The situation becomes more complicated in a multiprocessor environment where, in addition to maintaining internal registers, each of the CPUs also contains a local cache (Figure 1.6). In such an environment, a copy of A may exist simultaneously in several caches. Since the various CPUs can all execute

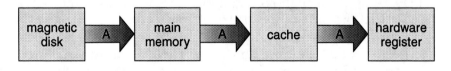

Figure 1.12   Migration of integer A from disk to register.

concurrently, we must make sure that an update to the value of A in one cache is immediately reflected in all other caches where A resides. This situation is called cache coherency, and it is usually a hardware problem (handled below the operating-system level).

1.8.4 I/O Systems

One of the purposes of an operating system is to hide the peculiarities of specific hardware devices from the user. For example, in UNIX, the peculiarities of I/O devices are hidden from the bulk of the operating system itself by the **I/O subsystem**. The I/O subsystem consists of several components:

* A memory-management component that includes buffering, caching, and spooling

* A general device-driver interface

* Drivers for specific hardware devices

Only the device driver knows the peculiarities of the specific device to which it is assigned.

We discussed in Section 1.2.3 how interrupt handlers and device drivers are used in the construction of efficient I/O subsystems. In Chapter 12, we discuss how the I/O subsystem interfaces to the other system components, manages devices, transfers data, and detects I/O completion.

1.9 Protection and Security

If a computer system has multiple users and allows the concurrent execution of multiple processes, then access to data must be regulated. For that purpose, mechanisms ensure that files, memory segments, CPU, and other resources can be operated on by only those processes that have gained proper authorization from the operating system. For example, memory-addressing hardware ensures that a process can execute only within its own address space. The timer ensures that no process can gain control of the CPU without eventually relinquishing control. Device-control registers are not accessible to users, so the integrity of the various peripheral devices is protected.

Protection, then, is any mechanism for controlling the access of processes or users to the resources defined by a computer system. This mechanism must provide means to specify the controls to be imposed and means to enforce the controls.

Protection can improve reliability by detecting latent errors at the interfaces between component subsystems. Early detection of interface errors can often prevent contamination of a healthy subsystem by another subsystem that is malfunctioning. Furthermore, an unprotected resource cannot defend against use (or misuse) by an unauthorized or incompetent user. A protection-oriented system provides a means to distinguish between authorized and unauthorized usage, as we discuss in Chapter 13.

A system can have adequate protection but still be prone to failure and allow inappropriate access. Consider a user whose authentication information (her means of identifying herself to the system) is stolen. Her data could be copied or deleted, even though file and memory protection are working. It is the job of security to defend a system from external and internal attacks. Such attacks spread across a huge range and include viruses and worms, denial-of-service attacks (which use all of a system's resources and so keep legitimate users out of the system), identity theft, and theft of service (unauthorized use of a system). Prevention of some of these attacks is considered an operating-system function on some systems, while other systems leave the prevention to policy or additional software. Due to the alarming rise in security incidents, operating-system security features represent a fast-growing area of research and implementation. Security is discussed in Chapter 14.

Protection and security require the system to be able to distinguish among all its users. Most operating systems maintain a list of user names and associated user identifiers (user IDs). In Windows Vista parlance, this is a security ID (SID). These numerical IDs are unique, one per user. When a user logs into the system, the authentication stage determines the appropriate user ID for the user. That user ID is associated with all of the user's processes and threads. When an ID needs to be user readable, it is translated back to the user name via the user name list.

In some circumstances, we wish to distinguish among sets of users rather than individual users. For example, the owner of a file on a UNIX system may be allowed to issue all operations on that file, whereas a selected set of users may only be allowed to read the file. To accomplish this, we need to define a group name and the set of users belonging to that group. Group functionality can be implemented as a system-wide list of group names and group identifiers. A user can be in one or more groups, depending on operating-system design decisions. The user's group IDs are also included in every associated process and thread.

In the course of normal use of a system, the user ID and group ID for a user are sufficient. However, a user sometimes needs to escalate privileges to gain extra permissions for an activity. The user may need access to a device that is restricted, for example. Operating systems provide various methods to allow privilege escalation. On UNIX, for example, the setuid attribute on a program causes that program to run with the user ID of the owner of the file, rather than the current user's ID. The process runs with this effective UID until it turns off the extra privileges or terminates.

1.10 Distributed Systems

A distributed system is a collection of physically separate, possibly heterogeneous, computer systems that are networked to provide the users with access to the various resources that the system maintains. Access to a shared resource increases computation speed, functionality, data availability, and reliability. Some operating systems generalize network access as a form of file access, with the details of networking contained in the network interface's device driver. Others make users specifically invoke network functions. Generally, systems contain a mix of the two modes—for example FTP and NFS. The protocols that create a distributed system can greatly affect that system's utility and popularity.

A network, in the simplest terms, is a communication path between two or more systems. Distributed systems depend on networking for their functionality. Networks vary in the protocols used, the distances between nodes, and the transport media. TCP/IP is the most common network protocol, although ATM and other protocols are in widespread use. Likewise, operating-system support of protocols varies. Most operating systems support TCP/IP, including the Windows and UNIX operating systems. Some systems support proprietary protocols to suit their needs. To an operating system, a network protocol simply needs an interface device—a network adapter, for example—with a device driver to manage it, as well as software to handle data. These concepts are discussed throughout this book.

Networks are characterized based on the distances between their nodes. A local-area network (LAN) connects computers within a room, a floor, or a building. A wide-area network (WAN) usually links buildings, cities, or countries. A global company may have a WAN to connect its offices worldwide. These networks may run one protocol or several protocols. The continuing advent of new technologies brings about new forms of networks. For example, a metropolitan-area network (MAN) can link buildings within a city. BlueTooth and 802.11 devices use wireless technology to communicate over a distance of several feet, in essence creating a small-area network such as might be found in a home.

The media to carry networks are equally varied. They include copper wires, fiber strands, and wireless transmissions between satellites, microwave dishes, and radios. When computing devices are connected to cellular phones, they create a network. Even very short-range infrared communication can be used for networking. At a rudimentary level, whenever computers communicate, they use or create a network. These networks also vary in their performance and reliability.

Some operating systems have taken the concept of networks and distributed systems further than merely providing network connectivity. A network operating system is an operating system that provides features such as file sharing across the network and includes a communication scheme that allows different processes on different computers to exchange messages. A computer running a network operating system acts autonomously from all other computers on the network, although it is aware of the network and is able to communicate with other networked computers. A distributed operating system provides a less autonomous environment: The different operating systems communicate closely enough to provide the illusion that only a single operating system controls the network.

We do not cover computer networks and distributed systems further in this text. We encourage the interested reader to consult the bibliographical notes at the end of this chapter for sources of further information.

1.11 Special-Purpose Systems

The discussion thus far has focused on the general-purpose computer systems that we are all familiar with. There are, however, other classes of computer systems whose functions are more limited and whose objective is to deal with limited computation domains.

1.11.1 Real-Time Embedded Systems

Embedded computers are the most prevalent form of computers in existence. These devices are found everywhere, from car engines and manufacturing robots to DVDs and microwave ovens. They tend to have very specific tasks. The systems they run on are usually primitive, and so the operating systems provide limited features. Usually, they have little or no user interface, preferring to spend their time monitoring and managing hardware devices, such as automobile engines and robotic arms.

These embedded systems vary considerably. Some are general-purpose computers, running standard operating systems—such as UNIX—with special-purpose applications to implement the functionality. Others are hardware devices with a special-purpose embedded operating system providing just the functionality desired. Yet others are hardware devices with application-specific integrated circuits (ASICs) that perform their tasks without an operating system.

The use of embedded systems continues to expand. The power of these devices, both as standalone units and as elements of networks and the Web, is sure to increase as well. Even now, entire houses can be computerized, so that a central computer—either a general-purpose computer or an embedded system—can control heating and lighting, alarm systems, and even coffee makers. Web access can enable a home owner to tell the house to heat up before she arrives home. Someday, the refrigerator may call the grocery store when it notices the milk is gone.

Embedded systems almost always run real-time operating systems. A real-time system is used when rigid time requirements have been placed on the operation of a processor or the flow of data; thus, it is often used as a control device in a dedicated application. Sensors bring data to the computer. The computer must analyze the data and possibly adjust controls to modify the sensor inputs. Systems that control scientific experiments, medical imaging systems, industrial control systems, and certain display systems are real-time systems. Some automobile-engine fuel-injection systems, home-appliance controllers, and weapon systems are also real-time systems.

A real-time system has well-defined, fixed time constraints. Processing *must* be done within the defined constraints, or the system will fail. For instance, it would not do for a robot arm to be instructed to halt *after* it had smashed into the car it was building. A real-time system functions correctly only if it returns the correct result within its time constraints. Contrast this system with a time-sharing system, where it is desirable (but not mandatory) to respond quickly, or a batch system, which may have no time constraints at all.

We do not cover real-time systems further in this text. We encourage the interested reader to consult the bibliographical notes at the end of this chapter for sources of further information.

1.11.2 Multimedia Systems

Most operating systems are designed to handle conventional data such as text files, programs, word-processing documents, and spreadsheets. However, a recent trend in technology is the incorporation of **multimedia data** into computer systems. Multimedia data consist of audio and video files as well as conventional files. These data differ from conventional data in that multimedia data—such as frames of video—must be delivered (streamed) according to certain time restrictions (for example, 30 frames per second).

Multimedia describes a wide range of applications in popular use today. These include audio files such as MP3, DVD movies, video conferencing, and short video clips of movie previews or news stories downloaded over the Internet. Multimedia applications may also include live webcasts (broadcasting over the World Wide Web) of speeches or sporting events and even live webcams that allow a viewer in Manhattan to observe customers at a Paris cafe. Multimedia applications need not be either audio or video; rather, a multimedia application often includes a combination of both. For example, a movie may consist of separate audio and video tracks. Nor must multimedia applications be delivered only to desktop personal computers. Increasingly, they are being directed toward smaller devices, including PDAs and cellular telephones. For example, a stock trader may have stock quotes delivered wirelessly and in real time to his PDA.

We do not cover multimedia systems in further this text. We encourage the interested reader to consult the bibliographical notes at the end of this chapter for sources of further information.

1.11.3 Handheld Systems

Handheld systems include personal digital assistants (PDAs), such as Palm and Pocket-PCs, and cellular telephones, many of which use special-purpose embedded operating systems. Developers of handheld systems and applications face many challenges, most of which are due to the limited size of such devices. For example, a PDA is typically about 5 inches in height and 3 inches in width, and it weighs less than one-half pound. Because of their size, most handheld devices have small amounts of memory, slow processors, and small display screens. We take a look now at each of these limitations.

The amount of physical memory in a handheld depends on the device, but typically it is somewhere between 1 MB and 1 GB. (Contrast this with a typical PC or workstation, which may have several gigabytes of memory.) As a result, the operating system and applications must manage memory efficiently. This includes returning all allocated memory to the memory manager when the memory is not being used. In Chapter 8, we explore virtual memory, which allows developers to write programs that behave as if the system has more memory than is physically available. Currently, not many handheld devices use virtual-memory techniques, so program developers must work within the confines of limited physical memory.

A second issue of concern to developers of handheld devices is the speed of the processor used in the devices. Processors for most handheld devices run at a fraction of the speed of a processor in a PC. Faster processors require more power. To include a faster processor in a handheld device would require a larger battery, which would take up more space and would have to be replaced (or recharged) more frequently. Most handheld devices use smaller, slower processors that consume less power. Therefore, the operating system and applications must be designed not to tax the processor.

The last issue confronting program designers for handheld devices is I/O. A lack of physical space limits input methods to small keyboards, handwriting recognition, or small screen-based keyboards. The small display screens limit output options. Whereas a monitor for a home computer may measure up to 30 inches, the display for a handheld device is often no more than 3 inches square. Familiar tasks, such as reading e-mail and browsing Web pages, must be condensed into smaller displays. One approach for displaying the content in Web pages is Web clipping, where only a small subset of a Web page is delivered and displayed on the handheld device.

Some handheld devices use wireless technology, such as BlueTooth or 802.11, allowing remote access to e-mail and Web browsing. Cellular telephones with connectivity to the Internet fall into this category. However, for PDAs that do not provide wireless access, downloading data typically requires the user first to download the data to a PC or workstation and then download the data to the PDA. Some PDAs allow data to be directly copied from one device to another using an infrared link.

Generally, the limitations in the functionality of PDAs are balanced by their convenience and portability. Their use continues to expand as network connections become more available and other options, such as digital cameras and MP3 players, expand their utility.

1.12 Computing Environments

So far, we have provided an overview of computer-system organization and major operating-system components. We conclude with a brief overview of how these are used in a variety of computing environments.

1.12.1 Traditional Computing

As computing matures, the lines separating many of the traditional computing environments are blurring. Consider the "typical office environment." Just a few years ago, this environment consisted of PCs connected to a network, with servers providing file and print services. Remote access was awkward, and portability was achieved by use of laptop computers. Terminals attached to mainframes were prevalent at many companies as well, with even fewer remote access and portability options.

The current trend is toward providing more ways to access these computing environments. Web technologies are stretching the boundaries of traditional computing. Companies establish portals, which provide Web accessibility to their internal servers. Network computers are essentially terminals that understand Web-based computing. Handheld computers can synchronize with PCs to allow very portable use of company information. Handheld PDAs can also connect to wireless networks to use the company's Web portal (as well as the myriad other Web resources).

At home, most users had a single computer with a slow modem connection to the office, the Internet, or both. Today, network-connection speeds once available only at great cost are relatively inexpensive, giving home users more access to more data. These fast data connections are allowing home computers to serve up Web pages and to run networks that include printers, client PCs, and servers. Some homes even have firewalls to protect their networks from security breaches. Those firewalls cost thousands of dollars a few years ago and did not even exist a decade ago.

In the latter half of the previous century, computing resources were scarce. (Before that, they were nonexistent!) For a period of time, systems were either batch or interactive. Batch systems processed jobs in bulk, with predetermined input (from files or other sources of data). Interactive systems waited for input from users. To optimize the use of the computing resources, multiple users shared time on these systems. Time-sharing systems used a timer and scheduling algorithms to cycle processes rapidly through the CPU, giving each user a share of the resources.

Today, traditional time-sharing systems are uncommon. The same scheduling technique is still in use on workstations and servers, but frequently the processes are all owned by the same user (or a single user and the operating system). User processes, and system processes that provide services to the user, are managed so that each frequently gets a slice of computer time. Consider the windows created while a user is working on a PC, for example, and the fact that they may be performing different tasks at the same time.

1.12.2 Client–Server Computing

As PCs have become faster, more powerful, and cheaper, designers have shifted away from centralized system architecture. Terminals connected to centralized systems are now being supplanted by PCs. Correspondingly, user-interface functionality once handled directly by centralized systems is increasingly being handled by PCs. As a result, many of today's systems act as server systems to satisfy requests generated by client systems. This form of specialized distributed system, called a client–server system, has the general structure depicted in Figure 1.13.

Server systems can be broadly categorized as compute servers and file servers:

* The compute-server system provides an interface to which a client can send a request to perform an action (for example, read data); in response, the server executes the action and sends back results to the client. A server running a database that responds to client requests for data is an example of such a system.

* The file-server system provides a file-system interface where clients can create, update, read, and delete files. An example of such a system is a Web server that delivers files to clients running Web browsers.

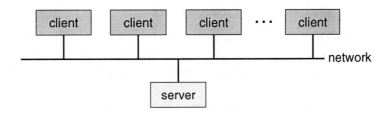

Figure 1.13 General structure of a client–server system.

1.12.3 Peer-to-Peer Computing

Another structure for a distributed system is the peer-to-peer (P2P) system model. In this model, clients and servers are not distinguished from one another; instead, all nodes within the system are considered peers, and each may act as either a client or a server, depending on whether it is requesting or providing a service. Peer-to-peer systems offer an advantage over traditional client-server systems. In a client-server system, the server is a bottleneck; but in a peer-to-peer system, services can be provided by several nodes distributed throughout the network.

To participate in a peer-to-peer system, a node must first join the network of peers. Once a node has joined the network, it can begin providing services to—and requesting services from—other nodes in the network. Determining what services are available is accomplished in one of two general ways:

* When a node joins a network, it registers its service with a centralized lookup service on the network. Any node desiring a specific service first contacts this centralized lookup service to determine which node provides the service. The remainder of the communication takes place between the client and the service provider.

* A peer acting as a client must first discover what node provides a desired service by broadcasting a request for the service to all other nodes in the network. The node (or nodes) providing that service responds to the peer making the request. To support this approach, a *discovery protocol* must be provided that allows peers to discover services provided by other peers in the network.

Peer-to-peer networks gained widespread popularity in the late 1990s with several file-sharing services, such as Napster and Gnutella, that enable peers to exchange files with one another. The Napster system uses an approach similar to the first type described above: a centralized server maintains an index of all files stored on peer nodes in the Napster network, and the actual exchanging of files takes place between the peer nodes. The Gnutella system uses a technique similar to the second type: a client broadcasts file requests to other nodes in the system, and nodes that can service the request respond directly to the client. The future of exchanging files remains uncertain because many of the files are copyrighted (music, for example), and there are laws governing the distribution of copyrighted material. In any case, though, peer-to-peer technology undoubtedly will play a role in the future of many services, such as searching, file exchange, and e-mail.

1.12.4 Web-Based Computing

The Web has become ubiquitous, leading to more access by a wider variety of devices than was dreamt of a few years ago. PCs are still the most prevalent access devices, with workstations, handheld PDAs, and even cell phones also providing access.

Web computing has increased the emphasis on networking. Devices that were not previously networked now include wired or wireless access. Devices that were networked now have faster network connectivity, provided by either improved networking technology, optimized network implementation code, or both.

The implementation of Web-based computing has given rise to new categories of devices, such as load balancers, which distribute network connections among a pool of similar servers. Operating systems like Windows 95, which acted as Web clients, have evolved into Linux and Windows XP and beyond, which can act as Web servers as well as clients. Generally, the Web has increased the complexity of devices because their users require them to be Web-enabled.

1.13 Open-Source Operating Systems

The study of operating systems, as noted earlier, is made easier by the availability of a vast number of open-source releases. Open-source operating systems are those made available in source-code format rather than as compiled binary code. Linux is the most famous open-source operating system, while Microsoft Windows is a well-known example of the opposite closed-source approach. Starting with the source code allows the programmer to produce binary code that can be executed on a system. Doing the opposite— reverse engineering the source code from the binaries—is quite a lot of work, and useful items such as comments are never recovered. Learning operating systems by examining the actual source code, rather than reading summaries of that code, can be extremely useful. With the source code in hand, a student can modify the operating system and then compile and run the code to try out those changes, which is another excellent learning tool. This text includes projects that involve modifying operating-system source code, while also describing algorithms at a high level to be sure all important operating system topics are covered. Throughout the text, we provide pointers to examples of open-source code for deeper study.

There are many benefits to open-source operating systems, including a community of interested (and usually unpaid) programmers who contribute to the code by helping to debug it, analyze it, provide support, and suggest changes. Arguably, open-source code is more secure than closed-source code because many more eyes are viewing the code. Certainly open-source code has bugs, but open-source advocates argue that bugs tend to be found and fixed faster owing to the number of people using and viewing the code. Companies that earn revenue from selling their programs tend to be hesitant to open-source their code, but Red Hat, SUSE, Sun, and a myriad of other companies are doing just that and showing that commercial companies benefit, rather than suffer, when they open-source their code. Revenue can be generated through support contracts and the sale of hardware on which the software runs, for example.

1.13.1 History

In the early days of modern computing (that is, the 1950s), a great deal of software was available in open-source format. The original hackers (computer enthusiasts) at MIT's Tech Model Railroad Club left their programs in drawers for others to work on. "Homebrew" user groups exchanged code during their meetings. Later, company-specific user groups, such as Digital Equipment

Corporation's DEC, accepted contributions of source-code programs, collected them onto tapes, and distributed the tapes to interested members.

Computer and software companies eventually sought to limit the use of their software to authorized computers and paying customers. Releasing only the binary files compiled from the source code, rather than the source code itself, helped them to achieve this goal, as well as protecting their code and their ideas from their competitors. Another issue involved copyrighted material. Operating systems and other programs can limit the ability to play back movies and music or display electronic books to authorized computers. Such copy protection or digital rights management (DRM) would not be effective if the source code that implemented these limits were published. Laws in many countries, including the U.S. Digital Millennium Copyright Act (DMCA), make it illegal to reverse-engineer DRM code or otherwise try to circumvent copy protection.

To counter the move to limit software use and redistribution, Richard Stallman in 1983 started the GNU project to create a free, open-source UNIX-compatible operating system. In 1985, he published the GNU Manifesto, which argues that all software should be free and open-sourced. He also formed the Free Software Foundation (FSF) with the goal of encouraging the free exchange of software source code and the free use of that software. Rather than copyright its software, the FSF "copylefts" the software to encourage sharing and improvement. The GNU General Public License (GPL) codifies copylefting and is a common license under which free software is released. Fundamentally, GPL requires that the source code be distributed with any binaries and that any changes made to the source code be released under the same GPL license.

1.13.2 Linux

As an example of an open-source operating system, consider GNU/Linux. The GNU project produced many UNIX-compatible tools, including compilers, editors, and utilities, but never released a kernel. In 1991, a student in Finland, Linus Torvalds, released a rudimentary UNIX-like kernel using the GNU compilers and tools and invited contributions worldwide. The advent of the Internet meant that anyone interested could download the source code, modify it, and submit changes to Torvalds. Releasing updates once a week allowed this so-called Linux operating system to grow rapidly, enhanced by several thousand programmers.

The resulting GNU/Linux operating system has spawned hundreds of unique distributions, or custom builds, of the system. Major distributions include RedHat, SUSE, Fedora, Debian, Slackware, and Ubuntu. Distributions vary in function, utility, installed applications, hardware support, user interface, and purpose. For example, RedHat Enterprise Linux is geared to large commercial use. PCLinuxOS is a LiveCD—an operating system that can be booted and run from a CD-ROM without being installed on a system's hard disk. One variant of PCLinuxOS, "PCLinuxOS Supergamer DVD," is a LiveDVD that includes graphics drivers and games. A gamer can run it on any compatible system simply by booting from the DVD. When the gamer is finished, a reboot of the system resets it to its installed operating system.

Access to the Linux source code varies by release. Here, we consider Ubuntu Linux. Ubuntu is a popular Linux distribution that comes in a variety of types, including those tuned for desktops, servers, and students. Its founder pays for the printing and mailing of DVDs containing the binary and source code (which helps to make it popular). The following steps outline a way to explore the Ubuntu kernel source code on systems that support the free "VMware Player" tool:

* Download the player from `http://www.vmware.com/download/player/` and install it on your system.

* Download a virtual machine containing Ubuntu. Hundreds of "appliances", or virtual machine images, pre-installed with oper-ating systems and applications, are available from VMware at `http://www.vmware.com/appliances/`.

* Boot the virtual machine within VMware Player.

* Get the source code of the kernel release of interest, such as 2.6, by executing `wget http://www.kernel.org/pub/linux/kernel/v2.6/linux-2.6.18.1.tar.bz2` within the Ubuntu virtual machine.

* Uncompress and untar the downloaded file via `tar xjf linux-2.6.18.1.tar.bz2`.

* Explore the source code of the Ubuntu kernel, which is now in `./linux-2.6.18.1`.

For more about Linux, see Chapter 15. For more about virtual machines, see Section 2.8.

1.13.3 BSD UNIX

BSD UNIX has a longer and more complicated history than Linux. It started in 1978 as a derivative of AT&T's UNIX. Releases from the University of California at Berkeley came in source and binary form, but they were not open-source because a license from AT&T was required. BSD UNIX's development was slowed by a lawsuit by AT&T, but eventually a fully functional open-source version, 4.4BSD-lite, was released in 1994.

Just as with Linux, there are many distributions of BSD UNIX, including FreeBSD, NetBSD, OpenBSD, and DragonflyBSD. To explore the source code of FreeBSD, simply download the virtual machine image of the version of interest and boot it within VMware, as described above for Ubuntu Linux. The source code comes with the distribution and is stored in `/usr/src/`. The kernel source code is in `/usr/src/sys`. For example, to examine the virtual-memory implementation code in the FreeBSD kernel, see the files in `/usr/src/sys/vm`.

Darwin, the core kernel component of Mac OS X, is based on BSD UNIX and is open-sourced as well. That source code is available from `http://www.opensource.apple.com/darwinsource/`. Every Mac OS X release has its open-source components posted at that site. The name of the pack-age that contains the kernel is "xnu." The source code for Mac OS X ker-nel revision 1228 (the source code to Mac OS X Leopard) can be found at www.opensource.apple.com/darwinsource/tarballs/apsl/xnu-1228.tar.gz. Apple also provides extensive developer tools, documentation, and support at `http://connect.apple.com`. For more information, see Appendix A.

1.13.4 Solaris

Solaris is the commercial UNIX-based operating system of Sun Microsystems. Originally, Sun's SunOS operating system was based on BSD UNIX. Sun moved to AT&T's System V UNIX as its base in 1991. In 2005, Sun open-sourced some of the Solaris code, and over time, the company has added more and more to that open-source code base. Unfortunately, not all of Solaris is open-sourced, because some of the code is still owned by AT&T and other companies. However, Solaris can be compiled from the open source and linked with binaries of the close-sourced components, so it can still be explored, modified, compiled, and tested.

The source code is available from http://opensolaris.org/os/downloads/. Also available there are pre-compiled distributions based on the source code, documentation, and discussion groups. It is not necessary to download the entire source-code bundle from the site, because Sun allows visitors to explore the source code on-line via a source code browser.

1.13.5 Utility

The free software movement is driving legions of programmers to create thousands of open-source projects, including operating systems. Sites like http://freshmeat.net/ and http://distrowatch.com/ provide portals to many of these projects. Open-source projects enable students to use source code as a learning tool. They can modify programs and test them, help find and fix bugs, and otherwise explore mature, full-featured operating systems, compilers, tools, user interfaces, and other types of programs. The availability of source code for historic projects, such as Multics, can help students to understand those projects and to build knowledge that will help in the implementation of new projects.

GNU/Linux, BSD UNIX, and Solaris are all open-source operating systems, but each has its own goals, utility, licensing, and purpose. Sometimes licenses are not mutually exclusive and cross-pollination occurs, allowing rapid improvements in operating-system projects. For example, several major components of Solaris have been ported to BSD UNIX. The advantages of free software and open sourcing are likely to increase the number and quality of open-source projects, leading to an increase in the number of individuals and companies that use these projects.

1.14 Summary

An operating system is software that manages the computer hardware, as well as providing an environment for application programs to run. Perhaps the most visible aspect of an operating system is the interface to the computer system it provides to the human user.

For a computer to do its job of executing programs, the programs must be in main memory. Main memory is the only large storage area that the processor can access directly. It is an array of words or bytes, ranging in size from millions to billions. Each word in memory has its own address. The main memory is usually a volatile storage device that loses its contents when power is turned off or lost. Most computer systems provide secondary storage as an extension of main memory. Secondary storage provides a form of nonvolatile storage that is capable of holding large quantities of data permanently. The most common secondary-storage device is a magnetic disk, which provides storage of both programs and data.

The wide variety of storage systems in a computer system can be organized in a hierarchy according to speed and cost. The higher levels are expensive, but they are fast. As we move down the hierarchy, the cost per bit generally decreases, whereas the access time generally increases.

There are several different strategies for designing a computer system. Uniprocessor systems have only a single processor, while multiprocessor systems contain two or more processors that share physical memory and peripheral devices. The most common multiprocessor design is symmetric multiprocessing (or SMP), where all processors are considered peers and run independently of one another. Clustered systems are a specialized form of multiprocessor systems and consist of multiple computer systems connected by a local area network.

To best utilize the CPU, modern operating systems employ multiprogramming, which allows several jobs to be in memory at the same time, thus ensuring that the CPU always has a job to execute. Time-sharing systems are an extension of multiprogramming wherein CPU scheduling algorithms rapidly switch between jobs, thus providing the illusion that each job is running concurrently.

The operating system must ensure correct operation of the computer system. To prevent user programs from interfering with the proper operation of the system, the hardware has two modes: user mode and kernel mode. Various instructions (such as I/O instructions and halt instructions) are privileged and can be executed only in kernel mode. The memory in which the operating system resides must also be protected from modification by the user. A timer prevents infinite loops. These facilities (dual mode, privileged instructions, memory protection, and timer interrupt) are basic building blocks used by operating systems to achieve correct operation.

A process (or job) is the fundamental unit of work in an operating system. Process management includes creating and deleting processes and providing mechanisms for processes to communicate and synchronize with each other. An operating system manages memory by keeping track of what parts of memory are being used and by whom. The operating system is also responsible for dynamically allocating and freeing memory space. Storage space is also managed by the operating system; this includes providing file systems for representing files and directories and managing space on mass-storage devices.

Operating systems must also be concerned with protecting and securing the operating system and users. Protection measures are mechanisms that control the access of processes or users to the resources made available by the computer system. Security measures are responsible for defending a computer system from external or internal attacks.

Distributed systems allow users to share resources on geographically dispersed hosts connected via a computer network. Services may be provided through either the client–server model or the peer-to-peer model. In a clustered system, multiple machines can perform computations on data residing on shared storage, and computing can continue even when some subset of cluster members fails.

LANs and WANs are the two basic types of networks. LANs enable processors distributed over a small geographical area to communicate, whereas WANs allow processors distributed over a larger area to communicate. LANs typically are faster than WANs.

There are several computer systems that serve specific purposes. These include real-time operating systems designed for embedded environments such as consumer devices, automobiles, and robotics. Real-time operating systems have well-defined fixed-time constraints. Processing *must* be done within the defined constraints, or the system will fail. Multimedia systems involve the delivery of multimedia data and often have special requirements of displaying or playing audio, video, or synchronized audio and video streams.

Recently, the influence of the Internet and the World Wide Web has encouraged the development of operating systems that include Web browsers and networking and communication software as integral features.

The free software movement has created thousands of open-source projects, including operating systems. Because of these projects, students are able to use source code as a learning tool. They can modify programs and test them, help find and fix bugs, and otherwise explore mature, full-featured operating systems, compilers, tools, user interfaces, and other types of programs.

GNU/Linux, BSD UNIX, and Solaris are all open-source operating systems. The advantages of free software and open sourcing are likely to increase the number and quality of open-source projects, leading to an increase in the number of individuals and companies that use these projects.

Practice Exercises

1.1 What are the three main purposes of an operating system?

1.2 What are the main differences between operating systems for mainframe computers and personal computers?

1.3 List the four steps that are necessary to run a program on a completely dedicated machine—a computer that is running only that program.

1.4 We have stressed the need for an operating system to make efficient use of the computing hardware. When is it appropriate for the operating system to forsake this principle and "waste" resources? Why is such a system not really wasteful?

1.5 What is the main difficulty that a programmer must overcome in writing an operating system for a real-time environment?

1.6 Consider the various definitions of *operating system*. Consider whether the operating system should include applications such as Web browsers and mail programs. Argue both that it should and that it should not, and support your answers.

1.7 How does the distinction between kernel mode and user mode function as a rudimentary form of protection (security) system?

1.8 Which of the following instructions should be privileged?

a.   Set value of timer.

b. Read the clock.

c. Clear memory.

d. Issue a trap instruction.

e. Turn off interrupts.

f. Modify entries in device-status table.

g. Switch from user to kernel mode.

h. Access I/O device.

1.9 Some early computers protected the operating system by placing it in a memory partition that could not be modified by either the user job or the operating system itself. Describe two difficulties that you think could arise with such a scheme.

1.10 Some CPUs provide for more than two modes of operation. What are two possible uses of these multiple modes?

1.11 Timers can be used to compute the current time. Provide a short description of how this could be accomplished.

1.12 Is the Internet a LAN or a WAN?

Exercises

1.13 In a multiprogramming and time-sharing environment, several users share the system simultaneously. This situation can result in various security problems.

a. What are two such problems?

b. Can we ensure the same degree of security in a time-shared machine as in a dedicated machine? Explain your answer.

1.14 The issue of resource utilization shows up in different forms in different types of operating systems. List what resources must be managed carefully in the following settings:

a. Mainframe or minicomputer systems

b. Workstations connected to servers

c. Handheld computers

1.15 Under what circumstances would a user be better off using a time-sharing system rather than a PC or a single-user workstation?

1.16 Identify which of the functionalities listed below need to be supported by the operating system for (a) handheld devices and (b) real-time systems.

a. Batch programming

b. Virtual memory

c. Time sharing

1.17   Describe the differences between symmetric and asymmetric multiprocessing. What are three advantages and one disadvantage of multiprocessor systems?

1.18   How do clustered systems differ from multiprocessor systems? What is required for two machines belonging to a cluster to cooperate to provide a highly available service?

1.19   Distinguish between the client–server and peer-to-peer models of distributed systems.

1.20   Consider a computing cluster consisting of two nodes running a database. Describe two ways in which the cluster software can manage access to the data on the disk. Discuss the benefits and disadvantages of each.

1.21   How are network computers different from traditional personal computers? Describe some usage scenarios in which it is advantageous to use network computers.

1.22   What is the purpose of interrupts? What are the differences between a trap and an interrupt? Can traps be generated intentionally by a user program? If so, for what purpose?

1.23   Direct memory access is used for high-speed I/O devices in order to avoid increasing the CPU's execution load.

    a.   How does the CPU interface with the device to coordinate the transfer?

    b.   How does the CPU know when the memory operations are complete?

    c.   The CPU is allowed to execute other programs while the DMA controller is transferring data. Does this process interfere with the execution of the user programs? If so, describe what forms of interference are caused.

1.24   Some computer systems do not provide a privileged mode of operation in hardware. Is it possible to construct a secure operating system for these computer systems? Give arguments both that it is and that it is not possible.

1.25   Give two reasons why caches are useful. What problems do they solve? What problems do they cause? If a cache can be made as large as the device for which it is caching (for instance, a cache as large as a disk), why not make it that large and eliminate the device?

1.26   Consider an SMP system similar to that shown in Figure 1.6. Illustrate with an example how data residing in memory could in fact have two different values in each of the local caches.

1.27   Discuss, with examples, how the problem of maintaining coherence of cached data manifests itself in the following processing environments:

    a.   Single-processor systems

      b.   Multiprocessor systems

      c.   Distributed systems

1.28 Describe a mechanism for enforcing memory protection in order to prevent a program from modifying the memory associated with other programs.

1.29 What network configuration would best suit the following environments?

      a.   A dormitory floor

      b.   A university campus

      c.   A state

      d.   A nation

1.30 Define the essential properties of the following types of operating systems:

      a.   Batch

      b.   Interactive

      c.   Time sharing

      d.   Real time

      e.   Network

      f.   Parallel

      g.   Distributed

      h.   Clustered

      i.   Handheld

1.31 What are the tradeoffs inherent in handheld computers?

1.32 Identify several advantages and several disadvantages of open-source operating systems. Include the types of users who would find each aspect to be an advantage or a disadvantage.

Bibliographical Notes

Brookshear [2003] provides an overview of computer science in general.

    An overview of the Linux operating system is presented in Bovet and Cesati [2006]. Solomon and Russinovich [2000] give an overview of Microsoft Windows and considerable technical detail about the system internals and components. Russinovich and Solomon [2009] update this information to WinSEVEN. McDougall and Mauro [2007] cover the internals of the Solaris operating system. Mac OS X is presented at http://www.apple.com/macosx. Mac OS X internals are discussed in Singh [2007].

    Coverage of peer-to-peer systems includes Parameswaran et al. [2001], Gong [2002], Ripeanu et al. [2002], Agre [2003], Balakrishnan et al. [2003], and

Loo [2003]. A discussion of peer-to-peer file-sharing systems can be found in Lee [2003]. Good coverage of cluster computing is provided by Buyya [1999]. Recent advances in cluster computing are described by Ahmed [2000]. A survey of issues relating to operating-system support for distributed systems can be found in Tanenbaum and Van Renesse [1985].

Many general textbooks cover operating systems, including Stallings [2000], Nutt [2004], and Tanenbaum [2001].

Hamacher et al. [2002] describe computer organization, and McDougall and Laudon [2006] discuss multicore processors. Hennessy and Patterson [2007] provide coverage of I/O systems and buses, and of system architecture in general. Blaauw and Brooks [1997] describe details of the architecture of many computer systems, including several from IBM. Stokes [2007] provides an illustrated introduction to microprocessors and computer architecture.

Cache memories, including associative memory, are described and analyzed by Smith [1982]. That paper also includes an extensive bibliography on the subject.

Discussions concerning magnetic-disk technology are presented by Freedman [1983] and by Harker et al. [1981]. Optical disks are covered by Kenville [1982], Fujitani [1984], O'Leary and Kitts [1985], Gait [1988], and Olsen and Kenley [1989]. Discussions of floppy disks are offered by Pechura and Schoeffler [1983] and by Sarisky [1983]. General discussions concerning mass-storage technology are offered by Chi [1982] and by Hoagland [1985].

Kurose and Ross [2005] and Tanenbaum [2003] provides general overviews of computer networks. Fortier [1989] presents a detailed discussion of networking hardware and software. Kozierok [2005] discuss TCP in detail. Mullender [1993] provides an overview of distributed systems. Wolf [2003] discusses recent developments in developing embedded systems. Issues related to handheld devices can be found in Myers and Beigl [2003] and Di Pietro and Mancini [2003].

A full discussion of the history of open sourcing and its benefits and challenges is found in Raymond [1999]. The history of hacking is discussed in Levy [1994]. The Free Software Foundation has published its philosophy on its Web site: `http://www.gnu.org/philosophy/free-software-for-freedom.html`. Detailed instructions on how to build the Ubuntu Linux kernel are on `http://www.howtoforge.com/kernel_compilation_ubuntu`. The open-source components of Mac OS X are available from `http://developer.apple.com/open-source/index.html`.

Wikipedia (`http://en.wikipedia.org/wiki/Richard_Stallman`) has an informative entry about Richard Stallman.

The source code of Multics is available at `http://web.mit.edu/multics-history/source/Multics_Internet_Server/Multics_sources.html`.

Operating-System Structures

CHAPTER

2

An operating system provides the environment within which programs are executed. Internally, operating systems vary greatly in their makeup, since they are organized along many different lines. The design of a new operating system is a major task. It is important that the goals of the system be well defined before the design begins. These goals form the basis for choices among various algorithms and strategies.

We can view an operating system from several vantage points. One view focuses on the services that the system provides; another, on the interface that it makes available to users and programmers; a third, on its components and their interconnections. In this chapter, we explore all three aspects of operating systems, showing the viewpoints of users, programmers, and operating-system designers. We consider what services an operating system provides, how they are provided, how they are debugged, and what the various methodologies are for designing such systems. Finally, we describe how operating systems are created and how a computer starts its operating system.

CHAPTER OBJECTIVES

- To describe the services an operating system provides to users, processes, and other systems.
- To discuss the various ways of structuring an operating system.
- To explain how operating systems are installed and customized and how they boot.

2.1 Operating-System Services

An operating system provides an environment for the execution of programs. It provides certain services to programs and to the users of those programs. The specific services provided, of course, differ from one operating system to another, but we can identify common classes. These operating-system services are provided for the convenience of the programmer, to make the programming

47

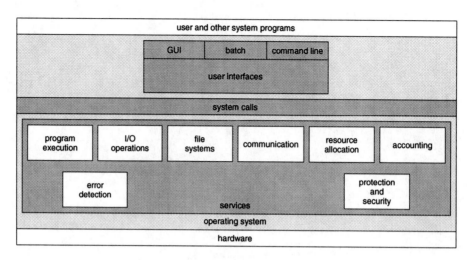

Figure 2.1 A view of operating system services.

task easier. Figure 2.1 shows one view of the various operating-system services and how they interrelate.

One set of operating-system services provides functions that are helpful to the user.

* **User interface**. Almost all operating systems have a user interface (UI). This interface can take several forms. One is a command-line interface (CLI), which uses text commands and a method for entering them (say, a program to allow entering and editing of commands). Another is a batch interface, in which commands and directives to control those commands are entered into files, and those files are executed. Most commonly, a graphical user interface (GUI) is used. Here, the interface is a window system with a pointing device to direct I/O, choose from menus, and make selections and a keyboard to enter text. Some systems provide two or all three of these variations.

* **Program execution**. The system must be able to load a program into memory and to run that program. The program must be able to end its execution, either normally or abnormally (indicating error).

* **I/O operations**. A running program may require I/O, which may involve a file or an I/O device. For specific devices, special functions may be desired (such as recording to a CD or DVD drive or blanking a display screen). For efficiency and protection, users usually cannot control I/O devices directly. Therefore, the operating system must provide a means to do I/O.

* **File-system manipulation**. The file system is of particular interest. Obviously, programs need to read and write files and directories. They also need to create and delete them by name, search for a given file, and list file information. Finally, some programs include permissions management to allow or deny access to files or directories based on file ownership. Many operating systems provide a variety of file systems, sometimes to allow personal choice, and sometimes to provide specific features or performance characteristics.

- **Communications**. There are many circumstances in which one process needs to exchange information with another process. Such communication may occur between processes that are executing on the same computer or between processes that are executing on different computer systems tied together by a computer network. Communications may be implemented via *shared memory* or through *message passing*, in which packets of information are moved between processes by the operating system.

- **Error detection**. The operating system needs to be constantly aware of possible errors. Errors may occur in the CPU and memory hardware (such as a memory error or a power failure), in I/O devices (such as a parity error on tape, a connection failure on a network, or lack of paper in the printer), and in the user program (such as an arithmetic overflow, an attempt to access an illegal memory location, or a too-great use of CPU time). For each type of error, the operating system should take the appropriate action to ensure correct and consistent computing. Of course, there is variation in how operating systems react to and correct errors. Debugging facilities can greatly enhance the user's and programmer's abilities to use the system efficiently.

Another set of operating-system functions exists not for helping the user but rather for ensuring the efficient operation of the system itself. Systems with multiple users can gain efficiency by sharing the computer resources among the users.

- **Resource allocation**. When there are multiple users or multiple jobs running at the same time, resources must be allocated to each of them. Many different types of resources are managed by the operating system. Some (such as CPU cycles, main memory, and file storage) may have special allocation code, whereas others (such as I/O devices) may have much more general request and release code. For instance, in determining how best to use the CPU, operating systems have CPU-scheduling routines that take into account the speed of the CPU, the jobs that must be executed, the number of registers available, and other factors. There may also be routines to allocate printers, modems, USB storage drives, and other peripheral devices.

- **Accounting**. We want to keep track of which users use how much and what kinds of computer resources. This record keeping may be used for accounting (so that users can be billed) or simply for accumulating usage statistics. Usage statistics may be a valuable tool for researchers who wish to reconfigure the system to improve computing services.

- **Protection and security**. The owners of information stored in a multiuser or networked computer system may want to control use of that information. When several separate processes execute concurrently, it should not be possible for one process to interfere with the others or with the operating system itself. Protection involves ensuring that all access to system resources is controlled. Security of the system from outsiders is also important. Such security starts with requiring each user to authenticate himself or herself to the system, usually by means of a password, to gain access to system resources. It extends to defending external I/O devices, including modems and network adapters, from invalid access attempts and to recording all such connections for detection of break-ins. If a system is to be protected and secure, precautions must be instituted throughout it. A chain is only as strong as its weakest link.

2.2 User Operating-System Interface

We mentioned earlier that there are several ways for users to interface with the operating system. Here, we discuss two fundamental approaches. One provides a command-line interface, or command interpreter, that allows users to directly enter commands to be performed by the operating system. The other allows users to interface with the operating system via a graphical user interface, or GUI.

2.2.1 Command Interpreter

Some operating systems include the command interpreter in the kernel. Others, such as Windows and UNIX, treat the command interpreter as a special program that is running when a job is initiated or when a user first logs on (on interactive systems). On systems with multiple command interpreters to choose from, the interpreters are known as shells. For example, on UNIX and Linux systems, a user may choose among several different shells, including the *Bourne shell, C shell, Bourne-Again shell, Korn shell*, and others. Third-party shells and free user-written shells are also available. Most shells provide similar functionality, and a user's choice of which shell to use is generally based on personal preference. Figure 2.2 shows the Bourne shell command interpreter being used on Solaris 10.

The main function of the command interpreter is to get and execute the next user-specified command. Many of the commands given at this level manipulate files: *create, delete, list, print, copy, execute,* and so on. The MS-DOS and UNIX shells operate in this way. These commands can be implemented in two general ways.

In one approach, the command interpreter itself contains the code to execute the command. For example, a command to delete a file may cause the command interpreter to jump to a section of its code that sets up the parameters and makes the appropriate system call. In this case, the number of commands that can be given determines the size of the command interpreter, since each command requires its own implementing code.

An alternative approach—used by UNIX, among other operating systems—implements most commands through system programs. In this case, the command interpreter does not understand the command in any way; it merely uses the command to identify a file to be loaded into memory and executed. Thus, the UNIX command to delete a file

```
rm file.txt
```

would search for a file called `rm`, load the file into memory, and execute it with the parameter `file.txt`. The function associated with the `rm` command would be defined completely by the code in the file `rm`. In this way, programmers can add new commands to the system easily by creating new files with the proper

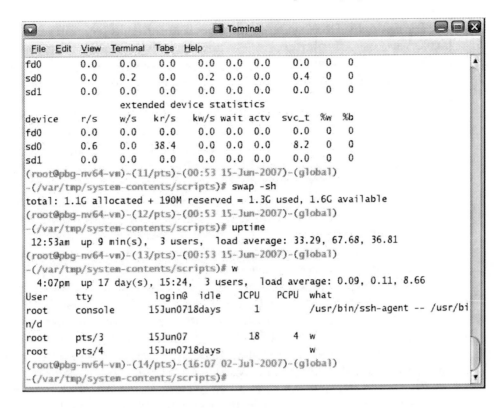

Figure 2.2 The Bourne shell command interpreter in Solaris 10.

names. The command-interpreter program, which can be small, does not have to be changed for new commands to be added.

2.2.2 Graphical User Interfaces

A second strategy for interfacing with the operating system is through a user-friendly graphical user interface, or GUI. Here, rather than entering commands directly via a command-line interface, users employ a mouse-based window-and-menu system characterized by a desktop metaphor. The user moves the mouse to position its pointer on images, or icons, on the screen (the desktop) that represent programs, files, directories, and system functions. Depending on the mouse pointer's location, clicking a button on the mouse can invoke a program, select a file or directory—known as a **folder**—or pull down a menu that contains commands.

Graphical user interfaces first appeared due in part to research taking place in the early 1970s at Xerox PARC research facility. The first GUI appeared on the Xerox Alto computer in 1973. However, graphical interfaces became more widespread with the advent of Apple Macintosh computers in the 1980s. The user interface for the Macintosh operating system (Mac OS) has undergone various changes over the years, the most significant being the adoption of the *Aqua* interface that appeared with Mac OS X. Microsoft's first version of Windows—Version 1.0—was based on the addition of a GUI interface to the MS-DOS operating system. Later versions of Windows have made cosmetic changes in the appearance of the GUI along with several enhancements in its functionality, including Windows Explorer.

Traditionally, UNIX systems have been dominated by command-line interfaces. Various GUI interfaces are available, however, including the Common Desktop Environment (CDE) and X-Windows systems, which are common on commercial versions of UNIX, such as Solaris and IBM's AIX system. In addition, there has been significant development in GUI designs from various open-source projects, such as *K Desktop Environment* (or *KDE*) and the *GNOME* desktop by the GNU project. Both the KDE and GNOME desktops run on Linux and various UNIX systems and are available under open-source licenses, which means their source code is readily available for reading and for modification under specific license terms.

The choice of whether to use a command-line or GUI interface is mostly one of personal preference. As a very general rule, many UNIX users prefer command-line interfaces, as they often provide powerful shell interfaces. In contrast, most Windows users are pleased to use the Windows GUI environment and almost never use the MS-DOS shell interface. The various changes undergone by the Macintosh operating systems provide a nice study in contrast. Historically, Mac OS has not provided a command-line interface, always requiring its users to interface with the operating system using its GUI. However, with the release of Mac OS X (which is in part implemented using a UNIX kernel), the operating system now provides both a new Aqua interface and a command-line interface. Figure 2.3 is a screenshot of the Mac OS X GUI.

The user interface can vary from system to system and even from user to user within a system. It typically is substantially removed from the actual system structure. The design of a useful and friendly user interface is therefore

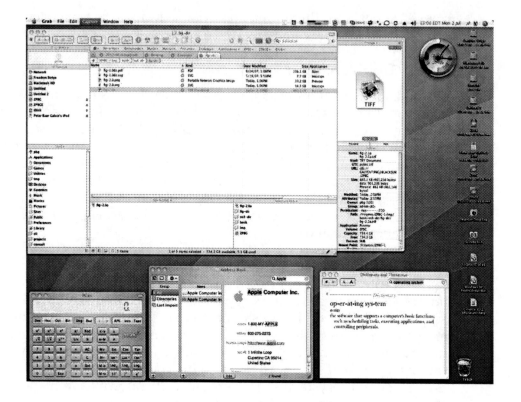

Figure 2.3 The Mac OS X GUI.

not a direct function of the operating system. In this book, we concentrate on the fundamental problems of providing adequate service to user programs. From the point of view of the operating system, we do not distinguish between user programs and system programs.

2.3 System Calls

System calls provide an interface to the services made available by an operating system. These calls are generally available as routines written in C and C++, although certain low-level tasks (for example, tasks where hardware must be accessed directly) may need to be written using assembly-language instructions.

Before we discuss how an operating system makes system calls available, let's first use an example to illustrate how system calls are used: writing a simple program to read data from one file and copy them to another file. The first input that the program will need is the names of the two files: the input file and the output file. These names can be specified in many ways, depending on the operating-system design. One approach is for the program to ask the user for the names of the two files. In an interactive system, this approach will require a sequence of system calls, first to write a prompting message on the screen and then to read from the keyboard the characters that define the two files. On mouse-based and icon-based systems, a menu of file names is usually displayed in a window. The user can then use the mouse to select the source name, and a window can be opened for the destination name to be specified. This sequence requires many I/O system calls.

Once the two file names are obtained, the program must open the input file and create the output file. Each of these operations requires another system call. There are also possible error conditions for each operation. When the program tries to open the input file, it may find that there is no file of that name or that the file is protected against access. In these cases, the program should print a message on the console (another sequence of system calls) and then terminate abnormally (another system call). If the input file exists, then we must create a new output file. We may find that there is already an output file with the same name. This situation may cause the program to abort (a system call), or we may delete the existing file (another system call) and create a new one (another system call). Another option, in an interactive system, is to ask the user (via a sequence of system calls to output the prompting message and to read the response from the terminal) whether to replace the existing file or to abort the program.

Now that both files are set up, we enter a loop that reads from the input file (a system call) and writes to the output file (another system call). Each read and write must return status information regarding various possible error conditions. On input, the program may find that the end of the file has been reached or that there was a hardware failure in the read (such as a parity error). The write operation may encounter various errors, depending on the output device (no more disk space, printer out of paper, and so on).

Finally, after the entire file is copied, the program may close both files (another system call), write a message to the console or window (more system calls), and finally terminate normally (the final system call). As we can see, even simple programs may make heavy use of the operating system. Frequently, systems execute thousands of system calls per second. This system-call sequence is shown in Figure 2.4.

Most programmers never see this level of detail, however. Typically, application developers design programs according to an application programming interface (API). The API specifies a set of functions that are available to an application programmer, including the parameters that are passed to each function and the return values the programmer can expect. Three of the most common APIs available to application programmers are the Win32 API for Windows systems, the POSIX API for POSIX-based systems (which include virtually all versions of UNIX, Linux, and Mac OS X), and the Java API for designing programs that run on the Java virtual machine. Note that—unless specified —the system-call names used throughout this text are generic examples. Each operating system has its own name for each system call.

Behind the scenes, the functions that make up an API typically invoke the actual system calls on behalf of the application programmer. For example, the Win32 function `CreateProcess()` (which unsurprisingly is used to create a new process) actually calls the `NTCreateProcess()` system call in the Windows kernel. Why would an application programmer prefer programming according to an API rather than invoking actual system calls? There are several reasons for doing so. One benefit of programming according to an API concerns program portability: An application programmer designing a program using an API can expect her program to compile and run on any system that supports the same API (although in reality, architectural differences often make this more difficult than it may appear). Furthermore, actual system calls can often be more detailed and difficult to work with than the API available to an application programmer. Regardless, there often exists a strong correlation between a function in the API and its associated system call within the kernel.

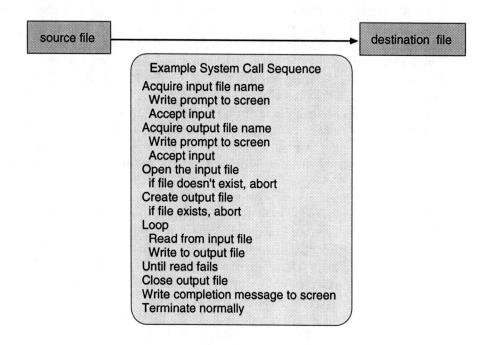

Figure 2.4   Example of how system calls are used.

EXAMPLE OF STANDARD API

As an example of a standard API, consider the `ReadFile()` function in the Win32 API—a function for reading from a file. The API for this function appears in Figure 2.5.

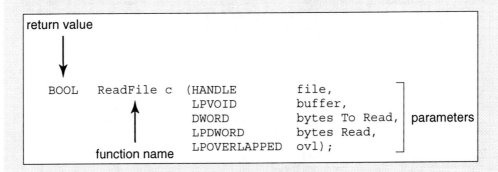

Figure 2.5 The API for the `ReadFile()` function.

A description of the parameters passed to `ReadFile()` is as follows:

* HANDLE file—the file to be read

* LPVOID buffer—a buffer where the data will be read into and written from

* DWORD bytesToRead—the number of bytes to be read into the buffer

* LPDWORD bytesRead—the number of bytes read during the last read

* LPOVERLAPPED ovl—indicates if overlapped I/O is being used

In fact, many of the POSIX and Win32 APIs are similar to the native system calls provided by the UNIX, Linux, and Windows operating systems.

The run-time support system (a set of functions built into libraries included with a compiler) for most programming languages provides a **system-call interface** that serves as the link to system calls made available by the operating system. The system-call interface intercepts function calls in the API and invokes the necessary system calls within the operating system. Typically, a number is associated with each system call, and the system-call interface maintains a table indexed according to these numbers. The system call interface then invokes the intended system call in the operating-system kernel and returns the status of the system call and any return values.

The caller need know nothing about how the system call is implemented or what it does during execution. Rather, it need only obey the API and understand what the operating system will do as a result of the execution of that system call. Thus, most of the details of the operating-system interface are hidden from the programmer by the API and are managed by the run-time support library. The relationship between an API, the system-call interface, and the operating

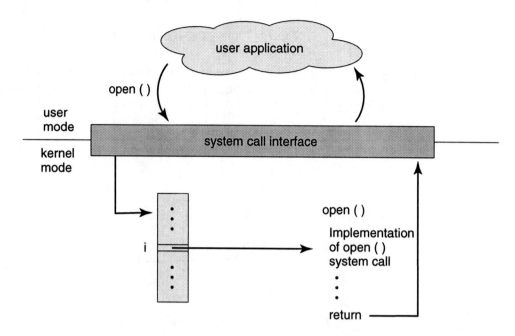

Figure 2.6 The handling of a user application invoking the open() system call.

system is shown in Figure 2.6, which illustrates how the operating system handles a user application invoking the open() system call.

System calls occur in different ways, depending on the computer in use. Often, more information is required than simply the identity of the desired system call. The exact type and amount of information vary according to the particular operating system and call. For example, to get input, we may need to specify the file or device to use as the source, as well as the address and length of the memory buffer into which the input should be read. Of course, the device or file and length may be implicit in the call.

Three general methods are used to pass parameters to the operating system. The simplest approach is to pass the parameters in *registers*. In some cases, however, there may be more parameters than registers. In these cases, the parameters are generally stored in a *block*, or table, in memory, and the address of the block is passed as a parameter in a register (Figure 2.7). This is the approach taken by Linux and Solaris. Parameters also can be placed, or *pushed*, onto the *stack* by the program and *popped* off the stack by the operating system. Some operating systems prefer the block or stack method because those approaches do not limit the number or length of parameters being passed.

2.4 Types of System Calls

System calls can be grouped roughly into six major categories: **process control**, **file manipulation**, **device manipulation**, **information maintenance**, **communications**, and **protection**. In Sections 2.4.1 through 2.4.6, we discuss briefly the types of system calls that may be provided by an operating system. Most of these system calls support, or are supported by, concepts and functions

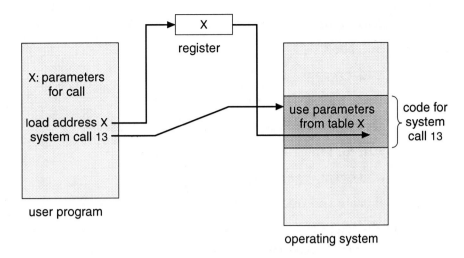

Figure 2.7 Passing of parameters as a table.

that are discussed in later chapters. Figure 2.8 summarizes the types of system calls normally provided by an operating system.

2.4.1 Process Control

A running program needs to be able to halt its execution either normally (end) or abnormally (abort). If a system call is made to terminate the currently running program abnormally, or if the program runs into a problem and causes an error trap, a dump of memory is sometimes taken and an error message generated. The dump is written to disk and may be examined by a debugger—a system program designed to aid the programmer in finding and correcting bugs—to determine the cause of the problem. Under either normal or abnormal circumstances, the operating system must transfer control to the invoking command interpreter. The command interpreter then reads the next command. In an interactive system, the command interpreter simply continues with the next command; it is assumed that the user will issue an appropriate command to respond to any error. In a GUI system, a pop-up window might alert the user to the error and ask for guidance. In a batch system, the command interpreter usually terminates the entire job and continues with the next job. Some systems allow control cards to indicate special recovery actions in case an error occurs. A control card is a batch-system concept. It is a command to manage the execution of a process. If the program discovers an error in its input and wants to terminate abnormally, it may also want to define an error level. More severe errors can be indicated by a higher-level error parameter. It is then possible to combine normal and abnormal termination by defining a normal termination as an error at level 0. The command interpreter or a following program can use this error level to determine the next action automatically.

A process or job executing one program may want to load and execute another program. This feature allows the command interpreter to execute a program as directed by, for example, a user command, the click of a mouse, or a batch command. An interesting question is where to return control when the loaded program terminates. This question is related to the problem of

- Process control
  - end, abort
  - load, execute
  - create process, terminate process
  - get process attributes, set process attributes
  - wait for time
  - wait event, signal event
  - allocate and free memory
- File management
  - create file, delete file
  - open, close
  - read, write, reposition
  - get file attributes, set file attributes
- Device management
  - request device, release device
  - read, write, reposition
  - get device attributes, set device attributes
  - logically attach or detach devices
- Information maintenance
  - get time or date, set time or date
  - get system data, set system data
  - get process, file, or device attributes
  - set process, file, or device attributes
- Communications
  - create, delete communication connection
  - send, receive messages
  - transfer status information
  - attach or detach remote devices

Figure 2.8 Types of system calls.

whether the existing program is lost, saved, or allowed to continue execution concurrently with the new program.

If control returns to the existing program when the new program terminates, we must save the memory image of the existing program; thus, we have effectively created a mechanism for one program to call another program. If both programs continue concurrently, we have created a new job or process to

EXAMPLES OF WINDOWS AND UNIX SYSTEM CALLS

	Windows	**Unix**
Process Control	`CreateProcess()`	`fork()`
	`ExitProcess()`	`exit()`
	`WaitForSingleObject()`	`wait()`
File Manipulation	`CreateFile()`	`open()`
	`ReadFile()`	`read()`
	`WriteFile()`	`write()`
	`CloseHandle()`	`close()`
Device Manipulation	`SetConsoleMode()`	`ioctl()`
	`ReadConsole()`	`read()`
	`WriteConsole()`	`write()`
Information Maintenance	`GetCurrentProcessID()`	`getpid()`
	`SetTimer()`	`alarm()`
	`Sleep()`	`sleep()`
Communication	`CreatePipe()`	`pipe()`
	`CreateFileMapping()`	`shmget()`
	`MapViewOfFile()`	`mmap()`
Protection	`SetFileSecurity()`	`chmod()`
	`InitializeSecurityDescriptor()`	`umask()`
	`SetSecurityDescriptorGroup()`	`chown()`

be multiprogrammed. Often, there is a system call specifically for this purpose (`create process` or `submit job`).

If we create a new job or process, or perhaps even a set of jobs or processes, we should be able to control its execution. This control requires the ability to determine and reset the attributes of a job or process, including the job's priority, its maximum allowable execution time, and so on (`get process attributes` and `set process attributes`). We may also want to terminate a job or process that we created (`terminate process`) if we find that it is incorrect or is no longer needed.

Having created new jobs or processes, we may need to wait for them to finish their execution. We may want to wait for a certain amount of time to pass (`wait time`); more probably, we will want to wait for a specific event to occur (`wait event`). The jobs or processes should then signal when that event has occurred (`signal event`). Quite often, two or more processes may share data. To ensure the integrity of the data being shared, operating systems often provide system calls allowing a process to **lock** shared data, thus preventing another process from accessing the data while it is locked. Typically such system calls include `acquire_lock` and `release_lock`. System calls of these

EXAMPLE OF STANDARD C LIBRARY

The standard C library provides a portion of the system-call interface for many versions of UNIX and Linux. As an example, let's assume a C program invokes the `printf()` statement. The C library intercepts this call and invokes the necessary system call(s) in the operating system—in this instance, the `write()` system call. The C library takes the value returned by `write()` and passes it back to the user program. This is shown in Figure 2.9.

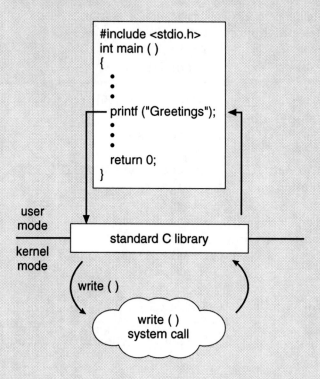

Figure 2.9 Standard C library handling of `write()`.

types, dealing with the coordination of concurrent processes, are discussed in great detail in Chapter 6.

   There are so many facets of and variations in process and job control that we next use two examples—one involving a single-tasking system and the other a multitasking system—to clarify these concepts. The MS-DOS operating system is an example of a single-tasking system. It has a command interpreter that is invoked when the computer is started (Figure 2.10(a)). Because MS-DOS is single-tasking, it uses a simple method to run a program and does not create a new process. It loads the program into memory, writing over most of itself to give the program as much memory as possible (Figure 2.10(b)). Next, it sets the instruction pointer to the first instruction of the program. The program then runs, and either an error causes a trap, or the program executes a system call to terminate. In either case, the error code is saved in the system memory for later use. Following this action, the small portion of the command interpreter that was not overwritten resumes execution. Its first task is to reload the rest

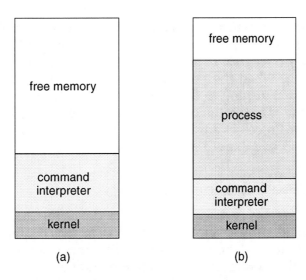

Figure 2.10 MS-DOS execution. (a) At system startup. (b) Running a program.

of the command interpreter from disk. Then the command interpreter makes the previous error code available to the user or to the next program.

FreeBSD (derived from Berkeley UNIX) is an example of a multitasking system. When a user logs on to the system, the shell of the user's choice is run. This shell is similar to the MS-DOS shell in that it accepts commands and executes programs that the user requests. However, since FreeBSD is a multitasking system, the command interpreter may continue running while another program is executed (Figure 2.11). To start a new process, the shell executes a `fork()` system call. Then, the selected program is loaded into memory via an `exec()` system call, and the program is executed. Depending on the way the command was issued, the shell then either waits for the process to finish or runs the process "in the background." In the latter case, the shell immediately requests another command. When a process is running in the background, it cannot receive input directly from the keyboard, because the

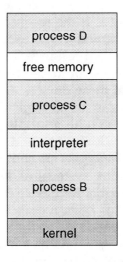

Figure 2.11 FreeBSD running multiple programs.

shell is using this resource. I/O is therefore done through files or through a GUI interface. Meanwhile, the user is free to ask the shell to run other programs, to monitor the progress of the running process, to change that program's priority, and so on. When the process is done, it executes an `exit()` system call to terminate, returning to the invoking process a status code of 0 or a nonzero error code. This status or error code is then available to the shell or other programs. Processes are discussed in Chapter 3 with a program example using the `fork()` and `exec()` system calls.

2.4.2 File Management

The file system is discussed in more detail in Chapters 9 and 10. We can, however, identify several common system calls dealing with files.

We first need to be able to `create` and `delete` files. Either system call requires the name of the file and perhaps some of the file's attributes. Once the file is created, we need to open it and to use it. We may also `read`, `write`, or `reposition` (rewinding or skipping to the end of the file, for example). Finally, we need to `close` the file, indicating that we are no longer using it.

We may need these same sets of operations for directories if we have a directory structure for organizing files in the file system. In addition, for either files or directories, we need to be able to determine the values of various attributes and perhaps to reset them if necessary. File attributes include the file name, file type, protection codes, accounting information, and so on. At least two system calls, `get file attribute` and `set file attribute`, are required for this function. Some operating systems provide many more calls, such as calls for file `move` and `copy`. Others might provide an API that performs those operations using code and other system calls, and others might just provide system programs to perform those tasks. If the system programs are callable by other programs, then each can be considered an API by other system programs.

2.4.3 Device Management

A process may need several resources to execute—main memory, disk drives, access to files, and so on. If the resources are available, they can be granted, and control can be returned to the user process. Otherwise, the process will have to wait until sufficient resources are available.

The various resources controlled by the operating system can be thought of as devices. Some of these devices are physical devices (for example, disk drives), while others can be thought of as abstract or virtual devices (for example, files). A system with multiple users may require us to first `request` the device, to ensure exclusive use of it. After we are finished with the device, we `release` it. These functions are similar to the open and `close` system calls for files. Other operating systems allow unmanaged access to devices. The hazard then is the potential for device contention and perhaps deadlock.

Once the device has been requested and allocated to us, we can `read`, `write`, and (possibly) `reposition` the device, just as we can with files. In fact, the similarity between I/O devices and files is so great that many operating systems, including UNIX, merge the two into a combined file–device structure. In this case, a set of system calls is used on both files and devices. Sometimes,

I/O devices are identified by special file names, directory placement, or file attributes.

The user interface can also make files and devices appear to be similar, even though the underlying system calls are dissimilar. This is another example of the many design decisions that go into building an operating system and user interface.

2.4.4 Information Maintenance

Many system calls exist simply for the purpose of transferring information between the user program and the operating system. For example, most systems have a system call to return the current time and date. Other system calls may return information about the system, such as the number of current users, the version number of the operating system, the amount of free memory or disk space, and so on.

Another set of system calls is helpful in debugging a program. Many systems provide system calls to dump memory. This provision is useful for debugging. A program trace lists each system call as it is executed. Even microprocessors provide a CPU mode known as *single step,* in which a trap is executed by the CPU after every instruction. The trap is usually caught by a debugger.

Many operating systems provide a time profile of a program to indicate the amount of time that the program executes at a particular location or set of locations. A time profile requires either a tracing facility or regular timer interrupts. At every occurrence of the timer interrupt, the value of the program counter is recorded. With sufficiently frequent timer interrupts, a statistical picture of the time spent on various parts of the program can be obtained.

In addition, the operating system keeps information about all its processes, and system calls are used to access this information. Generally, calls are also used to reset the process information (get process attributes and set process attributes). In Section 3.1.3, we discuss what information is normally kept.

2.4.5 Communication

There are two common models of interprocess communication: the message-passing model and the shared-memory model. In the **message-passing model**, the communicating processes exchange messages with one another to transfer information. Messages can be exchanged between the processes either directly or indirectly through a common mailbox. Before communication can take place, a connection must be opened. The name of the other communicator must be known, be it another process on the same system or a process on another computer connected by a communications network. Each computer in a network has a *host name* by which it is commonly known. A host also has a network identifier, such as an IP address. Similarly, each process has a *process name,* and this name is translated into an identifier by which the operating system can refer to the process. The get hostid and get processid system calls do this translation. The identifiers are then passed to the general-purpose open and close calls provided by the file system or to specific open connection and close connection system calls, depending on the system's model of communication. The recipient process usually must give its permission for communication to take place with an `accept connection` call. Most processes that will be receiving connections are special-purpose *daemons*, which are systems programs provided for that purpose. They execute a `wait for connection` call and are awakened when a connection is made. The source of the communication, known as the *client*, and the receiving daemon, known as a *server*, then exchange messages by using `read message` and `write message` system calls. The `close connection` call terminates the communication.

In the **shared-memory model**, processes use `shared memory create` and `shared memory attach` system calls to create and gain access to regions of memory owned by other processes. Recall that, normally, the operating system tries to prevent one process from accessing another process's memory. Shared memory requires that two or more processes agree to remove this restriction. They can then exchange information by reading and writing data in the shared areas. The form of the data is determined by the processes and is not under the operating system's control. The processes are also responsible for ensuring that they are not writing to the same location simultaneously. Such mechanisms are discussed in Chapter 6. In Chapter 4, we look at a variation of the process scheme—threads—in which memory is shared by default.

Both of the models just discussed are common in operating systems, and most systems implement both. Message passing is useful for exchanging smaller amounts of data, because no conflicts need be avoided. It is also easier to implement than is shared memory for intercomputer communication. Shared memory allows maximum speed and convenience of communication, since it can be done at memory transfer speeds when it takes place within a computer. Problems exist, however, in the areas of protection and synchronization between the processes sharing memory.

2.4.6 Protection

Protection provides a mechanism for controlling access to the resources provided by a computer system. Historically, protection was a concern only on multiprogrammed computer systems with several users. However, with the advent of networking and the Internet, all computer systems, from servers to PDAs, must be concerned with protection.

Typically, system calls providing protection include `set permission` and `get permission`, which manipulate the permission settings of resources such as files and disks. The `allow user` and `deny user` system calls specify whether particular users can—or cannot—be allowed access to certain resources.

We cover protection in Chapter 13 and the much larger issue of security in Chapter 14.

2.5 System Programs

Another aspect of a modern system is the collection of system programs. Recall Figure 1.1, which depicted the logical computer hierarchy. At the lowest level is hardware. Next is the operating system, then the system programs, and finally the application programs. **System programs**, also known as **system utilities**, provide a convenient environment for program development and execution.

Some of them are simply user interfaces to system calls; others are considerably more complex. They can be divided into these categories:

* **File management**. These programs create, delete, copy, rename, print, dump, list, and generally manipulate files and directories.

* **Status information**. Some programs simply ask the system for the date, time, amount of available memory or disk space, number of users, or similar status information. Others are more complex, providing detailed performance, logging, and debugging information. Typically, these programs format and print the output to the terminal or other output devices or files or display it in a window of the GUI. Some systems also support a registry, which is used to store and retrieve configuration information.

* **File modification**. Several text editors may be available to create and modify the content of files stored on disk or other storage devices. There may also be special commands to search contents of files or perform transformations of the text.

* **Programming-language support**. Compilers, assemblers, debuggers, and interpreters for common programming languages (such as C, C++, Java, Visual Basic, and PERL) are often provided to the user with the operating system.

* **Program loading and execution**. Once a program is assembled or compiled, it must be loaded into memory to be executed. The system may provide absolute loaders, relocatable loaders, linkage editors, and overlay loaders. Debugging systems for either higher-level languages or machine language are needed as well.

* **Communications**. These programs provide the mechanism for creating virtual connections among processes, users, and computer systems. They allow users to send messages to one another's screens, to browse Web pages, to send electronic-mail messages, to log in remotely, and to transfer files from one machine to another.

In addition to systems programs, most operating systems are supplied with programs that are useful in solving common problems or performing common operations. Such **application programs** include Web browsers, word processors and text formatters, spreadsheets, database systems, compilers, plotting and statistical-analysis packages, and games.

The view of the operating system seen by most users is defined by the application and system programs, rather than by the actual system calls. Consider a user's PC. When a user's computer is running the Mac OS X operating system, the user might see the GUI, featuring a mouse-and-windows interface. Alternatively, or even in one of the windows, the user might have a command-line UNIX shell. Both use the same set of system calls, but the system calls look different and act in different ways. Further confusing the user view, consider the user dual-booting from Mac OS X into Windows Vista. Now the same user on the same hardware has two entirely different interfaces and two sets of applications using the same physical resources. On the same hardware, then, a user can be exposed to multiple user interfaces sequentially or concurrently.

2.6 Operating-System Design and Implementation

In this section, we discuss problems we face in designing and implementing an operating system. There are, of course, no complete solutions to such problems, but there are approaches that have proved successful.

2.6.1 Design Goals

The first problem in designing a system is to define goals and specifications. At the highest level, the design of the system will be affected by the choice of hardware and the type of system: batch, time shared, single user, multiuser, distributed, real time, or general purpose.

Beyond this highest design level, the requirements may be much harder to specify. The requirements can, however, be divided into two basic groups: *user* goals and *system* goals.

Users desire certain obvious properties in a system. The system should be convenient to use, easy to learn and to use, reliable, safe, and fast. Of course, these specifications are not particularly useful in the system design, since there is no general agreement on how to achieve them.

A similar set of requirements can be defined by those people who must design, create, maintain, and operate the system. The system should be easy to design, implement, and maintain; and it should be flexible, reliable, error free, and efficient. Again, these requirements are vague and may be interpreted in various ways.

There is, in short, no unique solution to the problem of defining the requirements for an operating system. The wide range of systems in existence shows that different requirements can result in a large variety of solutions for different environments. For example, the requirements for VxWorks, a real-time operating system for embedded systems, must have been substantially different from those for MVS, a large multiuser, multiaccess operating system for IBM mainframes.

Specifying and designing an operating system is a highly creative task. Although no textbook can tell you how to do it, general principles have been developed in the field of **software engineering**, and we turn now to a discussion of some of these principles.

2.6.2 Mechanisms and Policies

One important principle is the separation of **policy** from **mechanism**. Mechanisms determine *how* to do something; policies determine *what* will be done. For example, the timer construct (see Section 1.5.2) is a mechanism for ensuring CPU protection, but deciding how long the timer is to be set for a particular user is a policy decision.

The separation of policy and mechanism is important for flexibility. Policies are likely to change across places or over time. In the worst case, each change in policy would require a change in the underlying mechanism. A general mechanism insensitive to changes in policy would be more desirable. A change in policy would then require redefinition of only certain parameters of the system. For instance, consider a mechanism for giving priority to certain types of programs over others. If the mechanism is properly separated from policy, it can be used either to support a policy decision that I/O-intensive programs should have priority over CPU-intensive ones or to support the opposite policy.

Microkernel-based operating systems (Section 2.7.3) take the separation of mechanism and policy to one extreme by implementing a basic set of primitive building blocks. These blocks are almost policy free, allowing more advanced mechanisms and policies to be added via user-created kernel modules or via user programs themselves. As an example, consider the history of UNIX. At first, it had a time-sharing scheduler. In the latest version of Solaris, scheduling is controlled by loadable tables. Depending on the table currently loaded, the system can be time shared, batch processing, real time, fair share, or any combination. Making the scheduling mechanism general purpose allows vast policy changes to be made with a single load-new-table command. At the other extreme is a system such as Windows, in which both mechanism and policy are encoded in the system to enforce a global look and feel. All applications have similar interfaces, because the interface itself is built into the kernel and system libraries. The Mac OS X operating system has similar functionality.

Policy decisions are important for all resource allocation. Whenever it is necessary to decide whether or not to allocate a resource, a policy decision must be made. Whenever the question is *how* rather than *what*, it is a mechanism that must be determined.

2.6.3 Implementation

Once an operating system is designed, it must be implemented. Traditionally, operating systems have been written in assembly language. Now, however, they are most commonly written in higher-level languages such as C or C++.

The first system that was not written in assembly language was probably the Master Control Program (MCP) for Burroughs computers. MCP was written in a variant of ALGOL. MULTICS, developed at MIT, was written mainly in PL/1. The Linux and Windows operating systems are written mostly in C, although there are some small sections of assembly code for device drivers and for saving and restoring the state of registers.

The advantages of using a higher-level language, or at least a systems-implementation language, for implementing operating systems are the same as those accrued when the language is used for application programs: the code can be written faster, is more compact, and is easier to understand and debug. In addition, improvements in compiler technology will improve the generated code for the entire operating system by simple recompilation. Finally, an operating system is far easier to *port*—to move to some other hardware—if it is written in a higher-level language. For example, MS-DOS was written in Intel 8088 assembly language. Consequently, it runs natively only on the Intel X86 family of CPUs. (Although MS-DOS runs natively only on Intel X86, emulators of the X86 instruction set allow the operating system to run non-natively— slower, with more resource use—on other CPUs. Emulators are programs that duplicate the functionality of one system with another system.) The Linux operating system, in contrast, is written mostly in C and is available natively on a number of different CPUs, including Intel X86, Sun SPARC, and IBMPowerPC.

The only possible disadvantages of implementing an operating system in a higher-level language are reduced speed and increased storage requirements. These, however, are no longer major issues in today's systems. Although an expert assembly-language programmer can produce efficient small routines, for large programs a modern compiler can perform complex analysis and apply sophisticated optimizations that produce excellent code. Modern processors have deep pipelining and multiple functional units that can handle the details of complex dependencies much more easily than can the human mind.

As is true in other systems, major performance improvements in operating systems are more likely to be the result of better data structures and algorithms than of excellent assembly-language code. In addition, although operating systems are large, only a small amount of the code is critical to high performance; the memory manager and the CPU scheduler are probably the most critical routines. After the system is written and is working correctly, bottleneck routines can be identified and can be replaced with assembly-language equivalents.

2.7   Operating-System Structure

A system as large and complex as a modern operating system must be engineered carefully if it is to function properly and be modified easily. A common approach is to partition the task into small components rather than have one monolithic system. Each of these modules should be a well-defined portion of the system, with carefully defined inputs, outputs, and functions. We have already discussed briefly in Chapter 1 the common components of operating systems. In this section, we discuss how these components are interconnected and melded into a kernel.

2.7.1 Simple Structure

Many commercial operating systems do not have well-defined structures. Frequently, such systems started as small, simple, and limited systems and then grew beyond their original scope. MS-DOS is an example of such a system. It was originally designed and implemented by a few people who had no idea that it would become so popular. It was written to provide the most functionality in the least space, so it was not divided into modules carefully. Figure 2.12 shows its structure.

In MS-DOS, the interfaces and levels of functionality are not well separated. For instance, application programs are able to access the basic I/O routines to write directly to the display and disk drives. Such freedom leaves MS-DOS vulnerable to errant (or malicious) programs, causing entire system crashes when user programs fail. Of course, MS-DOS was also limited by the hardware of its era. Because the Intel 8088 for which it was written provides no dual mode and no hardware protection, the designers of MS-DOS had no choice but to leave the base hardware accessible.

Another example of limited structuring is the original UNIX operating system. Like MS-DOS, UNIX initially was limited by hardware functionality. It consists of two separable parts: the kernel and the system programs. The kernel

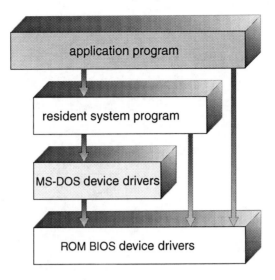

Figure 2.12 MS-DOS layer structure.

is further separated into a series of interfaces and device drivers that have been added and expanded over the years as UNIX has evolved. We can view the traditional UNIX operating system as being layered, as shown in Figure 2.13. Everything below the system-call interface and above the physical hardware is the kernel. The kernel provides the file system, CPU scheduling, memory management, and other operating-system functions through system calls. Taken in sum, that is an enormous amount of functionality to be combined into one level. This monolithic structure was difficult to implement and maintain.

2.7.2 Layered Approach

With proper hardware support, operating systems can be broken into pieces that are smaller and more appropriate than those allowed by the original

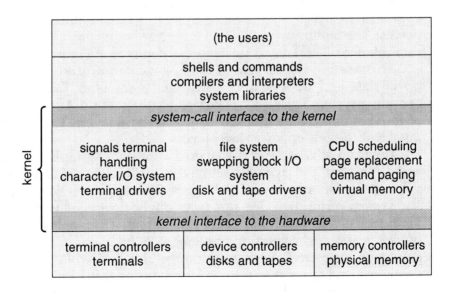

Figure 2.13 Traditional UNIX system structure.

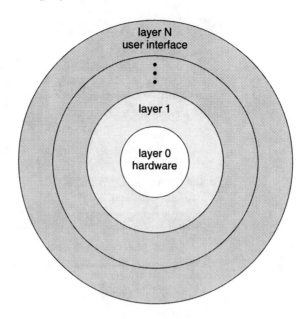

Figure 2.14   A layered operating system.

MS-DOS and UNIX systems. The operating system can then retain much greater control over the computer and over the applications that make use of that computer. Implementers have more freedom in changing the inner workings of the system and in creating modular operating systems. Under a top-down approach, the overall functionality and features are determined and are separated into components. Information hiding is also important, because it leaves programmers free to implement the low-level routines as they see fit, provided that the external interface of the routine stays unchanged and that the routine itself performs the advertised task.

A system can be made modular in many ways. One method is the **layered approach**, in which the operating system is broken into a number of layers (levels). The bottom layer (layer 0) is the hardware; the highest (layer N) is the user interface. This layering structure is depicted in Figure 2.14.

An operating-system layer is an implementation of an abstract object made up of data and the operations that can manipulate those data. A typical operating-system layer—say, layer M—consists of data structures and a set of routines that can be invoked by higher-level layers. Layer M, in turn, can invoke operations on lower-level layers.

The main advantage of the layered approach is simplicity of construction and debugging. The layers are selected so that each uses functions (operations) and services of only lower-level layers. This approach simplifies debugging and system verification. The first layer can be debugged without any concern for the rest of the system, because, by definition, it uses only the basic hardware (which is assumed correct) to implement its functions. Once the first layer is debugged, its correct functioning can be assumed while the second layer is debugged, and so on. If an error is found during the debugging of a particular layer, the error must be on that layer, because the layers below it are already debugged. Thus, the design and implementation of the system are simplified.

Each layer is implemented with only those operations provided by lower-level layers. A layer does not need to know how these operations are implemented; it needs to know only what these operations do. Hence, each layer hides the existence of certain data structures, operations, and hardware from higher-level layers.

The major difficulty with the layered approach involves appropriately defining the various layers. Because a layer can use only lower-level layers, careful planning is necessary. For example, the device driver for the backing store (disk space used by virtual-memory algorithms) must be at a lower level than the memory-management routines, because memory management requires the ability to use the backing store.

Other requirements may not be so obvious. The backing-store driver would normally be above the CPU scheduler, because the driver may need to wait for I/O and the CPU can be rescheduled during this time. However, on a large system, the CPU scheduler may have more information about all the active processes than can fit in memory. Therefore, this information may need to be swapped in and out of memory, requiring the backing-store driver routine to be below the CPU scheduler.

A final problem with layered implementations is that they tend to be less efficient than other types. For instance, when a user program executes an I/O operation, it executes a system call that is trapped to the I/O layer, which calls the memory-management layer, which in turn calls the CPU-scheduling layer, which is then passed to the hardware. At each layer, the parameters may be modified, data may need to be passed, and so on. Each layer adds overhead to the system call; the net result is a system call that takes longer than does one on a nonlayered system.

These limitations have caused a small backlash against layering in recent years. Fewer layers with more functionality are being designed, providing most of the advantages of modularized code while avoiding the difficult problems of layer definition and interaction.

2.7.3 Microkernels

We have already seen that as UNIX expanded, the kernel became large and difficult to manage. In the mid-1980s, researchers at Carnegie Mellon University developed an operating system called **Mach** that modularized the kernel using the **microkernel** approach. This method structures the operating system by removing all nonessential components from the kernel and implementing them as system and user-level programs. The result is a smaller kernel. There is little consensus regarding which services should remain in the kernel and which should be implemented in user space. Typically, however, microkernels provide minimal process and memory management, in addition to a communication facility.

The main function of the microkernel is to provide a communication facility between the client program and the various services that are also running in user space. Communication is provided by *message passing*, which was described in Section 2.4.5. For example, if the client program wishes to access a file, it must interact with the file server. The client program and service never interact directly. Rather, they communicate indirectly by exchanging messages with the microkernel.

One benefit of the microkernel approach is ease of extending the operating system. All new services are added to user space and consequently do not require modification of the kernel. When the kernel does have to be modified, the changes tend to be fewer, because the microkernel is a smaller kernel. The resulting operating system is easier to port from one hardware design to another. The microkernel also provides more security and reliability, since most services are running as user—rather than kernel—processes. If a service fails, the rest of the operating system remains untouched.

Several contemporary operating systems have used the microkernel approach. Tru64 UNIX (formerly Digital UNIX) provides a UNIX interface to the user, but it is implemented with a Mach kernel. The Mach kernel maps UNIX system calls into messages to the appropriate user-level services. The Mac OS X kernel (also known as *Darwin*) is also based on the Mach microkernel.

Another example is QNX, a real-time operating system. The QNX micro-kernel provides services for message passing and process scheduling. It also handles low-level network communication and hardware interrupts. All other services in QNX are provided by standard processes that run outside the kernel in user mode.

Unfortunately, microkernels can suffer from performance decreases due to increased system function overhead. Consider the history of Windows NT. The first release had a layered microkernel organization. However, this version delivered low performance compared with that of Windows 95. Windows NT 4.0 partially redressed the performance problem by moving layers from user space to kernel space and integrating them more closely. By the time Windows XP was designed, its architecture was more monolithic than microkernel.

2.7.4 Modules

Perhaps the best current methodology for operating-system design involves using object-oriented programming techniques to create a modular kernel. Here, the kernel has a set of core components and links in additional services either during boot time or during run time. Such a strategy uses dynamically loadable modules and is common in modern implementations of UNIX, such as Solaris, Linux, and Mac OS X. For example, the Solaris operating system structure, shown in Figure 2.15, is organized around a core kernel with seven types of loadable kernel modules:

1. Scheduling classes
2. File systems
3. Loadable system calls
4. Executable formats
5. STREAMS modules
6. Miscellaneous
7. Device and bus drivers

Such a design allows the kernel to provide core services yet also allows certain features to be implemented dynamically. For example, device and

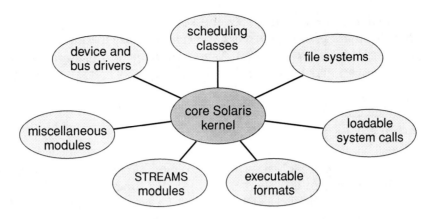

Figure 2.15 Solaris loadable modules.

bus drivers for specific hardware can be added to the kernel, and support for different file systems can be added as loadable modules. The overall result resembles a layered system in that each kernel section has defined, protected interfaces, but it is more flexible than a layered system in that any module can call any other module. Furthermore, the approach is like the microkernel approach in that the primary module has only core functions and knowledge of how to load and communicate with other modules, but it is more efficient, because modules do not need to invoke message passing in order to communicate.

The Apple Mac OS X operating system uses a hybrid structure. It is a layered system in which one layer consists of the Mach microkernel. The structure of Mac OS X appears in Figure 2.16. The top layers include application environments and a set of services providing a graphical interface to applications. Below these layers is the kernel environment, which consists primarily of the Mach microkernel and the BSD kernel. Mach provides memory management; support for remote procedure calls (RPCs) and interprocess communication (IPC) facilities, including message passing; and thread scheduling. The BSD component provides a BSD command line interface, support for networking and file systems, and an implementation of POSIX APIs, including Pthreads.

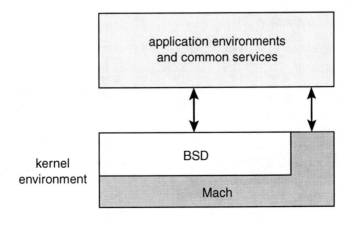

Figure 2.16 The Mac OS X structure.

In addition to Mach and BSD, the kernel environment provides an I/O kit for development of device drivers and dynamically loadable modules (which Mac OS X calls **kernel extensions**). As shown in the figure, applications and common services can make use of either the Mach or BSD facilities directly.

2.8 Virtual Machines

The layered approach described in Section 2.7.2 is taken to its logical conclusion in the concept of a virtual machine. The fundamental idea behind a virtual machine is to abstract the hardware of a single computer (the CPU, memory, disk drives, network interface cards, and so forth) into several different execution environments, thereby creating the illusion that each separate execution environment is running its own private computer.

By using CPU scheduling (Chapter 5) and virtual-memory techniques (Chapter 8), an operating system host can create the illusion that a process has its own processor with its own (virtual) memory. The virtual machine provides an interface that is *identical* to the underlying bare hardware. Each guest process is provided with a (virtual) copy of the underlying computer (Figure 2.17). Usually, the guest process is in fact an operating system, and that is how a single physical machine can run multiple operating systems concurrently, each in its own virtual machine.

2.8.1 History

Virtual machines first appeared commercially on IBM mainframes via the VM operating system in 1972. VM has evolved and is still available, and many of

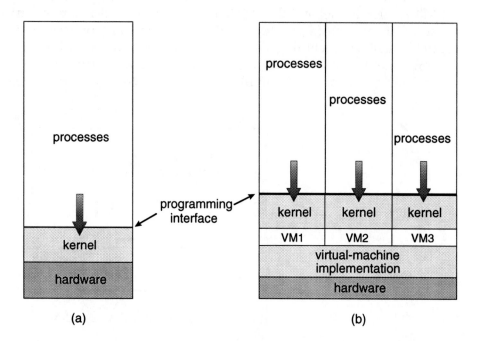

Figure 2.17   System models. (a) Nonvirtual machine. (b) Virtual machine.

the original concepts are found in other systems, making this facility worth exploring.

IBM VM370 divided a mainframe into multiple virtual machines, each running its own operating system. A major difficulty with the VM virtual-machine approach involved disk systems. Suppose that the physical machine had three disk drives but wanted to support seven virtual machines. Clearly, it could not allocate a disk drive to each virtual machine, because the virtual-machine software itself needed substantial disk space to provide virtual memory and spooling. The solution was to provide virtual disks—termed *minidisks* in IBM's VM operating system—that are identical in all respects except size. The system implemented each minidisk by allocating as many tracks on the physical disks as the minidisk needed.

Once these virtual machines were created, users could run any of the operating systems or software packages that were available on the underlying machine. For the IBM VM system, a user normally ran CMS—a single-user interactive operating system.

2.8.2 Benefits

There are several reasons for creating a virtual machine. Most of them are fundamentally related to being able to share the same hardware yet run several different execution environments (that is, different operating systems) concurrently.

One important advantage is that the host system is protected from the virtual machines, just as the virtual machines are protected from each other. A virus inside a guest operating system might damage that operating system but is unlikely to affect the host or the other guests. Because each virtual machine is completely isolated from all other virtual machines, there are no protection problems. At the same time, however, there is no direct sharing of resources. Two approaches to provide sharing have been implemented. First, it is possible to share a file-system volume and thus to share files. Second, it is possible to define a network of virtual machines, each of which can send information over the virtual communications network. The network is modeled after physical communication networks but is implemented in software.

A virtual-machine system is a perfect vehicle for operating-systems research and development. Normally, changing an operating system is a difficult task. Operating systems are large and complex programs, and it is difficult to be sure that a change in one part will not cause obscure bugs to appear in some other part. The power of the operating system makes changing it particularly dangerous. Because the operating system executes in kernel mode, a wrong change in a pointer could cause an error that would destroy the entire file system. Thus, it is necessary to test all changes to the operating system carefully.

The operating system, however, runs on and controls the entire machine. Therefore, the current system must be stopped and taken out of use while changes are made and tested. This period is commonly called *system-development time*. Since it makes the system unavailable to users, system-development time is often scheduled late at night or on weekends, when system load is low.

A virtual-machine system can eliminate much of this problem. System programmers are given their own virtual machine, and system development is done on the virtual machine instead of on a physical machine. Normal system operation seldom needs to be disrupted for system development.

Another advantage of virtual machines for developers is that multiple operating systems can be running on the developer's workstation concurrently. This virtualized workstation allows for rapid porting and testing of programs in varying environments. Similarly, quality-assurance engineers can test their applications in multiple environments without buying, powering, and maintaining a computer for each environment.

A major advantage of virtual machines in production data-center use is system consolidation, which involves taking two or more separate systems and running them in virtual machines on one system. Such physical-to-virtual conversions result in resource optimization, as many lightly used systems can be combined to create one more heavily used system.

If the use of virtual machines continues to spread, application deployment will evolve accordingly. If a system can easily add, remove, and move a virtual machine, then why install applications on that system directly? Instead, application developers could pre-install the application on a tuned and customized operating system in a virtual machine. That virtual environment would be the release mechanism for the application. This method would be an improvement for application developers; application management would become easier, less tuning would required, and technical support of the application would be more straightforward. System administrators would find the environment easier to manage as well. Installation would be simple, and redeploying the application to another system would be much easier than the usual steps of uninstalling and reinstalling. For widespread adoption of this methodology to occur, though, the format of virtual machines must be standardized so that any virtual machine will run on any virtualization platform. The "Open Virtual Machine Format" is an attempt to do just that, and it could succeed in unifying virtual-machine formats.

2.8.3 Simulation

System virtualization as discussed so far is just one of many system-emulation methodologies. Virtualization is the most common because it makes guest operating systems and applications "believe" they are running on native hardware. Because only the system's resources need to be virtualized, these guests run at almost full speed.

Another methodology is simulation, in which the host system has one system architecture and the guest system was compiled for a different architecture. For example, suppose a company has replaced its outdated computer system with a new system but would like to continue to run certain important programs that were compiled for the old system. The programs could be run in an emulator that translates each of the outdated system's instructions into the native instruction set of the new system. Emulation can increase the life of programs and allow us to explore old architectures without having an actual old machine, but its major challenge is performance. Instruction-set emulation can run an order of magnitude slower than native instructions. Thus, unless the new machine is ten times faster than the old, the program running on the new machine will run more slowly than it did on its native hardware. Another challenge is that it is difficult to create a correct emulator because, in essence, this involves writing an entire CPU in software.

2.8.4 Para-virtualization

Para-virtualization is another variation on this theme. Rather than try to trick a guest operating system into believing it has a system to itself, para-virtualization presents the guest with a system that is similar but not identical to the guest's preferred system. The guest must be modified to run on the paravirtualized hardware. The gain for this extra work is more efficient use of resources and a smaller virtualization layer.

Solaris 10 includes containers, or zones, that create a virtual layer between the operating system and the applications. In this system, only one kernel is installed, and the hardware is not virtualized. Rather, the operating system and its devices are virtualized, providing processes within a container with the impression that they are the only processes on the system. One or more containers can be created, and each can have its own applications, network stacks, network address and ports, user accounts, and so on. CPU resources can be divided up among the containers and the systemwide processes. Figure 2.18 shows a Solaris 10 system with two containers and the standard "global" user space.

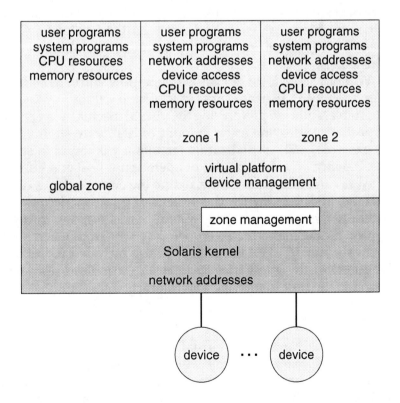

Figure 2.18 Solaris 10 with two containers.

2.8.5 Implementation

Although the virtual-machine concept is useful, it is difficult to implement. Much work is required to provide an *exact* duplicate of the underlying machine. Remember that the underlying machine typically has two modes: user mode and kernel mode. The virtual-machine software can run in kernel mode, since it is the operating system. The virtual machine itself can execute in only user mode. Just as the physical machine has two modes, however, so must the virtual machine. Consequently, we must have a virtual user mode and a virtual kernel mode, both of which run in a physical user mode. Those actions that cause a transfer from user mode to kernel mode on a real machine (such as a system call or an attempt to execute a privileged instruction) must also cause a transfer from virtual user mode to virtual kernel mode on a virtual machine.

Such a transfer can be accomplished as follows. When a system call, for example, is made by a program running on a virtual machine in virtual user mode, it will cause a transfer to the virtual-machine monitor in the real machine. When the virtual-machine monitor gains control, it can change the register contents and program counter for the virtual machine to simulate the effect of the system call. It can then restart the virtual machine, noting that it is now in virtual kernel mode.

The major difference, of course, is time. Whereas the real I/O might have taken 100 milliseconds, the virtual I/O might take less time (because it is spooled) or more time (because it is interpreted). In addition, the CPU is being multiprogrammed among many virtual machines, further slowing down the virtual machines in unpredictable ways. In the extreme case, it may be necessary to simulate all instructions to provide a true virtual machine. VM, discussed earlier, works for IBM machines because normal instructions for the virtual machines can execute directly on the hardware. Only the privileged instructions (needed mainly for I/O) must be simulated and hence execute more slowly.

Without some level of hardware support, virtualization would be impossible. The more hardware support available within a system, the more feature rich, stable, and well performing the virtual machines can be. All major general-purpose CPUs provide some amount of hardware support for virtualization. For example, AMD virtualization technology is found in several AMD processors. It defines two new modes of operation—host and guest. Virtual machine software can enable host mode, define the characteristics of each guest virtual machine, and then switch the system to guest mode, passing control of the system to the guest operating system that is running in the virtual machine. In guest mode, the virtualized operating system thinks it is running on native hardware and sees certain devices (those included in the host's definition of the guest). If the guest tries to access a virtualized resource, then control is passed to the host to manage that interaction.

2.8.6 Examples

Despite the advantages of virtual machines, they received little attention for a number of years after they were first developed. Today, however, virtual machines are coming into fashion as a means of solving system compatibility problems. In this section, we explore two popular contemporary virtual machines: the VMware Workstation and the Java virtual machine. As you will see, these virtual machines can typically run on top of operating systems of any of the design types discussed earlier. Thus, operating system design methods—simple layers, microkernels, modules, and virtual machines—are not mutually exclusive.

2.8.6.1 VMware

Most of the virtualization techniques discussed in this section require virtualization to be supported by the kernel. Another method involves writing the virtualization tool to run in user mode as an application on top of the operating system. Virtual machines running within this tool believe they are running on bare hardware but in fact are running inside a user-level application.

VMware Workstation is a popular commercial application that abstracts Intel X86 and compatible hardware into isolated virtual machines. VMware Workstation runs as an application on a host operating system such as Windows or Linux and allows this host system to concurrently run several different guest operating systems as independent virtual machines.

The architecture of such a system is shown in Figure 2.19. In this scenario, Linux is running as the host operating system and FreeBSD, Windows NT, and Windows XP are running as guest operating systems. The virtualization layer is the heart of VMware, as it abstracts the physical hardware into isolated virtual machines running as guest operating systems. Each virtual machine has its own virtual CPU, memory, disk drives, network interfaces, and so forth.

The physical disk the guest owns and manages is really just a file within the file system of the host operating system. To create an identical guest instance, we can simply copy the file. Copying the file to another location protects the guest instance against a disaster at the original site. Moving the file to another

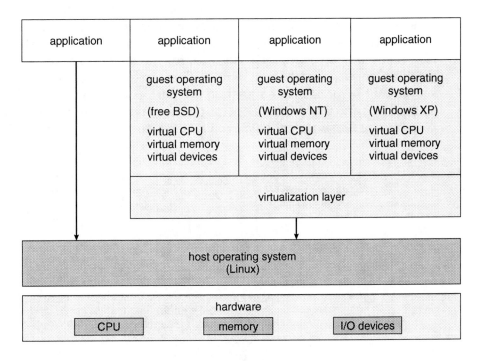

Figure 2.19 VMware architecture.

location moves the guest system. These scenarios show how virtualization can improve the efficiency of system administration as well as system resource use.

2.8.6.2 The Java Virtual Machine

Java is a popular object-oriented programming language introduced by Sun Microsystems in 1995. In addition to a language specification and a large API library, Java also provides a specification for a Java virtual machine—or JVM.

Java objects are specified with the `class` construct; a Java program consists of one or more classes. For each Java class, the compiler produces an architecture-neutral **bytecode** output (`.class`) file that will run on any implementation of the JVM.

The JVM is a specification for an abstract computer. It consists of a **class loader** and a Java interpreter that executes the architecture-neutral bytecodes, as diagrammed in Figure 2.20. The class loader loads the compiled `.class` files from both the Java program and the Java API for execution by the Java interpreter. After a class is loaded, the verifier checks that the `.class` file is valid Java bytecode and does not overflow or underflow the stack. It also ensures that the bytecode does not perform pointer arithmetic, which could provide illegal memory access. If the class passes verification, it is run by the Java interpreter. The JVM also automatically manages memory by performing **garbage collection**—the practice of reclaiming memory from objects no longer in use and returning it to the system. Much research focuses on garbage-collection algorithms for increasing the performance of Java programs in the virtual machine.

The JVM may be implemented in software on top of a host operating system, such as Windows, Linux, or Mac OS X, or as part of a Web browser. Alternatively, the JVM may be implemented in hardware on a chip specifically designed to run Java programs. If the JVM is implemented in software, the Java interpreter interprets the bytecode operations one at a time. A faster software technique is to use a **just-in-time (JIT)** compiler. Here, the first time a Java method is invoked, the bytecodes for the method are turned into native machine language for the host system. These operations are then cached so that subsequent invocations of a method are performed using the native machine instructions and the bytecode operations need not be interpreted all over again. A technique that is potentially even faster is to run the JVM in hardware on a

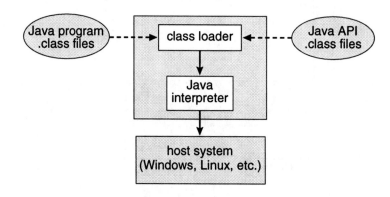

Figure 2.20 The Java virtual machine.

THE .NET FRAMEWORK

The .NET Framework is a collection of technologies, including a set of class libraries, and an execution environment that come together to provide a platform for developing software. This platform allows programs to be written to target the .NET Framework instead of a specific architecture. A program written for the .NET Framework need not worry about the specifics of the hardware or the operating system on which it will run. Thus, any architecture implementing .NET will be able to successfully execute the program. This is because the execution environment abstracts these details and provides a virtual machine as an intermediary between the executing program and the underlying architecture.

At the core of the .NET Framework is the Common Language Runtime (CLR). The CLR is the implementation of the .NET virtual machine. It provides an environment for execution of programs written in any of the languages targeted at the .NET Framework. Programs written in languages such as C# (pronounced *C-sharp*) and VB.NET are compiled into an intermediate, architecture-independent language called Microsoft Intermediate Language (MS-IL). These compiled files, called assemblies, include MS-IL instructions and metadata. They have file extensions of either .EXE or .DLL. Upon execution of a program, the CLR loads assemblies into what is known as the **Application Domain**. As instructions are requested by the executing program, the CLR converts the MS-IL instructions inside the assemblies into native code that is specific to the underlying architecture using just-in-time compilation. Once instructions have been converted to native code, they are kept and will continue to run as native code for the CPU. The architecture of the CLR for the .NET framework is shown in Figure 2.21.

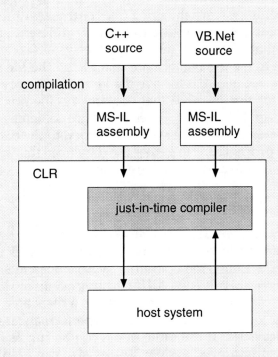

Figure 2.21 Architecture of the CLR for the .NET Framework.

special Java chip that executes the Java bytecode operations as native code, thus bypassing the need for either a software interpreter or a just-in-time compiler.

2.9 Operating-System Debugging

Broadly, debugging is the activity of finding and fixing errors, or bugs, in a system. Debugging seeks to find and fix errors in both hardware and software. Performance problems are considered bugs, so debugging can also include performance tuning, which seeks to improve performance by removing bottlenecks in the processing taking place within a system. A discussion of hardware debugging is outside of the scope of this text. In this section, we explore debugging kernel and process errors and performance problems.

2.9.1 Failure Analysis

If a process fails, most operating systems write the error information to a log file to alert system operators or users that the problem occurred. The operating system can also take a core dump—a capture of the memory (referred to as the "core" in the early days of computing) of the process. This core image is stored in a file for later analysis. Running programs and core dumps can be probed by a debugger, a tool designed to allow a programmer to explore the code and memory of a process.

Debugging user-level process code is a challenge. Operating-system kernel debugging is even more complex because of the size and complexity of the kernel, its control of the hardware, and the lack of user-level debugging tools. A kernel failure is called a crash. As with a process failure, error information is saved to a log file, and the memory state is saved to a crash dump.

Operating system debugging frequently uses different tools and techniques from process debugging due to the very different nature of these two tasks. Consider that a kernel failure in the file-system code would make it risky for the kernel to try to save its state to a file on the file system before rebooting. A common technique is to save the kernel's memory state to a section of disk set aside for this purpose that contains no file system. If the kernel detects an unrecoverable error, it writes the entire contents of memory, or at least the kernel-owned parts of the system memory, to the disk area. When the system reboots, a process runs to gather the data from that area and write it to a crash dump file within a file system for analysis.

2.9.2 Performance Tuning

To identify bottlenecks, we must be able to monitor system performance. Code must be added to compute and display measures of system behavior. In a number of systems, the operating system does this task by producing trace listings of system behavior. All interesting events are logged with their time and important parameters and are written to a file. Later, an analysis program can process the log file to determine system performance and to identify bottlenecks and inefficiencies. These same traces can be run as input for a simulation of a suggested improved system. Traces also can help people to find errors in operating-system behavior.

> **Kernighan's Law**
>
> "Debugging is twice as hard as writing the code in the first place. Therefore, if you write the code as cleverly as possible, you are, by definition, not smart enough to debug it."

Another approach to performance tuning is to include interactive tools with the system that allow users and administrators to question the state of various components of the system to look for bottlenecks. The UNIX command top displays resources used on the system, as well as a sorted list of the "top" resource-using processes. Other tools display the state of disk I/O, memory allocation, and network traffic. The authors of these single-purpose tools try to guess what a user would want to see while analyzing a system and to provide that information.

Making running operating systems easier to understand, debug, and tune is an active area of operating-system research and implementation. The cycle of enabling tracing as system problems occur and analyzing the traces later is being broken by a new generation of kernel-enabled performance analysis tools. Further, these tools are not single-purpose or merely for sections of code that were written to emit debugging data. The Solaris 10 DTrace dynamic tracing facility is a leading example of such a tool.

2.9.3 DTrace

DTrace is a facility that dynamically adds probes to a running system, both in user processes and in the kernel. These probes can be queried via the D programming language to determine an astonishing amount about the kernel, the system state, and process activities. For example, Figure 2.22 follows an application as it executes a system call (ioctl) and further shows the functional calls within the kernel as they execute to perform the system call. Lines ending with "U" are executed in user mode, and lines ending in "K" in kernel mode.

Debugging the interactions between user-level and kernel code is nearly impossible without a toolset that understands both sets of code and can instrument the interactions. For that toolset to be truly useful, it must be able to debug any area of a system, including areas that were not written with debugging in mind, and do so without affecting system reliability. This tool must also have a minimum performance impact—ideally it should have no impact when not in use and a proportional impact during use. The DTrace tool meets these requirements and provides a dynamic, safe, low-impact debugging environment.

Until the DTrace framework and tools became available with Solaris 10, kernel debugging was usually shrouded in mystery and accomplished via happenstance and archaic code and tools. For example, CPUs have a breakpoint feature that will halt execution and allow a debugger to examine the state of the system. Then execution can continue until the next breakpoint or termination. This method cannot be used in a multiuser operating-system kernel without negatively affecting all of the users on the system. Profiling, which periodically samples the instruction pointer to determine which code is being executed, can show statistical trends but not individual activities. Code can be included in the kernel to emit specific data under specific circumstances, but that code

```
# ./all.d `pgrep xclock` XEventsQueued
dtrace: script './all.d' matched 52377 probes
CPU FUNCTION
  0 -> XEventsQueued                         U
  0   -> _XEventsQueued                      U
  0     -> _X11TransBytesReadable            U
  0     <- _X11TransBytesReadable            U
  0     -> _X11TransSocketBytesReadable      U
  0     <- _X11TransSocketBytesreadable      U
  0     -> ioctl                             U
  0       -> ioctl                           K
  0         -> getf                          K
  0           -> set_active_fd               K
  0           <- set_active_fd               K
  0         <- getf                          K
  0         -> get_udatamodel                K
  0         <- get_udatamodel                K
...
  0         -> releasef                      K
  0           -> clear_active_fd             K
  0           <- clear_active_fd             K
  0           -> cv_broadcast                K
  0           <- cv_broadcast                K
  0         <- releasef                      K
  0       <- ioctl                           K
  0     <- ioctl                             U
  0   <- _XEventsQueued                      U
  0 <- XEventsQueued                         U
```

Figure 2.22   Solaris 10 dtrace follows a system call within the kernel.

slows down the kernel and tends not to be included in the part of the kernel where the specific problem being debugged is occurring.

In contrast, DTrace runs on production systems—systems that are running important or critical applications—and causes no harm to the system. It slows activities while enabled, but after execution it resets the system to its pre-debugging state. It is also a broad and deep tool. It can broadly debug everything happening in the system (both at the user and kernel levels and between the user and kernel layers). DTrace can also delve deeply into code, showing individual CPU instructions or kernel subroutine activities.

DTrace is composed of a compiler, a framework, providers of probes written within that framework, and consumers of those probes. DTrace providers create probes. Kernel structures exist to keep track of all probes that the providers have created. The probes are stored in a hash table data structure that is hashed by name and indexed according to unique probe identifiers. When a probe is enabled, a bit of code in the area to be probed is rewritten to call dtrace_probe(probe identifier) and then continue with the code's original operation. Different providers create different kinds of probes. For example, a kernel system-call probe works differently from a user-process probe, and that is different from an I/O probe.

DTrace features a compiler that generates a byte code that is run in the kernel. This code is assured to be "safe" by the compiler. For example, no loops are allowed, and only specific kernel state modifications are allowed when specifically requested. Only users with the DTrace "privileges" (or "root" users) are allowed to use DTrace, as it can retrieve private kernel data (and modify data if requested). The generated code runs in the kernel and enables probes. It also enables consumers in user mode and enables communications between the two.

A DTrace consumer is code that is interested in a probe and its results. A consumer requests that the provider create one or more probes. When a probe fires, it emits data that are managed by the kernel. Within the kernel, actions called enabling control blocks, or ECBs, are performed when probes fire. One probe can cause multiple ECBs to execute if more than one consumer is interested in that probe. Each ECB contains a predicate ("if statement") that can filter out that ECB. Otherwise, the list of actions in the ECB is executed. The most usual action is to capture some bit of data, such as a variable's value at that point of the probe execution. By gathering such data, a complete picture of a user or kernel action can be built. Further, probes firing from both user space and the kernel can show how a user-level action caused kernel-level reactions. Such data are invaluable for performance monitoring and code optimization.

Once the probe consumer terminates, its ECBs are removed. If there are no ECBs consuming a probe, the probe is removed. That involves rewriting the code to remove the dtrace_probe call and put back the original code. Thus, before a probe is created and after it is destroyed, the system is exactly the same, as if no probing occurred.

DTrace takes care to assure that probes do not use too much memory or CPU capacity, which could harm the running system. The buffers used to hold the probe results are monitored for exceeding default and maximum limits. CPU time for probe execution is monitored as well. If limits are exceeded, the consumer is terminated, along with the offending probes. Buffers are allocated per CPU to avoid contention and data loss.

An example of D code and its output shows some of its utility. The following program shows the DTrace code to enable scheduler probes and record the amount of CPU time for each process running with user ID 101 while those probes are enabled (that is, while the program runs):

```
sched:::on-cpu
uid == 101
{
    self->ts = timestamp;
}

sched:::off-cpu
self->ts
{
    @time[execname] = sum(timestamp - self->ts);
    self->ts = 0;
}
```

The output of the program, showing the processes and how much time (in nanoseconds) they spend running on the CPUs, is shown in Figure 2.23.

```
# dtrace -s sched.d
dtrace: script 'sched.d' matched 6 probes
^C
```

gnome-settings-d	142354
gnome-vfs-daemon	158243
dsdm	189804
wnck-applet	200030
gnome-panel	277864
clock-applet	374916
mapping-daemon	385475
xscreensaver	514177
metacity	539281
Xorg	2579646
gnome-terminal	5007269
mixer_applet2	7388447
java	10769137

Figure 2.23   Output of the D code.

Because DTrace is part of the open-source Solaris 10 operating system, it is being added to other operating systems when those systems do not have conflicting license agreements. For example, DTrace has been added to Mac OS X 10.5 and FreeBSD and will likely spread further due to its unique capabilities. Other operating systems, especially the Linux derivatives, are adding kernel-tracing functionality as well. Still other operating systems are beginning to include performance and tracing tools fostered by research at various institutions, including the Paradyn project.

2.10   Operating-System Generation

It is possible to design, code, and implement an operating system specifically for one machine at one site. More commonly, however, operating systems are designed to run on any of a class of machines at a variety of sites with a variety of peripheral configurations. The system must then be configured or generated for each specific computer site, a process sometimes known as **system generation (SYSGEN)**.

The operating system is normally distributed on disk, on CD-ROM or DVD-ROM, or as an "ISO" image, which is a file in the format of a CD-ROM or DVD-ROM. To generate a system, we use a special program. This SYSGEN program reads from a given file, or asks the operator of the system for information concerning the specific configuration of the hardware system, or probes the hardware directly to determine what components are there. The following kinds of information must be determined.

* What CPU is to be used? What options (extended instruction sets, floating-point arithmetic, and so on) are installed? For multiple CPU systems, each CPU may be described.

* How will the boot disk be formatted? How many sections, or "partitions," will it be separated into, and what will go into each partition?

* How much memory is available? Some systems will determine this value themselves by referencing memory location after memory location until an "illegal address" fault is generated. This procedure defines the final legal address and hence the amount of available memory.

* What devices are available? The system will need to know how to address each device (the device number), the device interrupt number, the device's type and model, and any special device characteristics.

* What operating-system options are desired, or what parameter values are to be used? These options or values might include how many buffers of which sizes should be used, what type of CPU-scheduling algorithm is desired, what the maximum number of processes to be supported is, and so on.

Once this information is determined, it can be used in several ways. At one extreme, a system administrator can use it to modify a copy of the source code of the operating system. The operating system then is completely compiled. Data declarations, initializations, and constants, along with conditional compilation, produce an output-object version of the operating system that is tailored to the system described.

At a slightly less tailored level, the system description can lead to the creation of tables and the selection of modules from a precompiled library. These modules are linked together to form the generated operating system. Selection allows the library to contain the device drivers for all supported I/O devices, but only those needed are linked into the operating system. Because the system is not recompiled, system generation is faster, but the resulting system may be overly general.

At the other extreme, it is possible to construct a system that is completely table driven. All the code is always part of the system, and selection occurs at execution time, rather than at compile or link time. System generation involves simply creating the appropriate tables to describe the system.

The major differences among these approaches are the size and generality of the generated system and the ease of modifying it as the hardware configuration changes. Consider the cost of modifying the system to support a newly acquired graphics terminal or another disk drive. Balanced against that cost, of course, is the frequency (or infrequency) of such changes.

2.11 System Boot

After an operating system is generated, it must be made available for use by the hardware. But how does the hardware know where the kernel is or how to load that kernel? The procedure of starting a computer by loading the kernel is known as *booting* the system. On most computer systems, a small piece of code known as the **bootstrap program** or **bootstrap loader** locates the kernel, loads it into main memory, and starts its execution. Some computer systems, such as PCs, use a two-step process in which a simple bootstrap loader fetches a more complex boot program from disk, which in turn loads the kernel.

When a CPU receives a reset event—for instance, when it is powered up or rebooted—the instruction register is loaded with a predefined memory location, and execution starts there. At that location is the initial bootstrap program. This program is in the form of **read-only memory (ROM)**, because the RAM is in an unknown state at system startup. ROM is convenient because it needs no initialization and cannot easily be infected by a computer virus.

The bootstrap program can perform a variety of tasks. Usually, one task is to run diagnostics to determine the state of the machine. If the diagnostics pass, the program can continue with the booting steps. It can also initialize all aspects of the system, from CPU registers to device controllers and the contents of main memory. Sooner or later, it starts the operating system.

Some systems—such as cellular phones, PDAs, and game consoles—store the entire operating system in ROM. Storing the operating system in ROM is suitable for small operating systems, simple supporting hardware, and rugged operation. A problem with this approach is that changing the bootstrap code requires changing the ROM hardware chips. Some systems resolve this problem by using **erasable programmable read-only memory (EPROM)**, which is read-only except when explicitly given a command to become writable. All forms of ROM are also known as **firmware**, since their characteristics fall somewhere between those of hardware and those of software. A problem with firmware in general is that executing code there is slower than executing code in RAM. Some systems store the operating system in firmware and copy it to RAM for fast execution. A final issue with firmware is that it is relatively expensive, so usually only small amounts are available.

For large operating systems (including most general-purpose operating systems like Windows, Mac OS X, and UNIX) or for systems that change frequently, the bootstrap loader is stored in firmware, and the operating system is on disk. In this case, the bootstrap runs diagnostics and has a bit of code that can read a single block at a fixed location (say block zero) from disk into memory and execute the code from that boot block. The program stored in the boot block may be sophisticated enough to load the entire operating system into memory and begin its execution. More typically, it is simple code (as it fits in a single disk block) and knows only the address on disk and length of the remainder of the bootstrap program. GRUB is an example of an open-source bootstrap program for Linux systems. All of the disk-bound bootstrap, and the operating system itself, can be easily changed by writing new versions to disk. A disk that has a boot partition (more on that in Section 11.5.1) is called a **boot disk** or **system disk**.

Now that the full bootstrap program has been loaded, it can traverse the file system to find the operating system kernel, load it into memory, and start its execution. It is only at this point that the system is said to be **running**.

2.12 Summary

Operating systems provide a number of services. At the lowest level, system calls allow a running program to make requests from the operating system directly. At a higher level, the command interpreter or shell provides a mechanism for a user to issue a request without writing a program. Commands may come from files during batch-mode execution or directly from a terminal when in an interactive or time-shared mode. System programs are provided to satisfy many common user requests.

The types of requests vary according to level. The system-call level must provide the basic functions, such as process control and file and device manipulation. Higher-level requests, satisfied by the command interpreter or system programs, are translated into a sequence of system calls. System services can be classified into several categories: program control, status requests, and I/O requests. Program errors can be considered implicit requests for service.

Once the system services are defined, the structure of the operating system can be developed. Various tables are needed to record the information that defines the state of the computer system and the status of the system's jobs.

The design of a new operating system is a major task. It is important that the goals of the system be well defined before the design begins. The type of system desired is the foundation for choices among various algorithms and strategies that will be needed.

Since an operating system is large, modularity is important. Designing a system as a sequence of layers or using a microkernel is considered a good technique. The virtual-machine concept takes the layered approach and treats both the kernel of the operating system and the hardware as though they were hardware. Even other operating systems may be loaded on top of this virtual machine.

Throughout the entire operating-system design cycle, we must be careful to separate policy decisions from implementation details (mechanisms). This separation allows maximum flexibility if policy decisions are to be changed later.

Operating systems are now almost always written in a systems-implementation language or in a higher-level language. This feature improves their implementation, maintenance, and portability. To create an operating system for a particular machine configuration, we must perform system generation.

Debugging process and kernel failures can be accomplished through the use of debuggers and other tools that analyze core dumps. Tools such as DTrace analyze production systems to find bottlenecks and understand other system behavior.

For a computer system to begin running, the CPU must initialize and start executing the bootstrap program in firmware. The bootstrap can execute the operating system directly if the operating system is also in the firmware, or it can complete a sequence in which it loads progressively smarter programs from firmware and disk until the operating system itself is loaded into memory and executed.

Practice Exercises

2.1 What is the purpose of system calls?

2.2 What are the five major activities of an operating system with regard to process management?

2.3 What are the three major activities of an operating system with regard to memory management?

2.4   What are the three major activities of an operating system with regard to secondary-storage management?

2.5   What is the purpose of the command interpreter? Why is it usually separate from the kernel?

2.6   What system calls have to be executed by a command interpreter or shell in order to start a new process?

2.7   What is the purpose of system programs?

2.8   What is the main advantage of the layered approach to system design? What are the disadvantages of the layered approach?

2.9   List five services provided by an operating system, and explain how each creates convenience for users. In which cases would it be impossible for user-level programs to provide these services? Explain your answer.

2.10   Why do some systems store the operating system in firmware, while others store it on disk?

2.11   How could a system be designed to allow a choice of operating systems from which to boot? What would the bootstrap program need to do?

Exercises

2.12   The services and functions provided by an operating system can be divided into two main categories. Briefly describe the two categories and discuss how they differ.

2.13   Describe three general methods for passing parameters to the operating system.

2.14   Describe how you could obtain a statistical profile of the amount of time spent by a program executing different sections of its code. Discuss the importance of obtaining such a statistical profile.

2.15   What are the five major activities of an operating system with regard to file management?

2.16   What are the advantages and disadvantages of using the same system-call interface for manipulating both files and devices?

2.17   Would it be possible for the user to develop a new command interpreter using the system-call interface provided by the operating system?

2.18   What are the two models of interprocess communication? What are the strengths and weaknesses of the two approaches?

2.19   Why is the separation of mechanism and policy desirable?

2.20   It is sometimes difficult to achieve a layered approach if two components of the operating system are dependent on each other. Identify a scenario in which it is unclear how to layer two system components that require tight coupling of their functionalities.

2.21   What is the main advantage of the microkernel approach to system design? How do user programs and system services interact in a microkernel architecture? What are the disadvantages of the microkernel approach?

2.22   In what ways is the modular kernel approach similar to the layered approach? In what ways does it differ from the layered approach?

2.23   What is the main advantage for an operating-system designer of using a virtual-machine architecture? What is the main advantage for a user?

2.24   Why is a just-in-time compiler useful for executing Java programs?

2.25   What is the relationship between a guest operating system and a host operating system in a system like VMware? What factors need to be considered in choosing the host operating system?

2.26   The experimental Synthesis operating system has an assembler incorporated in the kernel. To optimize system-call performance, the kernel assembles routines within kernel space to minimize the path that the system call must take through the kernel. This approach is the antithesis of the layered approach, in which the path through the kernel is extended to make building the operating system easier. Discuss the pros and cons of the Synthesis approach to kernel design and system-performance optimization.

Programming Problems

2.27   In Section 2.3, we described a program that copies the contents of one file to a destination file. This program works by first prompting the user for the name of the source and destination files. Write this program using either the Win32 or POSIX API. Be sure to include all necessary error checking, including ensuring that the source file exists.

Once you have correctly designed and tested the program, if you used a system that supports it, run the program using a utility that traces system calls. Linux systems provide the `ptrace` utility, and Solaris systems use the `truss` or `dtrace` command. On Mac OS X, the `ktrace` facility provides similar functionality. As Windows systems do not provide such features, you will have to trace through the Win32 version of this program using a debugger.

Programming Projects

Adding a system call to the Linux kernel.

In this project, you will study the system-call interface provided by the Linux operating system and learn how user programs communicate with the operating system kernel via this interface. Your task is to incorporate a new system call into the kernel, thereby expanding the functionality of the operating system.

Part 1: Getting Started

A user-mode procedure call is performed by passing arguments to the called procedure either on the stack or through registers, saving the current state and the value of the program counter, and jumping to the beginning of the code corresponding to the called procedure. The process continues to have the same privileges as before.

System calls appear as procedure calls to user programs but result in a change in execution context and privileges. In Linux on the Intel 386 architecture, a system call is accomplished by storing the system-call number into the EAX register, storing arguments to the system call in other hardware registers, and executing a trap instruction (which is the INT 0x80 assembly instruction). After the trap is executed, the system-call number is used to index into a table of code pointers to obtain the starting address for the handler code implementing the system call. The process then jumps to this address, and the privileges of the process are switched from user to kernel mode. With the expanded privileges, the process can now execute kernel code, which may include privileged instructions that cannot be executed in user mode. The kernel code can then carry out the requested services, such as interacting with I/O devices, and can perform process management and other activities that cannot be performed in user mode.

The system call numbers for recent versions of the Linux kernel are listed in `/usr/src/linux-2.x/include/asm-i386/unistd.h`. (For instance, `__NR_close` corresponds to the system call `close()`, which is invoked for closing a file descriptor and is defined as value 6.) The list of pointers to system-call handlers is typically stored in the file `/usr/src/linux-2.x/arch/i386/kernel/entry.S` under the heading `ENTRY(sys_call_table)`. Notice that `sys_close` is stored at entry number 6 in the table to be consistent with the system-call number defined in the `unistd.h` file. (The keyword `.long` denotes that the entry will occupy the same number of bytes as a data value of type `long`.)

Part 2: Building a New Kernel

Before adding a system call to the kernel, you must familiarize yourself with the task of building the binary for a kernel from its source code and booting the machine with the newly built kernel. This activity comprises the following tasks, some of which depend on the particular installation of the Linux operating system in use.

* Obtain the kernel source code for the Linux distribution. If the source code package has already been installed on your machine, the corresponding files may be available under `/usr/src/linux` or `/usr/src/linux-2.x` (where the suffix corresponds to the kernel version number). If the package has not yet been installed, it can be downloaded from the provider of your Linux distribution or from `http://www.kernel.org`.

* Learn how to configure, compile, and install the kernel binary. This will vary among the different kernel distributions, but some typical commands for building the kernel (after entering the directory where the kernel source code is stored) include:

- ○ `make xconfig`

- ○ `make dep`

- ○ `make bzImage`

* Add a new entry to the set of bootable kernels supported by the system. The Linux operating system typically uses utilities such as `lilo` and `grub` to maintain a list of bootable kernels from which the user can choose during machine boot-up. If your system supports `lilo`, add an entry to `lilo.conf`, such as:

```
image=/boot/bzImage.mykernel
label=mykernel
root=/dev/hda5
read-only
```

where `/boot/bzImage.mykernel` is the kernel image and `mykernel` is the label associated with the new kernel. This step will allow you to choose the new kernel during the boot-up process. You will then have the option of either booting the new kernel or booting the unmodified kernel if the newly built kernel does not function properly.

Part 3: Extending the Kernel Source

You can now experiment with adding a new file to the set of source files used for compiling the kernel. Typically, the source code is stored in the `/usr/src/linux-2.x/kernel` directory, although that location may differ in your Linux distribution. There are two options for adding the system call. The first is to add the system call to an existing source file in this directory. The second is to create a new file in the source directory and modify `/usr/src/linux-2.x/kernel/Makefile` to include the newly created file in the compilation process. The advantage of the first approach is that when you modify an existing file that is already part of the compilation process, the Makefile need not be modified.

Part 4: Adding a System Call to the Kernel

Now that you are familiar with the various background tasks corresponding to building and booting Linux kernels, you can begin the process of adding a new system call to the Linux kernel. In this project, the system call will have limited functionality; it will simply transition from user mode to kernel mode, print a message that is logged with the kernel messages, and transition back to user mode. We will call this the *helloworld* system call. While it has only limited functionality, it illustrates the system-call mechanism and sheds light on the interaction between user programs and the kernel.

* Create a new file called `helloworld.c` to define your system call. Include the header files `linux/linkage.h` and `linux/kernel.h`. Add the following code to this file:

```
#include <linux/linkage.h>
#include <linux/kernel.h>
asmlinkage int sys_helloworld() {
  printk(KERN_EMERG "hello world!");

  return 1;
}
```

This creates a system call with the name sys_helloworld(). If you choose to add this system call to an existing file in the source directory, all that is necessary is to add the sys_helloworld() function to the file you choose. In the code, asmlinkage is a remnant from the days when Linux used both C++ and C code and is used to indicate that the code is written in C. The printk() function is used to print messages to a kernel log file and therefore may be called only from the kernel. The kernel messages specified in the parameter to printk() are logged in the file /var/log/kernel/warnings. The function prototype for the printk() call is defined in /usr/include/linux/kernel.h.

* Define a new system call number for _NR_helloworld in /usr/src/linux-2.x/include/asm-i386/unistd.h. A user program can use this number to identify the newly added system call. Also be sure to increment the value for _NR_syscalls, which is stored in the same file. This constant tracks the number of system calls currently defined in the kernel.

* Add an entry .long sys_helloworld to the sys_call_table defined in the /usr/src/linux-2.x/arch/i386/kernel/entry.S file. As discussed earlier, the system-call number is used to index into this table to find the position of the handler code for the invoked system call.

* Add your file helloworld.c to the Makefile (if you created a new file for your system call.) Save a copy of your old kernel binary image (in case there are problems with your newly created kernel). You can now build the new kernel, rename it to distinguish it from the unmodified kernel, and add an entry to the loader configuration files (such as lilo.conf). After completing these steps, you can boot either the old kernel or the new kernel that contains your system call.

Part 5: Using the System Call from a User Program

When you boot with the new kernel, it will support the newly defined system call; you now simply need to invoke this system call from a user program. Ordinarily, the standard C library supports an interface for system calls defined for the Linux operating system. As your new system call is not linked into the standard C library, however, invoking your system call will require manual intervention.

As noted earlier, a system call is invoked by storing the appropriate value in a hardware register and performing a trap instruction. Unfortunately, these low-level operations cannot be performed using C language statements and instead require assembly instructions. Fortunately, Linux provides macros for instantiating wrapper functions that contain the appropriate assembly instructions. For instance, the following C program uses the _syscall0() macro to invoke the newly defined system call:

```
#include <linux/errno.h>
#include <sys/syscall.h>
#include <linux/unistd.h>

_syscall0(int, helloworld);

main()
{
    helloworld();
}
```

* The _syscall0 macro takes two arguments. The first specifies the type of the value returned by the system call; the second is the name of the system call. The name is used to identify the system-call number that is stored in the hardware register before the trap instruction is executed. If your system call requires arguments, then a different macro (such as _syscall0, where the suffix indicates the number of arguments) could be used to instantiate the assembly code required for performing the system call.

* Compile and execute the program with the newly built kernel. There should be a message "hello world!" in the kernel log file /var/log/kernel/warnings to indicate that the system call has executed.

As a next step, consider expanding the functionality of your system call. How would you pass an integer value or a character string to the system call and have it printed into the kernel log file? What are the implications of passing pointers to data stored in the user program's address space as opposed to simply passing an integer value from the user program to the kernel using hardware registers?

Bibliographical Notes

Dijkstra [1968] advocated the layered approach to operating-system design. Brinch-Hansen [1970] was an early proponent of constructing an operating system as a kernel (or nucleus) on which more complete systems can be built.

System instrumentation and dynamic tracing are described in Tamches and Miller [1999]. DTrace is discussed in Cantrill et al. [2004]. The DTrace source code is available at http://src.opensolaris.org/source/. Cheung and Loong [1995] explore issues of operating-system structure from microkernel to extensible systems.

MS-DOS, Version 3.1, is described in Microsoft [1986]. Windows NT and Windows 2000 are described by Solomon [1998] and Solomon and Russinovich [2000]. WinSEVEN internals are described in Russinovich and Solomon [2009]. Hart [2005] covers Windows systems programming in detail. BSD UNIX is described in McKusick et al. [1996]. Bovet and Cesati [2006] thoroughly discuss the Linux kernel. Several UNIX systems—including Mach—are treated in detail in Vahalia [1996]. Mac OS X is presented at `http://www.apple.com/macosx` and in Singh [2007]. Solaris is fully described in McDougall and Mauro [2007].

The first operating system to provide a virtual machine was the CP/67 on an IBM 360/67. The commercially available IBM VM/370 operating system was derived from CP/67. Details regarding Mach, a microkernel-based operating system, can be found in Young et al. [1987]. Kaashoek et al. [1997] present details regarding exokernel operating systems, wherein the architecture separates management issues from protection, thereby giving untrusted software the ability to exercise control over hardware and software resources.

The specifications for the Java language and the Java virtual machine are presented by Gosling et al. [1996] and by Lindholm and Yellin [1999], respectively. The internal workings of the Java virtual machine are fully described by Venners [1998]. Golm et al. [2002] highlight the JX operating system; Back et al. [2000] cover several issues in the design of Java operating systems. More information on Java is available on the Web at `http://www.javasoft.com`. Details about the implementation of VMware can be found in Sugerman et al. [2001]. Information about the Open Virtual Machine Format can be found at `http://www.vmware.com/appliances/learn/ovf.html`.

MODULE 2: Windows Operating System

Introducing, Installing, and Upgrading Windows 7

EXAM OBJECTIVE MATRIX

SKILLS/CONCEPTS	MTA EXAM OBJECTIVE DESCRIPTION	MTA EXAM OBJECTIVE NUMBER
Identifying Windows Operating System Editions	Identify Windows operating system editions.	2.1
Identifying Upgrade Paths	Identify upgrade paths.	2.2
	Identify Windows operating system editions.	2.1
Identifying Application Compatibility	Identify upgrade paths.	2.2
Understanding Product Identification Keys	Understand installation types.	2.3
Understanding Installation Types	Understand installation types.	2.3

KEY TERMS

32-bit computer

64-bit computer

activation

application compatibility

CD key

cloud

custom installation

High Touch Installation (HTI)

image

Lite Touch Installation (LTI)

product key

upgrade installation

upgrade path

Windows 7

Windows 7 Enterprise

Windows 7 Home Basic

Windows 7 Home Premium

Windows 7 Professional

Windows 7 Starter

Windows 7 Ultimate

Windows 7 Upgrade Advisor

Windows Deployment Services

Window Easy Transfer

Zero Touch Installation (ZTI)

1

You work as an IT technician for Interstate Snacks, Inc., a mid-market food service and vending company. Management has decided to standardize on Windows 7 Professional and has asked your IT group to evaluate all existing computers to determine if they can support the operating system. Any newly acquired computers should have Windows 7 Professional installed. You need to learn as much as possible about Windows 7 system requirements, types of installations, and upgrade paths.

■ Identifying Windows Operating System Editions

THE BOTTOM LINE

Windows 7 is the latest Windows client operating system by Microsoft. This operating system runs on desktop computers, workstations, laptops, and other computers. It was preceded by Microsoft Windows Vista and, before that, Windows XP.

Windows 7 is a desktop operating system and is an improvement over both Windows Vista and Windows XP in many ways: it's faster and easier to install and set up, it's more stable, it has improved Start menu search functionality, and lots more. Windows 7 includes some terrific new features as well, such as large and animated task thumbnails, homegroups, Jump Lists, libraries, and Windows XP Mode, all of which you'll learn about in this course.

If you've used Windows Vista, the Windows 7 interface should seem highly familiar. However, it's a big leap from Windows XP to Windows 7.

Regardless of your experience with Windows operating systems, one thing hasn't changed—Microsoft offers a variety of editions to serve the needs of different users and markets.

The following are the six main editions of Windows 7:

- Windows 7 Starter
- Windows 7 Home Basic
- Windows 7 Home Premium
- Windows 7 Professional
- Windows 7 Enterprise
- Windows 7 Ultimate

There are some common threads throughout all editions. For example, every edition contains the same integrated applications, such as Network and Sharing Center, Control Panel, and Windows Media Player. The different editions also include many of the same multimedia features. All editions support 32-bit systems, and all editions except Windows 7 Starter support 64-bit systems. (You'll learn about 32-bit and 64-bit systems later in the lesson.)

Of the six editions, only Home Premium, Professional, and Ultimate are widely available in the retail sector. The other editions are designed for certain types of computers or markets, or specifically for enterprise use.

Starter is a low-cost edition designed for small notebook PCs such as netbooks. Home Basic is sold in emerging markets (such as China, Mexico, and Russia), but not in the United States or Canada. Home Premium emphasizes the multimedia experience and is geared toward home users, students, and small office/home office (SOHO) users. The Professional and Enterprise editions include additional security features and are designed to meet the needs of the business sector. Professional is recommended for small businesses, and Enterprise is recommended for mid- and large-sized businesses. Ultimate includes all of the features offered in Windows 7.

➕ **MORE INFORMATION**

For more information about Windows 7 and its various editions, visit http://windows.microsoft.com/en-US/windows7/products/home and http://windows.microsoft.com/en-US/windows7/products/compare

Windows 7 Home Premium, Professional, and Ultimate

The most commonly used Windows 7 editions are Home Premium, Professional, and Ultimate. In this section, you'll learn about the key differences between these popular operating systems.

TAKE NOTE*

A "domain" is a collection of user and computer accounts that are grouped together to enable centralized management and to apply security. Small Windows environments might use workgroups rather than domains. You'll learn about workgroups, domains, and other networking topics in Lesson 4.

All Windows 7 editions are based on a foundational feature set, and each edition includes some unique features. The following are descriptions of the most common retail editions of Windows 7:

- *Windows 7 Home Premium* contains features aimed at the home market segment, such as Windows Aero, Windows Media Center, Remote Media Streaming, Internet TV, Backup and Restore, and multi-touch support. This edition provides adequate networking and security features to be useful in small office environments.
- *Windows 7 Professional* is targeted mainly toward small business users but appeals to power users as well. It includes all the features of Windows 7 Home Premium and adds the ability to join a Windows domain. Additional features include location-aware printing, acting as a Remote Desktop host (especially useful for tech support), Encrypting File System, and Windows XP Mode.
- *Windows 7 Ultimate* contains all of the same features as Windows 7 Home Premium and Windows 7 Professional, but also includes the applications BitLocker and AppLocker (which are advanced security features). Home Premium and Professional users may upgrade to Ultimate for a fee using Windows Anytime Upgrade.

Table 1-1 compares some features of Windows 7 Home Premium, Professional, and Ultimate.

Table 1-1

Comparing a Subset of Features of Windows 7 Home Premium, Professional, and Ultimate

WINDOWS 7 FEATURE	HOME PREMIUM	PROFESSIONAL	ULTIMATE
Aero interface	Yes	Yes	Yes
Windows Media Center	Yes	Yes	Yes
Backup and Restore	Yes	Yes	Yes
Windows Anytime Upgrade	Yes	Yes	No
Back up to network	No	Yes	Yes
Location-aware printing	No	Yes	Yes
Remote Desktop Host	No	Yes	Yes
Encrypting File System	No	Yes	Yes
Windows XP Mode	No	Yes	Yes
Support for joining domains	No	Yes	Yes
BitLocker and AppLocker	No	No	Yes

Other Windows 7 Editions: Starter, Home Basic, and Enterprise

Some Windows 7 editions—Windows 7 Starter, Home Basic, and Enterprise—don't have a large retail presence for a variety of reasons. These include limited functionality, geographical restrictions, or a focus on larger business environments.

You won't find the following Windows editions on a retail shelf but they nonetheless fill a demand niche:

- *Windows 7 Starter* is available only as a pre-installed operating system on netbook-class PCs. This edition is designed to run well with relatively low memory and disk space. It does not include some Windows 7 features such as 64-bit system support, the Windows Aero theme, or Windows domain support for business users. Because it's essentially a stripped down version of Windows 7 Home Premium, Windows 7 Starter is built mainly for mobile users who only need to browse the Internet, check e-mail, and use a word processor or spreadsheet program.

- *Windows 7 Home Basic* supports the Windows Aero theme but does not include all Aero features. This edition is not available to North American users or those in other "developed technology markets" (such as Australia, Western and Central Europe, Hong Kong, or Saudi Arabia). Microsoft controls the geographical restrictions through the activation process (discussed later in this lesson). If you attempt to activate a computer running Home Basic in a country or region that's restricted from use, the activation process fails.

- *Windows 7 Enterprise* is geared toward enterprise environments. This edition contains all of the same features as Windows 7 Ultimate, but unlike the Ultimate edition, it is not available to home users on an individual license basis. Enterprise is available only through special corporate licensing agreements. Companies must have a Software Assurance Agreement with Microsoft to purchase software licenses. As a result, it includes benefits that are unique to the Software Assurance program, such as allowing operation of diskless PCs (nodes) and running multiple virtual machines.

32-Bit Computing versus 64-Bit Computing

The terms 32-bit and 64-bit refer to the way a computer's central processing unit (CPU) processes data. One of the significant differences is that a 64-bit computer can use much more random access memory (RAM) than a 32-bit computer. Operating systems also come in 32-bit and 64-bit versions, and it's important to match the correct operating system to its corresponding computer processor.

More memory and a faster processor helps an operating system run more efficiently, especially when running multiple programs or graphics-intensive applications. The end user has a much better computing experience using a computer that has ample memory.

A *32-bit computer*, also designated as x86, can use up to 4 gigabytes (GB) of RAM. A *64-bit computer*, often designated as x64, can handle much more RAM—the maximum is limited by the computer's motherboard. For example, Windows 7 Home Premium supports up to 8 GB of memory, which is typically the maximum the motherboard supports on new computers designed for the Windows 7 Home Premium market. If you install Windows 7 Professional, Ultimate, or Enterprise on the same computer, although they support up to 192 GB of memory, the motherboard will still use only 8 GB even if you try to install more memory.

TAKE NOTE*

Some computers have a 64-bit-capable processor, which is a 32-bit processor that can run 64-bit user-mode code.

TAKE NOTE *

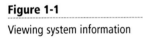

To check for the latest drivers, run Windows Update or go to Device Manager, double-click a specific hardware component, and click Update Driver on the Driver tab in the Properties dialog box. You can also visit the manufacturer's Web site and download the latest driver.

You can run a 32-bit operating system on a 64-bit computer, but you generally cannot run a 64-bit version of Windows on a 32-bit computer. (There are exceptions but they rarely apply nowadays.) In addition, a 64-bit computer requires 64-bit drivers for all of the hardware components. If you run a mix of 32-bit and 64-bit systems in an enterprise environment, you will need both types of drivers for networked printers, scanners, projectors, and other shared devices. You will also need to maintain multiple images—at least one image for the 32-bit computers and one for the 64-bit computers. An *image* is an exact replica of a computer system. You can use an image to quickly install an operating system with applications to a computer or to restore a crashed computer. You'll learn about images later in this lesson and in Lesson 8.

Finally, many computers today have multi-core processors. A 32-bit version of Windows 7 supports up to 32 processor cores; a 64-bit version of Windows 7 supports up to 256 processor cores.

DETERMINE IF YOUR PC IS RUNNING 32-BIT WINDOWS OR 64-BIT WINDOWS

GET READY. To find out if your computer is running a 32-bit or 64-bit version of Windows 7 or Windows Vista, perform the following steps:

1. Click the **Start** button, right-click **Computer**, and then click **Properties**. The System window displays.
2. Look in the System area to view the system type (see Figure 1-1).

Figure 1-1

Viewing system information

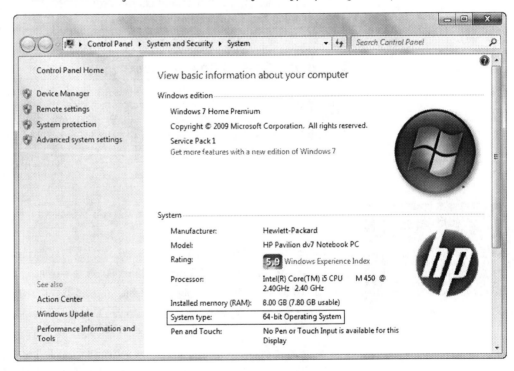

An alternative method is to check the System Information window. To do so, perform the following steps:

1. Click the **Start** button, type **system info** in the **Search programs and files** search box, and then click **System Information** in the resulting list.
2. Make sure **System Summary** is selected in the navigation pane on the left.
3. Look at the **System Type** value in the right pane (see Figure 1-2):
   - **x86-based PC** displays for a 32-bit operating system
   - **x64-based PC** displays for a 64-bit operating system

Figure 1-2

Viewing the System Type value on the System Information page

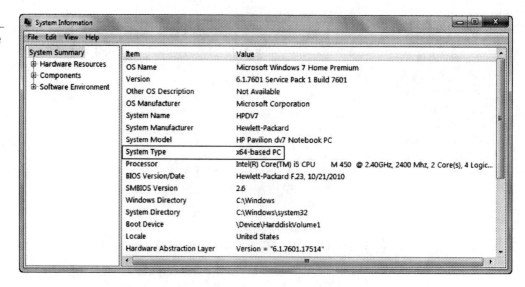

To check the operating system version in Windows XP:

1. Click **Start**.

2. Right-click **My Computer** and choose **Properties**. If "x64 Edition" is not listed, you're running the 32-bit version of Windows XP.

Windows 7 System Requirements

> Software manufacturers, including Microsoft, list the system requirements needed to run their products. The specifications are usually minimum requirements; recommended requirements—which allow for much better performance of the OS and applications—are often much higher (in the case of memory, processor speed, or hard disk space) or involve more recent technology.

CERTIFICATION READY
What is the minimum amount of RAM a computer must have in order to run Windows 7 on a 32-bit processor?
2.1

According to Microsoft, a computer that will run Windows 7 must meet the following system requirements:

- 1 gigahertz (GHz) or faster 32-bit (x86) or 64-bit (x64) processor
- 1 gigabyte (GB) RAM (32-bit) or 2 GB RAM (64-bit)
- 16 GB available hard disk space (32-bit) or 20 GB (64-bit)
- DirectX 9 graphics device with Windows Display Driver Model (WDDM) 1.0 or higher driver

Hardware specifications usually mean the software will run but might not result in an optimal user experience. When preparing to run Windows 7, it's best to exceed the processor, RAM, and hard disk space requirements, if possible. For example, a user who wants to simultaneously run a Web browser, an e-mail client, and productivity software (such as a word processor and a spreadsheet application) will have a good user experience on a computer with a 2 GHz processor, 4 GB of RAM, and at least a 250 GB hard drive. A user who needs to run memory-intensive graphic programs along with other applications will find the computer highly responsive with at least 8 GB of RAM and 500 GB or more of hard disk space. Computers that don't have access to shared storage space on a network may also need secondary storage, such as an external flash hard drive. This is especially important if the user has a large number of image, video, or audio files, which tend to consume much more disk space than ordinary document files.

In addition, Microsoft lists the following items as required for using specific features or for optimal performance:

- Internet access (be aware that you may need to pay for the service)
- Additional memory and advanced graphics hardware for video playback, depending on the resolution required or desired
- A graphics card compatible with DirectX 10 or higher for certain games and programs; DirectX enhances the multimedia capabilities of a computer by enabling the graphics card to process some multimedia functions rather than the CPU.
- A TV tuner and additional hardware for some Windows Media Center functionality
- Specific hardware for Windows Touch and Tablet PCs
- A network and PCs running Windows 7 for HomeGroup utilization
- A compatible optical drive to burn DVDs/CDs
- Trusted Platform Module (TPM) 1.2 for BitLocker; TPM is a security chip on some motherboards that helps protect a computer from being used when the computer has been lost, stolen, or attacked by a hacker.
- A universal serial bus (USB) flash drive for BitLocker To Go
- An additional 1 GB of RAM and an additional 15 GB of available hard disk space for Windows XP Mode
- Audio output for music and sound

If you're not sure whether your computer will run Windows 7, see the "Using Windows 7 Upgrade Advisor" section in this lesson.

TAKE NOTE*

Remember, some features of Windows 7, such as BitLocker, do not ship with every version of Windows 7.

+ MORE INFORMATION

For more information about the Windows 7 system requirements, visit http://windows.microsoft.com/en-US/windows7/products/system-requirements

■ Identifying Upgrade Paths

THE BOTTOM LINE

Can you upgrade to Windows 7 from your current operating system? If so, what type of upgrade you can perform? Those answers depend on many factors. Learn about Windows 7 upgrade paths to fully understand your options.

CERTIFICATION READY
What type of upgrade path is necessary for upgrading from Windows Vista to Windows 7?
2.2

A retail version of Windows 7 is available as a full version or an upgrade version. You install the full version on a clean hard disk. You should purchase an upgrade version if your computer is currently running Windows XP or Windows Vista. The full and upgrade versions are essentially the same—they have the same features and integrated programs.

In the context of this lesson, an *upgrade path* is the set of options you have to upgrade from one Windows operating system to another. When upgrading to Windows 7 from Windows Vista, you have two primary choices: a standard upgrade or a custom installation. Windows XP users must perform a custom installation when "upgrading" to Windows 7.

An *upgrade installation* replaces your current version of Windows with Windows 7 while retaining your files, settings, and programs. This type of installation is sometimes called an "in-place" installation. A *custom installation* replaces your current version of Windows with Windows 7 but overwrites your files, settings, and programs. This is also referred to as a "clean" installation.

TAKE NOTE*

You can use the upgrade or full version of Windows 7 to perform either a custom or upgrade installation. Regardless of the type of installation you plan to perform, you should first back up the files and settings on the computer to be upgraded as a safety precaution. Backups are covered in Lesson 8.

Table 1-2 shows the upgrade paths to Windows 7 Home Premium, Professional, and Ultimate.

Table 1-2

Windows 7 Upgrade Paths for Home Premium, Professional, and Ultimate

UPGRADING FROM	TO HOME PREMIUM	TO PROFESSIONAL	TO ULTIMATE
Windows XP	Custom	Custom	Custom
Windows Vista Home Basic	Upgrade	Custom	Upgrade
Windows Vista Home Premium	Upgrade	Custom	Upgrade
Windows Vista Business	Custom	Upgrade	Upgrade
Windows Vista Ultimate	Custom	Custom	Upgrade

+ MORE INFORMATION

For more information about upgrading to Windows 7, visit http://windows.microsoft.com/en-US/windows7/products/upgrade and http://windows.microsoft.com/en-US/windows7/upgrading-to-windows-7-frequently-asked-questions

Upgrade Paths from Windows XP

You don't have a lot of choices when upgrading from Windows XP. However, you can ease the process by following a few tips.

To upgrade from Windows XP to Windows 7, you must perform a custom installation. Because your files, programs, and settings will be overwritten, *back up all of your data files first*. A best practice is to create at least two backups and test both of them before proceeding with the upgrade.

You should also ensure you have the original installation media or downloaded installation files for all of the programs you plan to install after you upgrade to Windows 7.

You may be able to use Windows Easy Transfer to "move" files and settings from Windows XP to Windows 7. See the "Using Windows Easy Transfer" section in this lesson.

Upgrade Paths from Windows Vista

The upgrade path you must take from Windows Vista to Windows 7 depends on some key factors—mainly your current edition of Windows Vista and the edition of Windows 7 you want to run. There are a few other considerations too, such as 32-bit versus 64-bit environment and desired language.

If you want to upgrade from Windows Vista to Windows 7, knowing which version of Windows 7 to select can be daunting. The type of installation you perform—custom or upgrade—will depend on the edition of Windows Vista you're currently running and the edition of Windows 7 you want to install.

The main point to remember is that you can perform an upgrade installation if you're installing an equivalent or higher edition of Windows 7. Otherwise, you must perform a custom installation. Refer back to Table 1-2 to see which editions of Windows Vista map to which editions of Windows 7.

Here are some other situations that require a custom installation:

- If you're currently running a 32-bit version of Windows Vista and want to install a 64-bit version of Windows 7, or vice versa
- If you plan to use a different language in Windows 7 than the language you're using in Windows Vista

Upgrading directly to Windows 7 from Windows Vista can be a relatively quick and easy task. Your files, settings, and programs are preserved, which means you can be productive soon after the installation completes. Because a custom installation doesn't preserve your files, settings, and programs, you will need to spend some time installing programs and configuring Windows 7 after the upgrade.

 UPGRADE FROM WINDOWS VISTA TO WINDOWS 7

GET READY. To perform an upgrade installation from Windows Vista, perform the following steps:

1. In Windows Vista, start the upgrade installation:

   From a download: Locate the Windows 7 installation file and double-click it.

   From disc or USB flash drive: Insert the disc into your computer. If Setup doesn't start automatically, click **Start**, click **Computer**, double-click your disc or drive icon, and then double-click **setup.exe**.

2. On the Install Windows screen, click **Install now**.

3. On the Get important updates for installation screen, get the latest updates. Your computer must be connected to the Internet.

4. On the Please read the license terms screen, accept the license terms and click **Next**.

5. On the Which type of installation do you want? screen, click **Upgrade**.

6. Follow the instructions to finish installing Windows 7.

TAKE NOTE ✱ Once your computer restarts, you should check that your data files are accessible and that peripherals are working as expected. You may also want to personalize the desktop in Windows 7.

Upgrade Paths from Other Operating Systems

You can upgrade from one Windows 7 edition to an advanced edition fairly easily. Going from an old edition of Windows, such as Windows 95 or Windows 2000, to Windows 7 requires the purchase of a full version of Windows 7 and a custom installation.

To upgrade to Windows 7 from Windows 95 or Windows 2000, you need to purchase a full version of Windows 7 and perform a custom installation. You cannot "upgrade" from a non-Windows operating system such as UNIX, Linux, or Mac OS.

However, you can easily upgrade from one edition of Windows 7 to a more advanced edition using Windows Anytime Upgrade. Upgrading in this manner preserves your files, settings, and programs, so you can be up and running within minutes. Table 1-3 shows you the Windows 7 upgrade paths using Windows Anytime Upgrade.

Table 1-3

Windows Anytime Upgrade Options

Upgrade From	To Home Premium	To Professional	To Ultimate
Windows 7 Starter	Yes	Yes	Yes
Windows 7 Home Premium	No	Yes	Yes
Windows 7 Professional	No	No	Yes

To perform this type of in-place upgrade, you must buy an upgrade key from Microsoft or your preferred retailer.

Windows Anytime Upgrade (see Figure 1-3) will upgrade a 32-bit version of Windows 7 to a 32-bit version of Windows 7 and a 64-bit version to a 64-bit version. You cannot use Windows Anytime Upgrade when going from a 32-bit to a 64-bit version or vice versa.

Figure 1-3

The Windows Anytime Upgrade main window

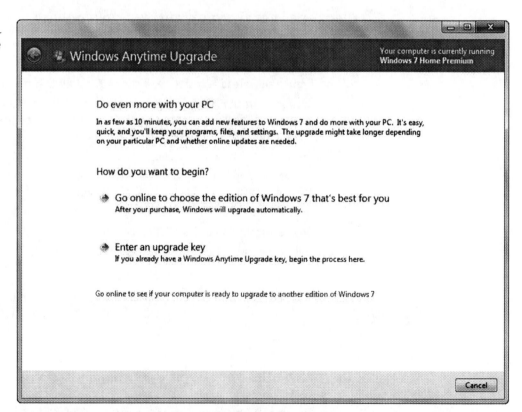

TAKE NOTE * Run Windows 7 Upgrade Advisor before purchasing an upgrade key to ensure your system is ready for the upgrade.

Once you install Windows 7 on a computer, all of the features for all editions of Windows 7 are stored on your computer. When you use Windows Anytime Upgrade to upgrade to an advanced edition of Windows 7, you are simply unlocking the features of that edition.

Using Windows 7 Upgrade Advisor

Windows 7 Upgrade Advisor helps you determine if your computer can run Windows 7, which editions and features will work, and whether your computer has any compatibility issues. You may download the utility for free from the Microsoft Web site at http://windows.microsoft.com/en-US/windows/downloads/upgrade-advisor

CERTIFICATION READY
What tool is used to check your computer's hardware, attached devices, and installed programs for compatibility issues with Windows 7?
2.1

If you've been running Windows Vista on your computer without any hardware problems, you'll probably be able to run Windows 7 too. The two operating systems run well on similar equipment. Upgrading from Windows XP to Windows 7 may result in more compatibility issues simply because the equipment may be older.

You should find out ahead of time if you need to upgrade hardware components or peripherals. *Windows 7 Upgrade Advisor* is a good preparation tool that checks your computer's hardware, attached devices, and installed programs for compatibility issues with Windows 7. The tool creates reports that list potential issues, such as an incompatible printer or a legacy application, and either recommends solutions or points to resources for further information. You also find out which version of Windows 7 is best for your computer.

INSTALL WINDOWS 7 UPGRADE ADVISOR

GET READY. To download and install Windows 7 Upgrade Advisor, perform the following steps:

1. Using a Web browser, go to the Windows 7 Upgrade Advisor Web page at http://windows.microsoft.com/en-us/windows/downloads/upgrade-advisor
2. Click the **Download** button to begin the download process. You may have to click two Download buttons on two different pages (just follow the on-screen instructions).
3. In the dialog box that displays, click **Save** and then save the setup file to a folder on your computer, such as the Downloads folder.
4. Open the folder and double-click **Windows7UpgradeAdvisorSetup.exe**.
5. If a Security Warning dialog box displays, click **Run** when prompted to start the installer.

TAKE NOTE *
If prompted to provide an administrator password or to click a button to continue, do so.

TAKE NOTE *
You might be prompted to install .NET Framework or another program before continuing. Click Yes to install the program and follow the prompts. If using Windows XP, you may need to log on as an administrator to complete the installation.

6. The Windows 7 Upgrade Advisor Setup Wizard starts. Accept the license terms and then click **Install**.
7. When the installation is complete, click **Close**.

RUN WINDOWS 7 UPGRADE ADVISOR

GET READY. To run Windows 7 Upgrade Advisor and scan your computer for upgrade and compatibility issues, perform the following steps:

1. Plug in and power on external hard disks, printers, or any other peripheral devices that you use regularly with your computer.
2. Click **Start > All Programs > Windows 7 Upgrade Advisor**. The Windows 7 Upgrade Advisor window displays, as shown in Figure 1-4. (This example shows Windows 7 Upgrade Advisor running in Windows XP.)

The Windows 7 Upgrade
Advisor window

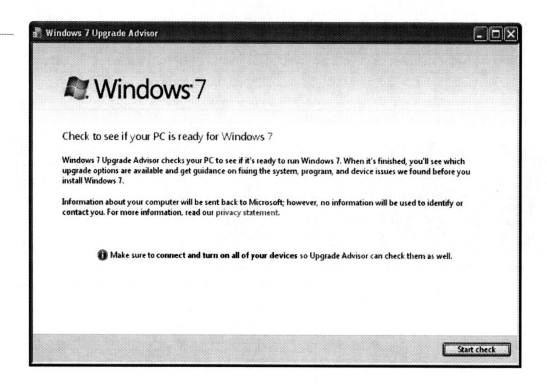

If prompted to provide
an administrator pass-
word or to click a but-
ton to continue, do so.

3. Click the **Start check** button to begin the scan process.
4. While the Upgrade Advisor scans your computer, you can click the displayed links to learn more about Windows 7 and compatibility issues. See Figure 1-5.

Figure 1-5

Upgrade Advisor provides
learning links while the scan is
underway

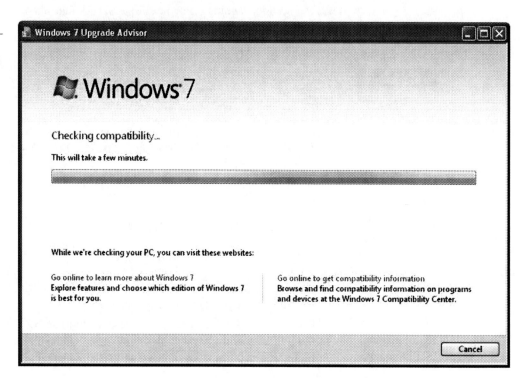

5. When the scan is complete, Upgrade Advisor displays the results of the scan. Parts of an example report are shown in Figure 1-6 and Figure 1-7.

Figure 1-6

The results of an Upgrade Advisor scan (displaying software issues)

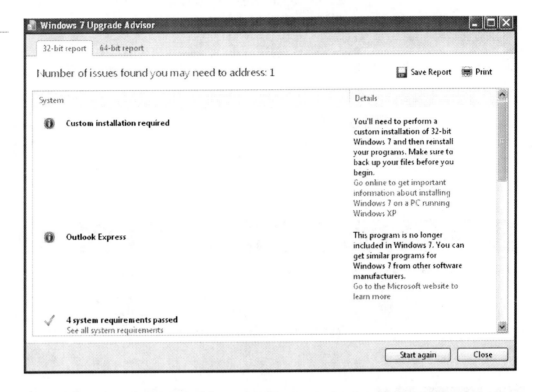

Figure 1-7

The results of an Upgrade Advisor scan (displaying device issues)

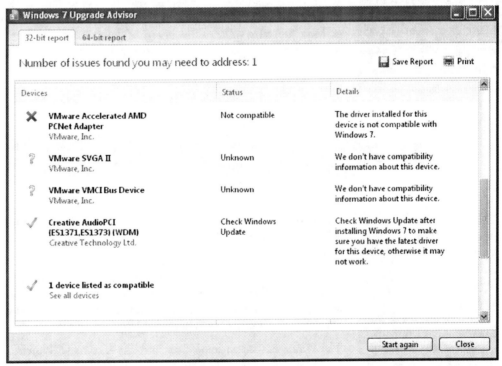

6. Click on any live links that appear in the window to see whether Upgrade Advisor has identified solutions to specific problems or to get more information about an action to be taken.

7. Print or save the list of the actions you must perform to install or upgrade Windows 7. To save the list, click the **Save Report** button.

8. In the **File name** text box, type a name for the report file and then click **Save**.

9. Click **Close** to close Upgrade Advisor.

Based on the results of the Windows 7 Upgrade Advisor scan, you should know which issues, if any, you'll encounter when you install or upgrade to Windows 7 on your computer.

➕ MORE INFORMATION

For more information about Windows 7 Upgrade Advisor and to download the program, visit http://windows. microsoft.com/en-US/windows/downloads/upgrade-advisor

■ Identifying Application Compatibility

↓
THE BOTTOM LINE

Operating system upgrades can result in one or more programs not working properly or not working at all. To identify and resolve issues, use the resources available at the Windows 7 Compatibility Center online as well as the Windows 7 Application Compatibility List for IT Professionals.

CERTIFICATION READY
What are two resources that help you identify and resolve application compatibility issues?
2.2

When you upgrade from one version of Windows to another (for example, from Windows XP or Windows Vista to Windows 7), the potential for *application compatibility* issues arises. Most programs will run fine in any of the operating systems, but some won't. For example, some programs might often crash or freeze, or they might not start at all.

TAKE NOTE*

Antivirus programs tend to be highly specific to operating system versions. You should usually upgrade your antivirus software when upgrading your operating system.

X REF

Windows XP Mode is built into some editions of Windows 7. It lets you run legacy programs in a virtual environment to avoid compatibility issues. You'll learn about Windows XP Mode in Lesson 2.

Two resources to help you identify and resolve application compatibility issues are the Windows 7 Compatibility Center and the Windows 7 Application Compatibility List for IT Professionals.

The Windows 7 Compatibility Center (see Figure 1-8) provides software programs, updates, downloads, drivers, and more that are compatible with Windows 7. Browse this site in advance of upgrading to Windows 7. You can also use this site to research software issues you encounter while using the Windows 7 Upgrade Advisor.

The Windows 7 Application Compatibility List for IT Professionals is a downloadable Microsoft Excel spreadsheet that lists commonly used programs, whether they are 32-bit or 64-bit, and information on compatibility. You can download this spreadsheet at http://www. microsoft.com/download/en/details.aspx?displaylang=en&id=2394. Much of the information in the spreadsheet is a result of the Windows 7 Logo Program, which tests software to determine if it meets Windows 7 requirements.

Figure 1-8

The Windows 7 Compatibility
Center web site

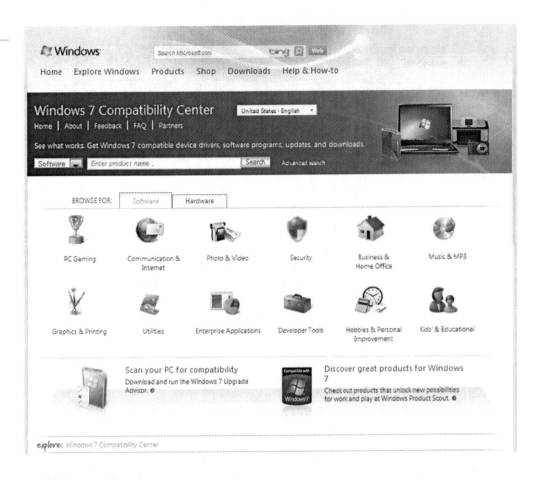

➕ MORE INFORMATION

For more information about application compatibility with Windows 7, visit the Windows 7 Compatibility Center
at http://www.microsoft.com/windows/compatibility/windows-7/en-us/default.aspx. The Windows 7 Application
Compatibility List for IT Professionals may be downloaded from http://www.microsoft.com/download/en/details.
aspx?displaylang=en&id=2394

■ Understanding Product Identification Keys

THE BOTTOM LINE

A product key is essential to installing any Windows operating system. This digital key
ensures you have a legal installation of the Windows software.

CERTIFICATION READY
What term is used
to describe a unique,
alphanumeric code
required by many
software programs
during installation?
2.3

The product identification key, often called a ***product key*** or ***CD key***, is a unique, alphanumeric code required by many software programs during installation. The purpose of a product
key is to help avoid illegal product installations. The product key you enter during Windows 7
installation is checked by Microsoft for legitimacy and whether it is already being used on a
different computer.

When you buy a retail copy of Windows 7, 32-bit and 64-bit versions are included on the same installation media. The product key you enter during setup determines which version of Windows 7 is installed.

A Windows 7 product key looks similar to xxxxx-xxxxx-xxxxx-xxxxx-xxxxx, but is composed of letters and numbers. It is usually located:

- On the installation disc holder inside the Windows package
- On a sticker on the back or bottom of your computer if the operating system came pre-installed on the computer
- In a confirmation e-mail if you purchased and downloaded Windows 7 online

During installation, you must enter the product key exactly as printed. (If you are off by even one character the installation fails.) After you enter the product key correctly, the product key is then written to the Windows registry in an encrypted format, making it unreadable for security purposes. Therefore, it's important to keep your Windows 7 installation media and printed product key in a safe location after initial installation, in case you need to reinstall or repair the operating system at some point.

If you lose your product key, contact Microsoft to request a replacement key.

After a certain period of time post-installation, you will need to activate Windows 7 to continue using the operating system.

You can use the same product key to install Windows on many different computers. However, to meet legal requirements, you won't be able to activate Windows on more than one computer at a time or for the number of computers for which you own Windows licenses. Other software companies, such as Adobe, use this method of product control as well.

Activating Windows 7

Microsoft uses activation to prevent the use of counterfeit copies or otherwise illegal use of its software products, including Windows 7. You must activate Windows 7 within 30 days of installation.

Activation is the process of verifying that your copy of Windows is genuine and that it is not in use on other computers than the number for which you own a license. If you purchased a single copy of Windows 7 from a retailer, for example, you can activate the software on only one computer at a time. Within 30 days of installing Windows 7, activate the software over the Web or by calling Microsoft. Once your Windows 7 installation is activated, you can use all features of the operating system.

If you installed Windows 7 on another computer, you must deactivate it on the original computer before activating it on the other computer. Deactivation may require a call to Microsoft Technical Support.

Registration is different from activation. You *must* activate an installation of Windows 7 but registration is optional. During registration, you give your contact information to Microsoft to sign up for technical support and other benefits.

■ Understanding Installation Types

There are many different types of Windows 7 installations, from the manual DVD method to a fully automated setup effort over a network. Learn the various ways in which you can install Windows 7 and select the most efficient method for your needs.

CERTIFICATION READY
What is a cloud installation?
2.3

CERTIFICATION READY
What are the types of removable media installations?
2.3

TAKE NOTE*

An image file is an exact replica of the contents of a hard disk, saved to a file with an .iso extension, or a .wim extension if it's a Windows Imaging Format image.

TAKE NOTE*

For more information on building a WinPE image, visit http://technet.microsoft.com/en-us/library/dd799244(WS.10).aspx

Microsoft provides many different ways to install Windows 7, from manual methods like inserting a DVD to fully automated, "non-touch" installations performed over a network or even via the cloud. (The **cloud** generally refers to the Internet or to a server accessible over the Internet.) The method you choose depends mainly on the number of computers on which you need to install Windows and how much time you have to devote to the project.

Installing Windows 7 from removable media is common in smaller enterprise or home environments. When you think of removable media, you might think of DVDs, but many installations are performed from USB drives as well. Using a DVD or USB drive is considered a manual method of installation. If you're installing Windows on one, two, or even 10 computers, a manual method works well. If you must install Windows on many computers, you'll want to understand automated methods, in order to save time (and, thus, money).

The following are categories that correspond to the level of interaction required during an installation:

- High Touch Installation (HTI)
- Lite Touch Installation (LTI)
- Zero Touch Installation (ZTI)

High Touch Installation (HTI) may include retail media or a standard image (ISO file). Using this method, you use an installation DVD or USB drive and manually install the operating system on every computer. You must then also manually configure each system.

In a larger environment, where you have, say, 25 or more computers that require Windows 7 installations, you could use a tool called ImageX to create bootable media. The Windows Automated Installation Kit (AIK) includes ImageX. You would perform these general steps:

1. Install Windows 7 on a clean hard disk.
2. Configure it with settings that will apply to all computers.
3. Use the Sysprep utility to create an image of the installation.
4. Boot to the Windows Preinstallation Environment (WinPE) and use ImageX to save the image to a DVD, a USB drive, or whatever type of media you plan to use.
5. Install the image on the remaining computers.

Lite Touch Installation (LTI) requires some human intervention in the early phase of the installation, but is automated (or unattended) from that point on. This installation method works well in environments with more than 150 computers.

You need the Windows AIK, Windows Deployment Services, and the Microsoft Deployment Toolkit 2010 for LTIs. **Windows Deployment Services** is a server role for Windows Server 2008 or Windows Server 2008 R2. It allows a user to press the F12 key, log on, and select an image for installation. After that, the installation can be automated. For example, you can use an answer file to configure Windows settings during installation. The answer file contains all the settings that are required for an unattended installation. The Microsoft Deployment Toolkit 2010 is a free download used to automate high-volume operating system deployments.

Zero Touch Installation (ZTI) is a fully automated, "touchless" method of installing Windows. You need System Center Configuration Manager (SCCM) for ZTIs. You use SCCM to deploy and update servers, client computers, and all kinds of devices on a network.

The ZTI method is geared for environments with more than 500 computers, involves a fairly steep learning curve, and requires a considerable budget compared to HTIs.

 TAKE NOTE *

Another form of automated installation is to use a cloud service such as Windows Intune. This particular service is geared toward business environments and enables you to manage and secure networked computers. In addition, you can upgrade client computers to Windows 7 Enterprise Edition. You need a Web browser and Internet connection along with appropriate licensing to deploy Windows 7 Enterprise Edition via Windows Intune.

➔ INSTALL WINDOWS 7

GET READY. There are many ways to install Windows 7. This exercise shows you how to install Windows 7 from removable media. Perform the following steps:

1. Turn on your computer and start the installation:

   From a download: Locate the Windows 7 installation file and double-click it.

   From disc or USB flash drive: Insert the disc into your computer. If Setup doesn't start automatically, click the **Start** button, click **Computer**, double-click your disc or drive icon, and then double-click **setup.exe**.

2. On the Install Windows screen, click **Install now.** The installation program shows you its progress as it install files (see Figure 1-9).

Figure 1-9

The Install Windows screen

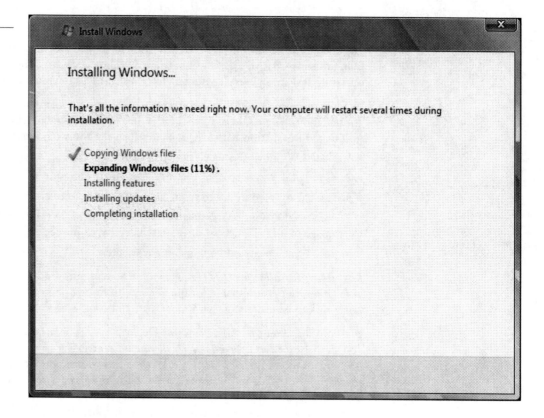

3. On the Get important updates for installation screen, if you have a live Internet connection, choose to get the latest updates to protect your PC.
4. On the Please read the license terms screen, accept the license terms and click **Next**.
5. On the Which type of installation do you want? screen, click **Custom.**

6. On the Where do you want to install Windows? screen, choose the partition that contains your previous version of Windows. Click **Next**.

7. In the Windows.old dialog box, click **OK**.

8. Follow any instructions and respond to prompts that appear, such as for naming your computer, creating a user account, and selecting a type of network (see Figure 1-10).

Figure 1-10

Selecting a type of network

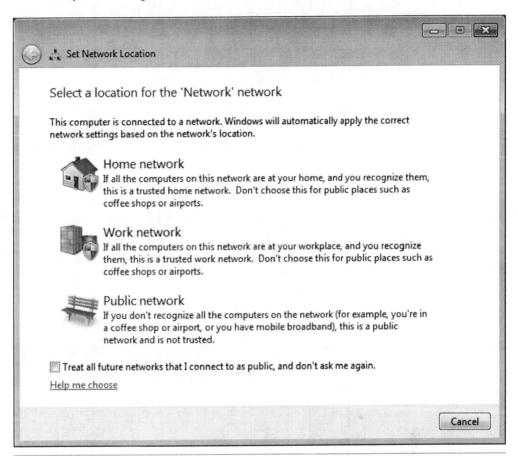

Be sure to run Windows Update immediately after installing Windows 7.

TAKE NOTE＊ For more information on installing Windows 7, visit http://windows.microsoft.com/en-US/windows7/Installing-Windows-7-recommended-links and http://windows.microsoft.com/en-US/windows7/Installing-and-reinstalling-Windows-7

Using Windows Easy Transfer

Windows Easy Transfer helps you move files and settings from one computer running Windows to another. The "move" can occur on the same computer if you're upgrading to a different version of Windows that requires a custom installation. Either way, by transferring your files and settings, you get a jump start on your productivity.

If you've used your computer for a long time, you've probably accumulated hundreds or thousands of files, especially if you take photos or collect digital music. You've also, over time, tweaked user settings so they're most efficient for accomplishing work and running software. You shouldn't have to lose files or settings—and your efforts—to upgrade to Windows 7.

Use *Windows Easy Transfer* to save your files and settings on an external hard drive, and then "transfer" them to the new installation of Windows 7. You cannot transfer your programs, so make sure you have the original installation media so you can manually install them in Windows 7.

TAKE NOTE*

For more information on Windows Easy Transfer, visit http://windows.microsoft.com/en-US/windows7/transfer-files-and-settings-from-another-computer

→ USE WINDOWS EASY TRANSFER

GET READY. This exercise uses Windows XP as the example operating system. To perform the transfer with an external hard drive, perform the following steps:

1. Download the latest Windows Easy Transfer program from Microsoft.com and install it on your computer.
2. Reboot your computer and log on as an administrator. Make sure no programs are running.
3. Click the **Start** button, click **All Programs**, and then click **Windows Easy Transfer for Windows 7**. The Windows Easy Transfer Wizard starts.
4. Read the information on the opening screen, and then click **Next**.
5. Select a transfer method (see Figure 1-11). For this example, click **An external hard disk or USB flash drive**.

TAKE NOTE*

If prompted to provide an administrator password or to click a button to continue, do so.

Figure 1-11

Selecting a transfer method

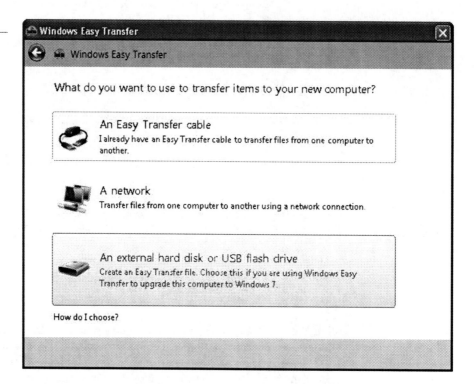

6. On the next screen, select **This is my old computer. I want to transfer files and settings from this computer.**
7. Windows Easy Transfer checks all user accounts, then displays a summary of what can be transferred (see Figure 1-12). Click **Next**.

Figure 1-12

Viewing content that can be transferred

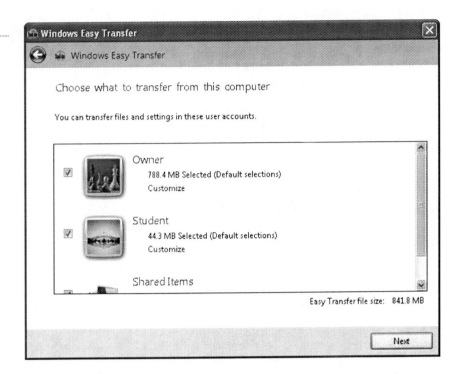

8. On the next screen, Windows Easy Transfer states it will save all files and settings to an Easy Transfer file. If you want to include a password, type it now. Otherwise, just click **Save**.

9. The Save your Easy Transfer file window displays. Select the external drive you are using for the transfer and click **Save**. A file with a .MIG extension is saved to the location you selected. The Save process may take several minutes or hours, depending on the amount of content you are transferring.

10. When the file is saved, click **Next**.

11. The Your transfer file is complete screen displays. Write down the location of the transfer file on your external drive. Click **Next**.

12. The Windows Easy Transfer is complete on this computer screen displays. Click **Close**.

After you install Windows 7 on the computer, perform the following steps:

1. Log on as an administrator and close any open programs.

2. Connect the external drive to your PC. You should be prompted to run Windows Easy Transfer. If not, open Windows Explorer, browse to your external drive, and then double-click the .MIG file. Windows Easy Transfer starts. If the program detects any open programs, it prompts you to close them. Click **Close all**.

3. The Choose what to transfer to this computer screen displays (see Figure 1-13). All items are checked by default. Uncheck any items you don't want transferred (if any) and click **Transfer**.

4. If you chose to password-protect your .MIG file, enter the password when prompted. The transfer process may take several minutes or several hours, depending on the amount of content you are transferring. A progress screen indicates at what stage the transfer is at. Do not close the window until the transfer is complete.

5. The Your Transfer is complete screen displays. To view the transferred files in Windows 7, click **See what was transferred** (see Figure 1-14).

Figure 1-13

Choosing what to transfer to the computer running Windows 7

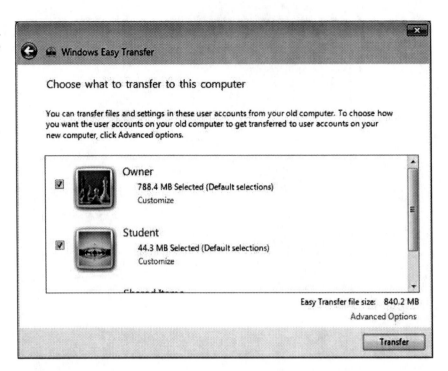

Figure 1-14

The Your Transfer is complete screen

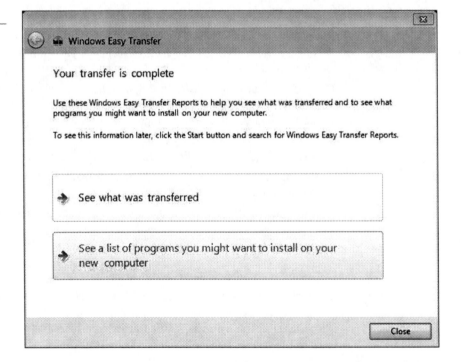

6. The Windows Easy Transfer Reports window displays with the Transfer report tab displayed (see Figure 1-15). Browse the list and click **Details** in any of the categories for more information. Click the Close icon (X) in the upper-right corner when you're done.

7. Windows Easy Transfer remembers the programs you used previously and recommends those that should run in Windows 7. Click **See a list of programs you might want to install on your new computer**. The Windows Easy Transfer Reports window reappears, with the Program report tab displayed (see Figure 1-16). Browse the list of programs and note the recommendations. Click the **Close** icon in the upper-right corner.

Figure 1-15

The Transfer report tab

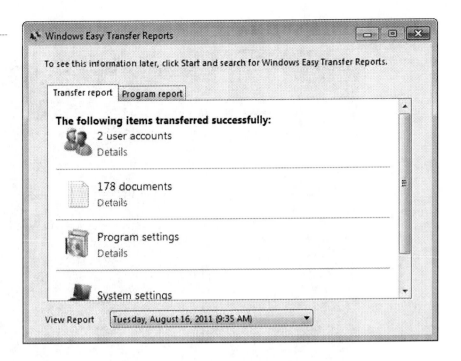

Figure 1-16

The Program report tab

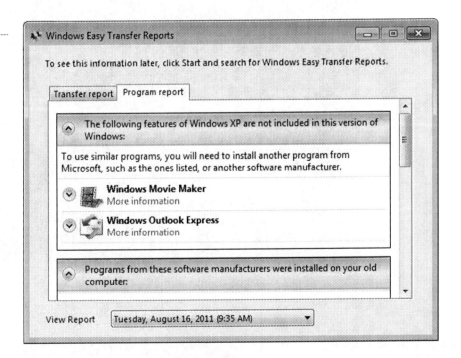

8. To end Windows Easy Transfer, click **Close**.

9. You're prompted to restart your computer. Click **Restart now** or **Restart later**.

The steps in this procedure will vary if you select different options; however, the basic process is the same.

SKILL SUMMARY

IN THIS LESSON YOU LEARNED:

- Windows 7 is a desktop operating system that improves on many aspects of its direct predecessors, Windows Vista and Windows XP.
- Windows 7 includes several new features, such as large and animated task thumbnails, homegroups, Jump Lists, libraries, and Windows XP Mode.
- The six main editions of Windows 7 are Starter, Home Basic, Home Premium, Professional, Ultimate, and Enterprise.
- Common computer architectures are 32-bit and 64-bit. A 32-bit computer can address up to 4 GB of RAM. A 64-bit computer can use much more RAM than a 32-bit computer. Operating systems also come in 32-bit and 64-bit versions, and it's important to match the correct operating system to the computer processor.
- You can run a 32-bit operating system on a 64-bit computer, but you generally cannot run a 64-bit version of Windows on a 32-bit computer.
- The main system requirements for running Windows 7 are: 1 GHz or faster 32-bit (x86) or 64-bit (x64) processor, 1 GB RAM (32-bit) or 2 GB RAM (64-bit), 16 GB available hard disk space (32-bit) or 20 GB (64-bit), and a DirectX 9 graphics device with Windows Display Driver Model (WDDM) 1.0 or higher driver.
- Windows 7 Upgrade Advisor helps you determine if your computer can run Windows 7, which editions and features will work, and whether your computer has any compatibility issues.
- The Windows 7 Compatibility Center provides software programs that are compatible with Windows 7, including updates, downloads, drivers, and more.
- An upgrade installation replaces your current version of Windows with Windows 7 while retaining your files, settings, and programs. A custom installation replaces your current version of Windows with Windows 7 but overwrites your files, settings, and programs. A custom installation is also referred to as a clean installation.
- The upgrade path you must take from Windows Vista to Windows 7 depends on some key factors, mainly your current edition of Windows Vista and the edition of Windows 7 you want to run. There are a few other considerations too, such as 32-bit versus 64-bit environment and desired language. You can easily upgrade from one edition of Windows 7 to a more advanced edition using Windows Anytime Upgrade.
- Installation methods fall into three main categories: High Touch Installation (HTI), Lite Touch Installation (LTI), and Zero Touch Installation (ZTI). HTI is mostly manual, and ZTI is almost completely automated.
- Windows Easy Transfer helps you move files and settings from one computer running Windows to another, or to a new installation of Windows 7 on the same computer.

■ Knowledge Assessment

Fill in the Blank

Complete the following sentences by writing the correct word or words in the blanks provided.

1. A(n) _____ is the set of options you have to upgrade from one Windows operating system to another.

2. _____ is the process of verifying that your copy of Windows is genuine and that it is not in use on more computers than the number for which you own licenses.

3. A _____-bit computer is also designated as x86.

4. A(n) _____ installation replaces your current version of Windows with Windows 7 while retaining your files, settings, and programs.

5. The _____ method involves manual installation of Windows 7 from media such as a DVD or USB drive.

6. Windows 7 _____ is targeted mainly toward small business users.

7. Windows 7 _____ is a retail version that includes BitLocker and AppLocker.

8. _____ is a fully automated, touchless method of installing Windows.

9. _____ is a server role for Windows Server 2008 or Windows Server 2008 R2 that allows for mostly automated installation of Windows 7 over a network.

10. To use Windows Anytime Upgrade to perform an in-place upgrade, you must buy an _____ from Microsoft or your preferred retailer.

Multiple Choice

Circle the letter that corresponds to the best answer.

1. Which edition of Windows 7 does *not* support x64 CPUs?
   a. Starter
   b. Home Basic
   c. Home Premium
   d. Professional

2. Which editions of Windows 7 are widely available in the retail sector? (Choose all that apply.)
   a. Home Premium
   b. Professional
   c. Ultimate
   d. Enterprise

3. Which edition of Windows 7 requires a Software Assurance Agreement with Microsoft?
   a. Home Premium
   b. Professional
   c. Ultimate
   d. Enterprise

4. Which of the following features is *not* included in Windows 7 Professional?
   a. Encrypting File System
   b. Windows XP Mode
   c. Support for joining domains
   d. BitLocker

5. Which tool scans your computer and produces a report of any Windows 7 compatibility issues with your computer?
   a. Windows 7 Compatibility Center
   b. Windows 7 Upgrade Advisor
   c. Windows Easy Transfer
   d. Windows Anytime Upgrade

6. Which Windows 7 installation method uses System Center Configuration Manager for deployment across a network?
   a. HTI
   b. LTI
   c. ZTI
   d. Windows Anytime Upgrade

7. Which Windows 7 installation method requires some human interaction but uses Windows Deployment Services to automate most of the installation?
   a. HTI
   b. LTI
   c. ZTI
   d. Windows Anytime Upgrade

8. You can use the upgrade installation method when upgrading from Windows Vista Business to which of the following? (Choose all that apply.)
   a. Windows 7 Home Basic
   b. Windows 7 Home Premium
   c. Windows 7 Professional
   d. Windows 7 Ultimate

9. What are two common methods for determining if your computer is running a 32-bit or 64-bit version of Windows 7 or Windows Vista? (Choose all that apply.)
   a. Run Windows 7 Upgrade Advisor.
   b. Open the Computer window.
   c. Open the System window.
   d. Run the System Information utility.

10. Where might a Windows 7 product key be located? (Choose all that apply.)
    a. On the installation disc holder inside the Windows package
    b. On a sticker on the back or bottom of your computer
    c. On the installation media itself
    d. In a confirmation e-mail if you purchased and downloaded Windows 7 online

True / False

Circle T if the statement is true or F if the statement is false.

T F 1. You must perform a custom installation to upgrade from Windows XP to Windows 7.

T F 2. A 1 GHz or faster 32-bit (x86) processor is required to run Windows 7.

T F 3. You must register Windows 7 to run it.

T F 4. The purpose of a Windows 7 product key is to help avoid illegal installations.

T F 5. The Windows 7 Logo Program tests software to determine if it meets Windows 7 requirements.

■ Competency Assessment

Scenario 1-1: Troubleshooting a Compatibility Problem

A remote employee reports that after he upgraded his computer to Windows 7, he is unable to use his USB printer. He says Windows 7 hangs whenever he plugs in his printer. How do you respond?

Scenario 1-2: Creating a Plan to Upgrade to Windows 7

The IT manager for your company informs you that senior management approved the budget for upgrading 20 networked client computers from Windows Vista Business to Windows 7. He asked you how to determine whether the computers can be upgraded to Windows 7 Professional, and which installation method will be most efficient and cost-effective. How do you answer?

■ Proficiency Assessment

Scenario 1-3: Converting a Small Office to Windows 7

Danielle provides IT support for Swish It Away, a small cleaning service in the Pacific Northwest. The company has eight computers. Four of the computers run Windows XP Professional Edition and the other four run Windows Vista Business Edition. The company president has asked her to make sure all eight computers are running Windows 7 Professional by the beginning of the next quarter. What type of installations must Danielle perform, and which additional steps (if any) must Danielle take to retain the users' files and settings?

Scenario 1-4: Selecting the Right Computer and Operating System

Swish It Away is beginning to grow. The president now wants Danielle to acquire computers for three new staff members. Randi has been hired as the president's personal assistant and will need to run a word processor, spreadsheet application, a Web browser, and an e-mail client. Pooja will provide marketing and graphics services, such as press releases, brochures, flyers, advertisements, and graphics for the new Web site. Stan is the new salesperson who will travel locally each day. When he's in the office, he will share a desktop computer with another salesperson, but Stan needs to be able to check e-mail and access the Internet while he's out of the office. What computer specifications should Danielle look for, and which editions of Windows 7 should run on each computer?

LESSON 2

Understanding Operating System Configurations

EXAM OBJECTIVE MATRIX

SKILLS/CONCEPTS	MTA EXAM OBJECTIVE DESCRIPTION	MTA EXAM OBJECTIVE NUMBER
Understanding User Accounts and User Account Control (UAC)	Understand user account control (UAC).	3.2
Configuring Control Panel Options	Configure Control Panel options.	1.1
Configuring Desktop Settings	Configure desktop settings.	1.2
Understanding Virtualized Clients	Understand virtualized clients.	2.4
Understanding Application Virtualization	Understand application virtualization.	3.5

KEY TERMS

accessibility options

Administrative Tools

Administrator account

Aero

Aero Peek

Aero Shake

Aero Snap

application virtualization

authentication

cached credentials

color depth

Control Panel

desktop settings

display settings

Ease of Access Center

elevated permissions

font size

gadget

Guest account

guest operating system (guest OS)

Jump List

live preview

Microsoft Enterprise Desktop Virtualization (Med-V or MED-V)

Microsoft Management Console (MMC) snap-ins

permissions

28

pin	**user profile**
Quick Start definitions	**virtualization**
resolution	**virtual computer**
shortcuts	**virtual desktop infrastructure (VDI)**
Standard user account	**virtual machine (VM)**
user account	**virtualized client**
User Account Control (UAC)	**Windows XP Mode**

As an IT technician at Interstate Snacks, you're responsible for setting up new computers and helping users adjust their existing computer settings. Your duties include creating user accounts, optimizing display settings, creating shortcuts, and so on. In addition, because your company uses a legacy program that doesn't run in Windows 7, some of your employees need an alternative way to access the program. So, you plan to show those employees how to use Windows XP Mode.

■ Understanding User Accounts and User Account Control (UAC)

THE BOTTOM LINE

Microsoft introduced the security feature User Account Control (UAC) in Windows Vista and improved the feature in Windows 7. UAC constantly monitors activity on your computer and notifies you when changes are about to be made that affect your computer's security or that affect other user accounts on the computer.

A *user account* is a collection of information that defines the actions that can be taken on a computer and which files and folders can be accessed (rights, policies, and *permissions*). An account also keeps track of user preferences, such as the desktop background, window color, and screen saver. Several users can share a computer and each user should have her own account. With separate accounts, each user can personalize her desktop, keep her files and settings protected from other users, and so on.

There are three types of user accounts in Windows 7:

- Administrator
- Standard user
- Guest

Each account has a different level of control over the computer.

Understanding Standard User Accounts and Administrative User Accounts

The two most commonly used account types in Windows 7 are Standard user and Administrator. A standard account is generally used for everyday tasks, and an administrative-level account is used for troubleshooting, installation, and similar tasks that require more rights and permissions.

The *Guest account* type is simply an account with few permissions and no password that allows a user to use a computer without requiring a unique user account. The Guest account is intended mainly for a user who needs temporary use of a computer, and is disabled by default.

The *Standard user account* type has fewer permissions than an administrative-level account but enough permissions to be productive. You should use a standard account for day-to-day work. When you're logged on as a standard user, you can surf the Web, read e-mail, create documents, and listen to music, as well as perform other rather basic tasks.

The *Administrator account* type provides the broadest permissions and therefore the most control over the computer. This includes changing all settings, installing programs, and modifying the Windows registry. Use an administrative-level account only when you need to make changes or perform maintenance that requires elevated permissions. (*Elevated permissions* generally refer to administrative-level permissions.) Using an administrative account for ordinary (Standard-level) computing tasks leaves the computer at a much greater risk of attack. For example, if you visit a malicious Web site by accident, the site can easily install and execute a Trojan horse program on the computer because of the broad permissions of the administrative account.

A computer administrator can use a Standard user account for most tasks and use the Run as administrator command to start certain tasks or programs with full administrator-level permissions. For example, let's say you want to run a program but get an Access denied error message. Depending on the program, you might be able to right-click the program's menu item or icon and then select Run as administrator from the shortcut menu. The program will run with full administrator rights. Before running any tasks or programs with elevated privileges, make sure the computer is protected by a firewall and up-to-date antivirus program or that it's disconnected from the Internet.

There's another, special account to be aware of: the default Administrator account. It is the name of the default administrative-level account that's created when you install Windows. Think of it as the ultimate master local (i.e., non-domain) account in Windows. You shouldn't use this account for anything other than troubleshooting or for specific activities that you can't perform with any other account.

The default Administrator account is automatically hidden (disabled) in Windows 7, but you can enable it if necessary. You must first open a command prompt window in administrator mode by clicking the Start button, typing **cmd** in the *Search programs and files* search box, right-clicking cmd.exe in the resulting list, and then selecting *Run as administrator*. In the command prompt window that displays, type **net user administrator /active:yes** and press Enter. When you're finished using the account and want to disable it, open a command prompt window as described and type **net user administrator /active:no**.

When you create a new user account or modify an existing account, you can choose Standard or you can choose Administrator. The Guest account type does not show up as an option in the Create a New Account window.

➔ CREATE A USER ACCOUNT

GET READY. To create a new user account, perform the following steps:

1. Click **Start** and then click **Control Panel.** In the main Control Panel window, in the User Accounts and Family Safety section, click **Add or remove user accounts** (see Figure 2-1).

2. If you're logged on as a standard user, a User Account Control dialog displays. Enter an administrator password and click **Yes.**

3. The Manage Accounts window displays (see Figure 2-2). Click **Create a new account.**

Figure 2-1

Selecting Add or remove user accounts in Control Panel

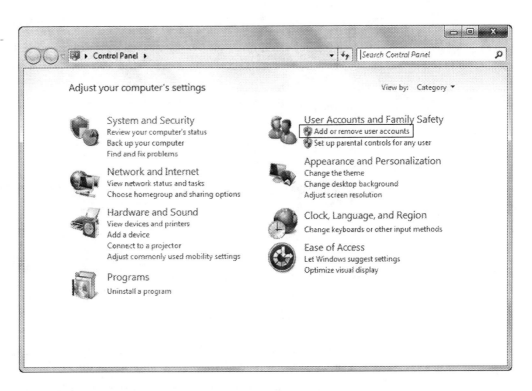

Figure 2-2

The Manage Accounts window

4. In the Create New Account window (Figure 2-3), in the **New account name** text box, type a name. Use just letters, numbers, and optionally spaces or hyphens.

5. If you want to create an administrative-level account, select **Administrator**; otherwise, leave **Standard user** selected.

Figure 2-3

The Create New Account window

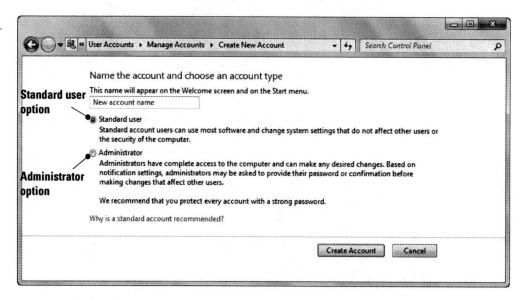

6. Click **Create Account.**

The new user displays in the Manage Accounts window. To change an account's settings, click an account name. The Change an Account screen displays and lists the following tasks:

- **Change the account name:** Edits the account's username. (This changes the name of the user's profile folder in the \Users folder. You will learn about user profiles later in the lesson.)
- **Create the password:** Creates or changes the account's password. For security purposes, it's recommended that you set a password on every user account.
- **Remove the password:** Deletes the password from this user's account.
- **Change the picture:** Selects a different picture to appear on the Start menu and the Welcome screen.
- **Set up Parental Controls:** Controls which applications and games the user can use and which days and times this user can use the computer.
- **Change the account type:** Changes the account type from Standard user to Administrator or vice versa.
- **Delete the account:** Removes the user account. You can choose to keep or delete a user account's files (such as pictures, music, documents, and so on).
- **Manage another account:** Returns to the Manage Accounts window and click another account.

Understanding User Account Control (UAC)

User Account Control (UAC) is a security feature in Windows Vista and Windows 7 that helps protect a computer from unauthorized changes. When a user, application, or even an attacker or malicious software attempts to modify certain system settings, a dialog box displays that requires confirmation or an administrative-level password to continue.

User Account Control (UAC) is a feature in Windows Vista and Windows 7 that requires administrative-level permission to make changes to your computer that affect security or affect settings for other user accounts. If you're logged on as a standard user and you attempt to make a change that requires administrative-level permissions, UAC displays a dialog box. A user with an administrator account on the computer must enter his password for you to continue (see Figure 2-4). You are then temporarily given the rights of an administrator to

Figure 2-4

A User Account Control dialog box requesting an administrative-level password

complete the task. Once you're finished, your permissions as a standard user once again apply. If you are logged on as an administrator and the UAC dialog box appears, click Continue or Yes to continue (see Figure 2-5).

Figure 2-5

A User Account Control dialog box requesting permission to continue

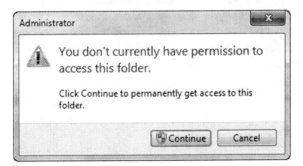

Some of the actions that can trigger a User Account Control dialog box include the following:

- Installing and uninstalling programs
- Changing system-wide settings
- Changing UAC settings
- Adding or removing user accounts
- Changing a user's account type
- Viewing or changing another user's folders and files
- Configuring Windows Update
- Running a program as Administrator (right-clicking a program name and selecting Run as administrator)
- Installing device drivers
- Changing settings for Windows Firewall

The point of UAC is to prevent potentially damaging, unauthorized changes to a computer, whether the changes are made accidentally, by malicious software, or by hackers accessing your system.

Understanding Types of UAC Prompts and Levels

There are four levels of UAC control. Each produces different sets of alerts or notifications to users. Any user can choose the level that works best for her, although the default settings are highly recommended.

In Windows 7, UAC has four notification levels, each of which has a different prompt (which means it displays a different dialog box). Each notification level varies slightly depending on whether you're logged on as a standard user or whether you're logged on as an administrator. The following levels pertain to an administrator account, unless noted otherwise:

- **Always notify me:** This is the most secure setting, which results in the most notifications. You are notified when programs try to install software or make changes to the computer, or when you make changes to Windows settings. (This is the default for a standard user account in Windows 7.)

- **Notify me only when programs try to make changes to my computer:** A UAC dialog box displays when installing software or making changes to system-wide computer settings, but no notification occurs when changing Windows settings. (This setting is the default for administrator Windows 7 accounts.)

- **Notify me only when programs try to make changes to my computer (do not dim my desktop):** Dimming the desktop is a visual indicator that an important change is pending. This setting does not open a UAC dialog box if you're making changes to your Windows settings. You must be logged on as an administrator to select this setting. This option is less secure but might be used by an administrator if the computer is highly secure.

- **Never notify me of installations or changes:** This is the least secure setting. You must be logged on as an administrator to select this setting. After restarting your computer, UAC is turned off. If you log on as a standard user, changes that require administrative-level permissions are denied (you are not prompted for an administrator password). This option should be used only in highly controlled and secure environments, such as test environments.

Microsoft highly recommends leaving UAC turned on for the safety and security of your computer.

 CHANGE UAC SETTINGS

GET READY. To modify UAC settings, perform the following steps:

1. Click **Start > Control Panel > System and Security > Change User Account Control settings** (see Figure 2-6). (Or, click the **Action Center** icon (the flag) on the right side of the Windows taskbar along the bottom of the screen, click **Open Action Center**, and then, in the left pane, click **Change User Account Control settings**.)

2. The User Account Control Settings window displays (see Figure 2-7). Move the slider up or down to raise or lower the number of UAC notifications you receive.

3. Click **OK** to save your changes.

Although Microsoft highly recommends that you leave UAC enabled, some users choose to turn it off to avoid the UAC notifications, especially if they're performing tasks (safely) that trigger UAC prompts. To turn off UAC, move the slider to the *Never notify* position and click OK. If you're prompted for an administrator password or confirmation, type the password or provide confirmation, and then restart your computer.

Figure 2-6

The System and Security window in Control Panel

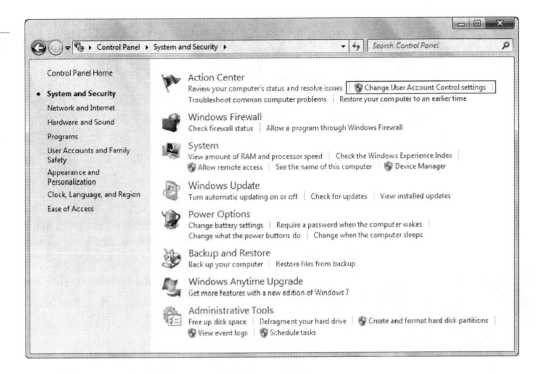

Figure 2-7

The User Account Control Settings window

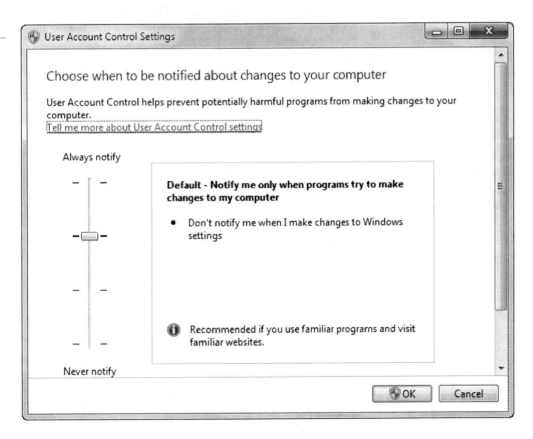

➕ MORE INFORMATION

For more information about User Account Control, visit http://windows.microsoft.com/en-US/windows7/products/features/user-account-control or http://technet.microsoft.com/en-us/library/cc709691(WS.10).aspx

■ Configuring Control Panel Options

THE BOTTOM LINE The Windows 7 Control Panel provides access to the primary tools and utilities used to manage devices, settings, and system behaviors on Windows PCs. You'll find control applets (small applications) for everything from system administration to Windows Update; you will also find specific controls for system devices, displays, and more.

You've already seen the Control Panel in action in this lesson, but you will learn more about it now. The *Control Panel* is a utility that allows you to configure operating system features, set up hardware, install and uninstall software, create and modify users, and perform system maintenance.

Each "program" in Control Panel is called an applet. Applets are organized by categories. Categories and applets are hyperlinked, so clicking a category or applet link in Control Panel opens a new window. One of Control Panel's most convenient aspects is that you can access many applets from multiple categories.

The default view in Control Panel is called Category view (see Figure 2-8). You can open the pull-down list in the upper-right corner of the Control Panel window to select two other views: Large icons and Small icons. The views are shown in Figure 2-9 and Figure 2-10, respectively. Choosing a different view can sometimes help you navigate through Control Panel applets more easily.

The preference settings you make in Control Panel applets are stored in the Windows registry. Therefore, you must have administrative-level access to modify many of the settings (such as uninstalling software and other system-wide settings) in the Control Panel.

Figure 2-8

The Category view in the Control Panel window

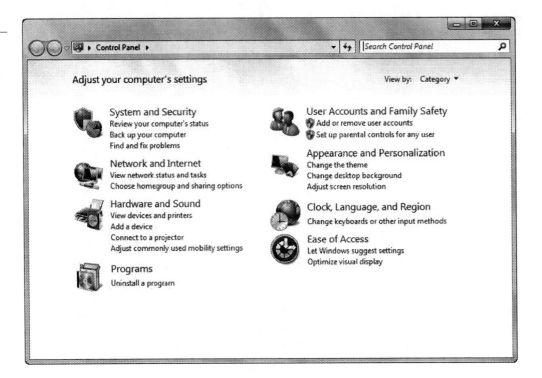

Figure 2-9

The Large icons view in the Control Panel window

Figure 2-10

The Small icons view in the Control Panel window

Table 2-1

Control Panel Categories

Category	Description
System and Security	Provides applets for maintaining the system and configuring security. This category includes Action Center, Windows Firewall, System, Windows Update, Power Options, Backup and Restore, Windows Anytime Upgrade, and Administrative Tools. Windows 7 Ultimate and Enterprise editions also offer BitLocker Drive Encryption (if installed).
Network and Internet	Provides applets for connecting to the Internet and other networks, setting up a local network (HomeGroup), and configuring wireless settings.
Hardware and Sound	Provides applets for configuring hardware (including printers), audio settings, power options, display settings, mobile options, and more.
Programs	Provides applets for installing/uninstalling software, setting default programs, and managing desktop gadgets.
User Accounts and Family Safety	Provides applets for creating and managing user accounts, configuring parental controls, and managing Windows credentials.
Appearance and Personalization	Provides applets for changing the Windows theme, desktop background, screen saver, display settings, desktop gadgets, and taskbar and Start menu. You can also open the Ease of Access Center, change folder options, and install fonts.
Clock, Language, and Region	Provides applets for changing your computer's date and time, time zone, language, and region/location.
Ease of Access	Provides access to the Ease of Access Center, where you can configure accessibility options; also provides access to the speech recognition feature.

Table 2-1 summarizes the categories in Windows 7 Control Panel.

Let's look at a few Control Panel applets in more detail.

Configuring Administrative Tools

Think of Administrative Tools as a well-rounded toolkit of utilities for power users and administrators. These utilities can help resolve most computer problems you may encounter and keep your system running optimally.

Administrative Tools is a set of utilities for managing advanced Windows features and diagnosing system problems. You can access the tools from the System and Security category of Control Panel. You can also click Start, type **admin tools** in the *Search programs and files* search box, and then select Administrative Tools from the resulting list. Figure 2-11 shows the Administrative Tools window on a Windows 7 Home Premium system. Windows 7 Professional, Ultimate, and Enterprise editions include the Local Security Policy and Print Management tools as well.

Within Administrative Tools, you can defragment your hard disk, monitor system performance, start and stop services, determine which programs run when Windows starts, and much more. Table 2-2 summarizes the tools.

Figure 2-11

The Administrative Tools window in Windows 7 Home Premium

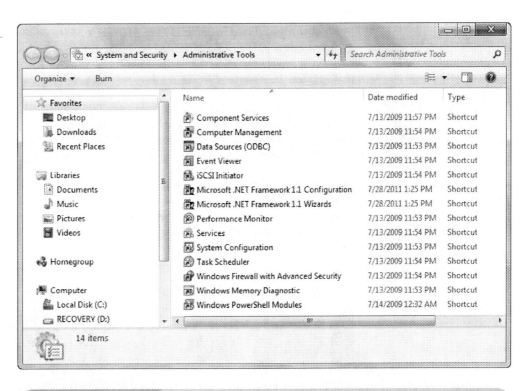

Table 2-2

Administrative Tools Utilities

CATEGORY	DESCRIPTION
Component Services	Used mainly by software developers; allows you to manage COM+/DCOM objects.
Computer Management	Allows you to manage local or remote computers by configuring hard disks and their partitions, monitoring system events, and managing system performance.
Data Sources (ODBC)	Used mainly by program developers and network database integrators, allows you to use ODBC to move data from one type of database to another.
Event Viewer	Allows you to view computer event information, such as program starting and stopping (including program crashes), security problems, and more.
iSCSI Initiator	Allows your computer to connect to network-attached storage.
Microsoft .NET Framework 1.1 Configuration/Wizards	Allows you to configure assemblies, services, and code access security policies related to .NET Framework. The Wizards tool gives you one-click access to configuration wizards.
Performance Monitor	Allows you to view and track system performance.
Services	Allows you to manage software and hardware services that work in the background.
System Configuration	Allows you to manage programs that run when Windows starts or when you log on.
Task Scheduler	Allows you to schedule programs and other tasks to run at certain times, automatically.
Windows Firewall with Advanced Security	Allows you to configure the built-in Windows Firewall.
Windows PowerShell Modules	Allows you to open a Windows PowerShell window and runs diagnostics.

Many of the tools listed in Table 2-2 are *Microsoft Management Console (MMC) snap-ins*. An MMC snap-in is a utility provided by Microsoft or a third party that's accessible through a common interface such as Administrative Tools. You can also access MMC by typing **MMC** in the *Search programs and files* search box.

> **TAKE NOTE** ★
>
> To show Administrative Tools in the Start menu, right-click the Start button, click Properties, and then click Customize. Scroll down the list and select *Display on the All Programs menu* (under the System administrative tools heading).

➕ MORE INFORMATION

For more information about Administrative Tools, visit http://windows.microsoft.com/en-US/windows-vista/ What-are-Administrative-Tools

Configuring Accessibility Options

> Microsoft has built many features into Windows 7 that work with assistive technologies or as stand-alone features that make the user experience better for the visually and hearing impaired. Most features can be configured in the Ease of Access Center.

CERTIFICATION READY
What is the primary purpose of Windows 7's accessibility options?
1.1

The *Ease of Access Center* (see Figure 2-12) provides many *accessibility options*, which help visually and hearing impaired users use Windows more easily and efficiently. The primary tools include Magnifier, Narrator, On-Screen Keyboard, and High Contrast.

Magnifier helps visually impaired users see a selected portion of the screen or the entire screen more clearly by increasing the size of text and graphics. The Magnifier application window

Figure 2-12

The Ease of Access Center tools

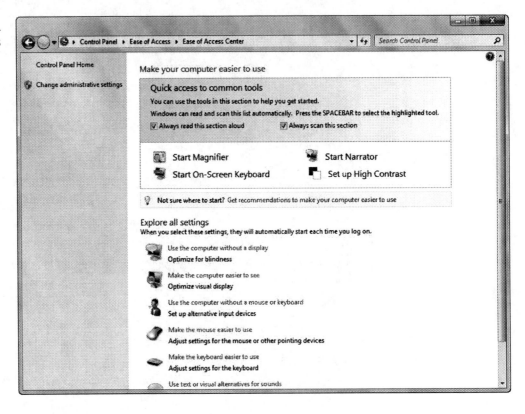

is quite small and provides you with access to Magnifier settings. Here you can set a certain magnification level and choose how the magnification "lens" follows the mouse pointer and text cursor. The lens looks like a magnifying glass icon on the screen.

Narrator is a text-to-speech program that reads aloud the actions you take, such as clicking and typing. This feature can also narrate certain events, such as error messages.

On-Screen Keyboard (see Figure 2-13) presents a keyboard on your screen from which you can type and enter data (rather than using a keyboard). You can use a mouse, stylus, or another pointing device to "press" keys.

Figure 2-13

The On-Screen Keyboard presents a fully functional keyboard

Another accessibility feature is the High Contrast theme (see Figure 2-14), a color scheme that makes some text easier to read and some images easier to identify on-screen.

Figure 2-14

The High Contrast settings

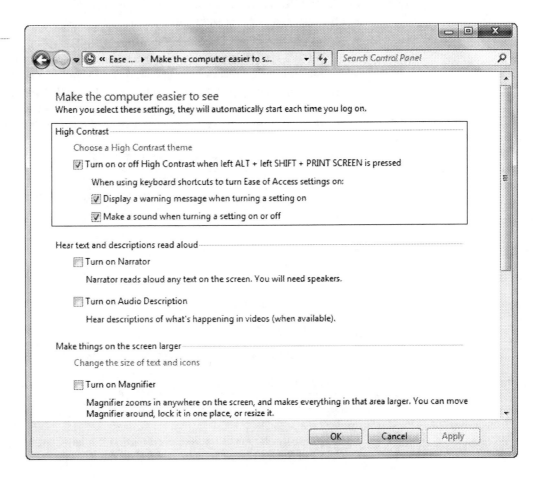

The bottom portion of the Ease of Access Center window includes other accessibility options you can configure for visually or hearing impaired users, including:

- Using the computer without a display
- Making the computer easier to see
- Using the computer without a mouse or keyboard
- Making the mouse easier to use
- Making the keyboard easier to use
- Using text or visual alternatives for sounds
- Making it easier to focus on tasks

Speech Recognition is an accessibility feature that you access in the Ease of Access category in Control Panel. This tool allows a user to speak commands into a microphone, which Windows then processes. All speech recognition programs require a sometimes lengthy training period in which the user "teaches" the computer to recognize the user's voice. You can learn more about the Windows Speech Recognition feature in Help and Support (click the Start button, click Help and Support, type **speech recognition** in the search box, and then press Enter).

＋ MORE INFORMATION

For more information about accessibility options and the Ease of Access Center, visit http://windows.microsoft.com/en-US/windows7/introducing-accessibility-in-windows or http://www.microsoft.com/enable/training/windowsvista/eoa.aspx

---

⊙ USE ACCESSIBILITY FEATURES

GET READY. To enable accessibility features, open the Ease of Access Center in Control Panel and then perform the following steps:

1. To use Magnifier, click **Start Magnifier**. When the application name displays, click it. A small application window displays a magnifier glass icon. Select the level of magnification in the window and then move the magnifier glass icon around the screen.

2. To use Narrator, click **Start Narrator**. The Microsoft Narrator dialog box displays (see Figure 2-15). Now when you type text or navigate text on the screen, Narrator reads it aloud. To turn Narrator off, click **Exit** in the Microsoft Narrator and then click **OK**.

Figure 2-15

The Microsoft Narrator dialog box

The steps are similar for On-Screen Keyboard and High Contrast. Just click Start On-Screen Keyboard or Set up High Contrast and follow the prompts.

■ Configuring Desktop Settings

THE BOTTOM LINE

Windows *desktop settings* is a broad term that refers to many different settings you can configure to personalize Windows, such as the Windows theme, the desktop background, mouse clicks and pointer speeds, gadgets, shortcuts, and more. All settings are customizable—choosing the right mix will make your Windows experience more enjoyable and more productive.

The Windows desktop is a flexible, configurable part of the Windows environment. You can grab the taskbar and move it to either side of the screen, to the top, or back to its default location at the bottom (the taskbar must be unlocked to move it—right-click the taskbar and, if Lock the taskbar is checked, select the box to deselect it). You can also choose which items appear in the notification area on the right side of the taskbar by configuring the taskbar Properties dialog box. To access this dialog box, right-click the taskbar and select Properties.

CERTIFICATION READY
How are desktop settings configured?
1.2

New in Windows 7 is the ability to *pin* program shortcuts directly to the taskbar; when you pin a program, the icon for that program displays on the taskbar even when the program isn't running. This provides you with quick access to your frequently used programs. Shortcuts for Internet Explorer, Windows Explorer, and Windows Media Player appear there by default. You can unpin programs from the taskbar as well. You'll learn about shortcuts later in the lesson.

When you open a program in Windows 7, an icon for that program displays on the taskbar. To activate a program, just click its icon on the taskbar. When you right-click a program's icon on the taskbar, a menu appears above the icon that contains a list of recently used files (if the application has an associated file type). The menu is called a *Jump List*. If you have several programs open at once, you can press and hold the Alt key and then press the Tab key repeatedly to switch between windows and see *live previews* of the window for each open program (see Figure 2-16).

Figure 2-16

Viewing live previews of open programs with Alt+Tab

Figure 2-17

The Windows 7 Personalization window

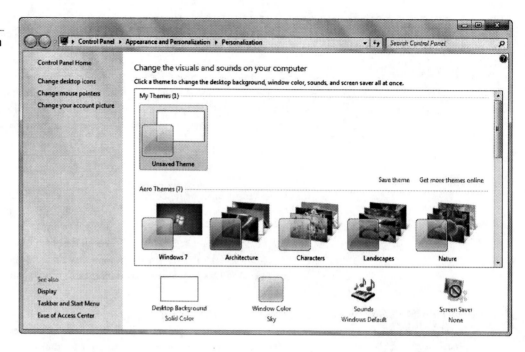

Many Windows 7 desktop settings are available when you right-click a blank area of the desktop and choose Personalize. The Personalization window is shown in Figure 2-17.

The main part of the window displays various themes you can use. Although there are many themes to choose from, a few of the most commonly used themes include the following:

- **Windows 7:** This is the default theme in Windows 7, which is an Aero theme. The Aero interface includes translucent borders and animations. You'll learn about the Aero interface in detail in the next section.

- **Windows Classic:** This theme is the same user interface used in Windows 2000 and earlier versions. The Windows Classic theme disables some of the high-end graphic features to provide better performance.

- **Windows 7 Basic:** This theme looks like Aero but doesn't include the semitransparent effect that can tax some older video cards. Selecting Windows 7 Basic can make the operating system seem more responsive.

Just click the theme of your choice and see the changes take effect immediately.

You can also change the background of any theme. Just click Desktop Background. In the Desktop Background window, open the **Picture location** drop-down list, and then select a different background image, a solid color, or a picture from your digital picture collection.

Clicking the Sounds link opens the Sound dialog box (see Figure 2-18). From here you can choose different sounds to accompany Windows events, such as when you connect a device or when you close Windows. The computer's sound volume must be set at an appropriate level to actually hear the sound.

Click the Screen Saver link to open the Screen Saver Settings dialog box. Then open the Screen saver drop-down list, select a screen saver, and click OK.

You'll learn about the Window Color link in the next section.

Figure 2-18

The Sound dialog box

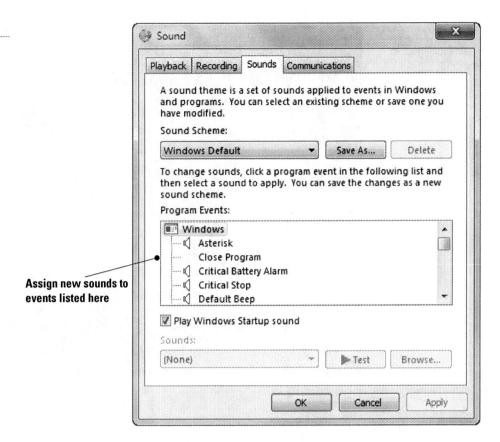

Assign new sounds to
events listed here

Exploring and Configuring the Aero Interface

The Aero interface was introduced in Windows Vista and has been improved in
Windows 7 with new features such as Aero Shake, Aero Peek, and Aero Snap. You
can tweak some Aero settings to improve computer performance and customize it for
personal appeal.

The default theme in Windows is Windows 7, which is an *Aero* theme. Aero themes have a
translucent "glass" design and provide your display with a three-dimensional look.

When you apply an Aero theme, window borders are partially transparent, allowing you to see
what lies beneath them (see Figure 2-19). Aero themes also provide some animation within
the interface. If you run the mouse over a button, the button glows. When you minimize a
window, it fades and shrinks downward. The Aero theme is also customizable, as you'll learn
in the exercise that follows. First, let's looks at some of the Aero features.

Aero Shake allows you to quickly minimize all open windows except the active one. Point the
mouse at the title bar of the active window, click the hold and left mouse button, and then
quickly move the mouse back and forth to shake it. (If you're new to Aero Shake, it can take
a little practice to use it properly.)

To minimize all open windows at once, click the Show Desktop button. This button is the
small shaded rectangle at the far right end of the taskbar. Pointing at it with your mouse

Figure 2-19

The translucent quality of an Aero theme

Show Desktop button

pointer displays a preview of the desktop. This is called peeking at the desktop and is part of the **Aero Peek** feature. If you click the Show Desktop button, all open windows are minimized.

Windows 7 Aero also includes **Aero Snap**, which allows you to quickly resize and arrange windows on the desktop. To use Aero Snap, drag the title bar of an open window to either side of the desktop to align it there, or drag it to the top of the desktop to maximize the window.

⊖ CHANGE AERO SETTINGS

GET READY. You can modify many settings to affect Aero behavior. For example, to change the color of the Aero interface, perform the following steps:

1. Right-click an empty part of the desktop, select **Personalize**, then click **Window Color**. The Window Color and Appearance window displays (see Figure 2-20).
2. Click a color box to change the color of Windows borders.
3. Uncheck the **Enable transparency** check box if you want to retain most of the Aero look and feel but you want to disable the semi-transparent effect.
4. Move the **Color intensity** slider to make the Windows border color more or less intense.
5. To create your own border color, click the **Show color mixer** arrow and then adjust the Hue, Saturation, and Brightness sliders (see Figure 2-21).
6. Click **Save changes**.

Figure 2-20

The Window Color and
Appearance window

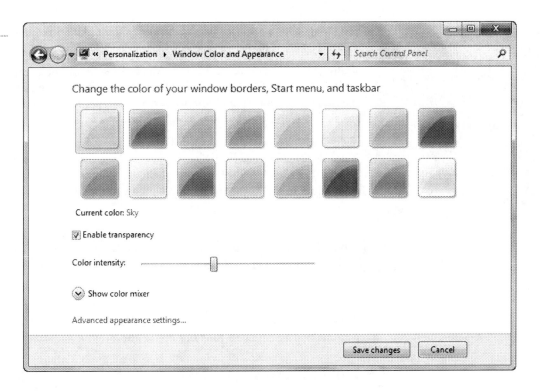

Figure 2-21

Adjusting the color mixer
settings

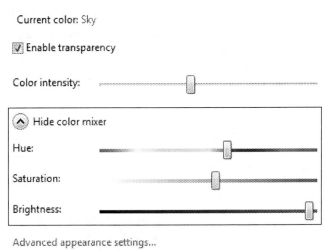

Configuring Display Settings

> Windows 7 has several *display settings*, but you're likely to modify the resolution, color
> depth, and font size most often. You can modify each setting to suit a particular application.

CERTIFICATION READY
What are some of the
display-related settings you
can adjust using the Screen
Resolution window?
1.2

The Windows 7 Screen Resolution window allows you to configure many display-related settings.
This is where you choose which monitor to use (if your computer is connected to two or more
monitors) and whether to display content in a landscape or portrait orientation. You can also
configure settings to connect a projector to your computer. Three other important display settings you might want to adjust for specific purposes are resolution, color depth, and font size.

Resolution refers to the number of pixels that create the "image," that is, everything you see
on the screen. **Resolution** has a horizontal value and a vertical value, such as 1200 x 768 or
1600 x 900. The Windows desktop expands itself to fit whichever resolution you select, so

X REF

If Windows 7 does not have the appropriate driver for the display, you might need to download and install a new driver to make the best use of your monitor. Lesson 5 covers drivers and how to install them.

you always have a full background. Similarly, the taskbar stretches across the bottom of the screen, regardless of the resolution you choose.

You might need to change a computer's screen resolution for a variety of reasons, such as when you're accommodating a visually impaired user or when you're using an external projector. Your computer's monitor has a minimum and a maximum resolution it can display, so Windows 7 gives you a range of resolutions to choose from.

Color depth refers to the number of bits that represents the color for each pixel on the screen. Color depths are generally 8 bits, 16 bits, 24 bits, and 32 bits; newer systems offer only 24 or 32 bits. The higher the color depth, the better photos and similar objects will look. You set color depth in the Advanced settings window of the Display control.

TAKE NOTE You seldom need to change resolution or color depth settings. Windows chooses the best settings for your monitor. The two primary monitor types are LCD and CRT.

Screen fonts are usually measured in dots per inch (dpi). You can enhance the appearance of your desktop by adjusting ***font size*** dpi to improve the readability of pixelated or illegible fonts.

➡ ADJUST DISPLAY SETTINGS

GET READY. To adjust display settings, perform the following steps:

1. To set screen resolution, right-click the desktop and select **Screen resolution**. Click the **Resolution** drop-down arrow and then drag the slider to change the resolution (see Figure 2-22).

Figure 2-22

Selecting a screen resolution

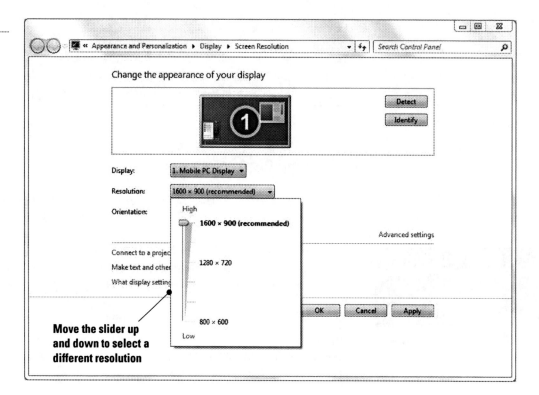

Move the slider up and down to select a different resolution

2. To adjust color depth, right-click the desktop, choose **Screen resolution,** and then click **Advanced settings**. Click the **Monitor** tab in the resulting properties window, click the **Colors** drop-down arrow, and then select the color depth of your choice (see Figure 2-23).

Figure 2-23

Selecting a color depth

3. To adjust screen font size, right-click the desktop, select **Personalize**, and then click **Display** in the left pane. The options are **Smaller**, **Medium**, and **Larger**.

Windows might prompt you to confirm your selections. The changes should take effect without requiring you to restart Windows.

Creating and Managing Shortcuts

Shortcuts are icons you can click to start a program or go to a location without requiring any extra steps. Shortcuts save time because you don't have to use several keystrokes or click several menus or commands.

CERTIFICATION READY
What is a shortcut?
1.2

An icon is a small, visual symbol of a computer resource, such as a program, folder, file, or drive. To access an actual computer resource, click or double-click its icon. Some icons are located on the desktop, others are in the Start menu, and still others might appear in the list of files and folders in Windows Explorer.

A *shortcut* (see Figure 2-24) is an icon or link that gives you quick access to an original resource. The links you see in Control Panel are also considered shortcuts. Because a shortcut only points to a resource, deleting a shortcut does not delete the actual item. You can usually distinguish a shortcut icon from the original item it refers to because the shortcut has a small arrow in the shortcut icon's lower-left corner.

Figure 2-24

An example of a shortcut icon

If you regularly access a particular folder, you can create a shortcut to that folder on the desktop. Whenever you want to open that folder, double-click the icon instead of launching Windows Explorer and navigating to the folder to open it.

 CREATE AND DELETE A SHORTCUT

GET READY. To create a folder shortcut on the desktop, perform the following steps:

1. In Windows Explorer, point to the folder for which you want to create a shortcut.
2. Right-click the folder and choose **Send To > Desktop (create shortcut)** (see Figure 2-25). The shortcut now displays on your desktop.

To delete a shortcut icon:

1. Right-click it, choose **Delete**, and then click **OK**. The shortcut is removed and sent to the Recycle Bin.

Figure 2-25

Creating a shortcut on the desktop

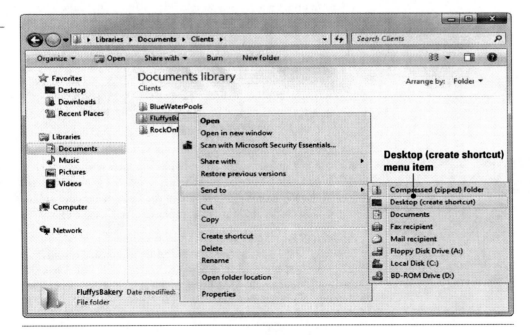

Configuring Gadgets

> Gadgets are small, versatile applications that are run from the Windows 7 desktop. Gadgets are similar to mobile apps on a smartphone. A *gadget* is a small, single-purpose application that can be installed on the Windows 7 desktop. There are all kinds of gadgets available, such as calendars, clocks, games, newsfeeds, and weather reports and forecasts.

CERTIFICATION READY
What is a gadget?
1.2

In Windows Vista, gadgets were displayed in the Windows Sidebar, which by default was located on the right side of the desktop. Windows 7 doesn't use the Windows Sidebar, so you can spread gadgets around your desktop wherever they're convenient to use. If open windows cover your gadgets, you can use Aero Peek to quickly reveal the desktop.

To open the Windows 7 gadget gallery, right-click an empty portion of the desktop and select Gadgets. The Windows 7 gadget gallery displays, as shown in Figure 2-26. The number of gadgets that install with Windows 7 is limited, but you can add gadgets to your gallery. Just click the *Get more gadgets online* link in the lower-right corner of the window. Your default Web browser opens to the Microsoft desktop gadgets Web site; the gadgets are free to download and install. Many gadgets are geared toward consumers, such as consumer shopping and auction sites and horoscope gadgets. However, some gadgets are useful in a business setting, such as the CPU meter, drive meter, and battery meter gadgets. As your gadget gallery grows, you can use the right and left arrows in the upper-left corner to scroll through available gadgets.

Figure 2-26

The Windows 7 gadget gallery

Click these arrows to scroll through available gadgets

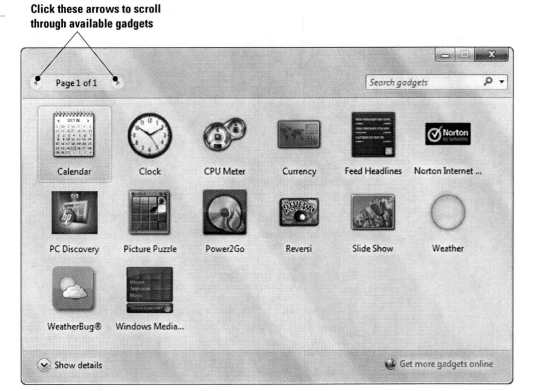

➕ **MORE INFORMATION**

For more information about Windows gadgets, visit http://windows.microsoft.com/en-US/windows7/products/features/gadgets

ADD A GADGET TO YOUR DESKTOP

GET READY. To add a gadget to your desktop, perform the following steps.

1. Right-click a blank area of the desktop and select **Gadgets**.

2. Browse the gadget gallery. To get information about a particular gadget, click the gadget and then click the **Show details** link in the lower-left corner of the gallery.

3. Right-click a gadget of your choosing and click **Add** (see Figure 2-27). That gadget displays on your desktop. You can also drag-and-drop a gadget onto your desktop.

Figure 2-27

Adding a gadget to your desktop

4. To move a gadget or change its size, hover your mouse pointer over the gadget and then use the menu that displays next to the gadget (see Figure 2-28).

Figure 2-28

A menu displays alongside a gadget when you hover your mouse pointer over the gadget

To remove a gadget from the desktop (but leave it in the gallery for later use), click the X at the top of the menu next to the gadget.

Configuring Profiles

All of a user's personal preferences—from theme choice to screen saver to shortcuts—are saved in a user profile. Windows relates a user's preferences to the user account. Each time a user logs on to Windows, the user's profile is loaded.

Now that you've learned how to change all kinds of desktop settings, create shortcuts, and add gadgets, you might wonder how Windows remembers all of those settings. Windows uses user profiles to do so. Your *user profile* contains your desktop settings (your theme, desktop background, screen saver, and so on) and other personal preferences. The purpose of a user profile is to maintain your preferences so they appear each time you log on to Windows.

User profiles can be local or roaming. A local profile is available only on the computer on which it was created. A roaming profile enables a user to use any computer to connect to a Windows domain and access her profile. (Remember, a domain is a collection of user and computer accounts that enable an administrator to manage and apply security to them as a group.) User preferences load upon domain log-on, giving the user a consistent desktop experience. A user with a lot of data and many personalized settings can experience a delay while the roaming profile loads.

In a domain, a server called a domain controller authenticates users at log on. *Authentication* means the domain controller checks the user's credentials, which are generally a user name and password. The user name entered must match the password on file. The domain controller also checks the permissions a user has to resources on the network. The credentials are saved to the computer's hard disk—referred to as *cached credentials*—which allow the user to access resources when a domain controller is unavailable. A domain controller might be unavailable because the server is down or because a user is attempting to access the network from a remote location.

Don't confuse a user profile with a user account. A user account is used to log on to Windows. Every user account has a subfolder in the C:\Users folder and each account has at least one user profile associated with it.

Understanding Virtualized Clients

THE BOTTOM LINE

Virtualization is a technology that creates an abstract version of a complete operating environment (including a processor, memory, storage, network links, a display, and so forth) entirely in software. Because the resulting runtime environment is completely software-based, the software produces what's called a *virtual computer* or a *virtual machine* (*VM*). Virtualization is a term used to describe the work involved in setting up all the data structures necessary to represent and run a VM on a physical computer of some kind.

In Windows, a *virtualized client* is a VM that's set up specifically to run some kind of application that typically runs in an older version of Windows (such as Windows 2000 or Windows XP). On a Windows 7 PC, a virtualized client runs as a VM inside what's called a *guest operating system* or *guest OS* within a virtual runtime environment (such as Windows Virtual PC or VMware Workstation).

Virtualization becomes necessary when users need to run applications that won't work on modern Windows operating systems. By running an older version of Windows (such as Windows XP) in a VM on Windows 7, users can continue to work with software that's incompatible with the host OS inside a compatible guest OS.

Understanding Windows XP Mode

As presented in the lesson case for Interstate Snacks at the outset of this chapter, users need access to a legacy program that doesn't work in Windows 7. Fortunately, it does work in Windows XP and that builds an ironclad case to make Windows XP Mode available to the Interstate Snacks user community. Although Windows Virtual PC runs on all Windows 7 versions, Windows XP Mode works only on Windows 7 Professional, Enterprise, or Ultimate. Be sure to factor that into your OS selection and deployment plans!

Windows XP Mode is an add-on that Microsoft makes available as an extension to Windows Virtual PC. When you install this virtual machine environment on a Windows 7 computer, users can run applications inside the VM that won't work on Windows 7.

CERTIFICATION READY
What is Windows XP Mode?
2.4

Visit http://www.microsoft.com/windows/virtual-pc/download.aspx to grab a copy for your users' PCs. Figure 2-29 shows the download page with a download for 64-bit Windows 7 Professional selected. The download confers a free Windows XP Mode license to those who put it to work, which helps companies avoid license infringement trouble with Microsoft.

Figure 2-29

Selecting the Windows XP Mode download to match a Windows 7 version

Once Windows XP Mode is installed, you must then install the applications that are not compatible with Windows 7 into the Windows XP VM that's created. Users can launch this VM directly from their desktops or menus to access the applications they need.

 INSTALL WINDOWS XP MODE

GET READY. Visit the Microsoft Web page where you'll download the files you need to install Windows XP mode on your user machines. To install Windows XP Mode, perform the following steps:

1. Check the system requirements prior to downloading Windows XP Mode.
2. Select the appropriate Windows version and language for your target PC or PCs. As shown in Figure 2-29, our example is 64-bit Windows 7 Professional and English.

3. On the Web page shown in Figure 2-30, for **Step 2**, click **Download**. Once Windows validation completes successfully, Internet Explorer requests permission to download a file named **WindowsXPMode_en-us.exe**. Grant permission and run the file. This sets the stage for WindowsVirtual PC to be installed in a subsequent step.

Figure 2-30

Once you download the XP Mode file, you'll step through its installation process

4. In stepping through the Windows XP Mode install, you'll work through a Setup program. You'll start by clicking **Next** to start the installation, designating a target directory (the Program Files default target is usually suitable, as shown in Figure 2-31), waiting through a virtual hard disk install, and then clicking **Finish** to complete the XP Mode setup.

5. With XP Mode installed, you must return to the Web page and move on to Step 3. This is where you download and install Windows Virtual PC. When you click the **Download** button for Step 3, you grant permission to download and run the file named Windows6.1-KB9598559-x64-RefreshPkg.msu. (Refer to Figure 2-30 if necessary).

6. When you execute the Windows Virtual PC file, you run a standalone Windows Update file. Once it gets going, it looks like any other ordinary Windows Update file. And, like many other such updates, it forces a restart of your system when it completes; it also goes through an update configuration before and after the reboot.

7. When the PC reboots, click **Start** and in the **Search programs and files** search box, type **XP**. In the results list displayed, click the Windows XP Mode entry. This completes the Windows XP Mode installation and initialization process and usually takes

Figure 2-31

Designating a target directory while installing Windows XP Mode software

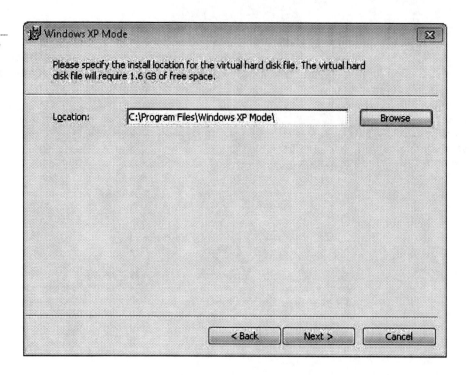

at least several minutes to complete. During this process, you'll need to agree to license terms and define a login password for the default xpmuser account that the program creates to finalize installation.

Now XP Mode is up and running and available as an entry named Windows XP Mode through the Virtual PC element in the Start Menu program listings. Before users can take advantage of this environment, you must complete your normal installation processes—which usually means installing anti-malware applications, standard programs, and of course the legacy applications that don't work under Windows 7.

Windows XP Mode makes it easy for users to run legacy applications, even on newer computers and inside otherwise incompatible operating systems. Programs installed inside the Windows XP Mode environment also show up in the standard Windows 7 Program menus, so users can access them without first launching the XP Mode Virtual Machine. Shortcuts to these programs can even be dropped on the desktop, if that's how users like to run things.

+ MORE INFORMATION

For more information about Windows XP Mode, visit http://windows.microsoft.com/en-us/windows7/products/features/windows-xp-mode

■ Understanding Application Virtualization

THE BOTTOM LINE

Application virtualization adds the ability to install and manage legacy applications and virtual machines centrally. This capability sometimes relies on additional Microsoft technologies, including a *virtual desktop infrastructure* (*VDI*) that runs a desktop OS within a virtual machine (VM) running on a server.

Microsoft and several third parties support remote access tools whereby users load and display carefully constructed VMs on their desktops, and these VMs provide them with remote access to tools that are located on servers that might be located off site. This approach simplifies the management and deployment of legacy applications for IT professionals, but still makes them readily accessible to end users, on and off corporate networks.

Microsoft's Remote Desktop Services (RDS) permit users to access and run VMs in a variety of situations. This includes obtaining access to remote servers designed to create and deliver VMs to users on corporate networks, as needed. These same technologies can also provide remote access to mobile workers in the field or telecommuters in their homes. You will learn more about RDS in Lesson 3.

Understanding Med-V

Microsoft Enterprise Desktop Virtualization (aka *Med-V* or *MED-V*) is the part of the Microsoft Desktop Optimization Pack (MDOP), which delivers legacy applications to Windows 7 users in the form of Windows-XP based virtual machines. It provides a mechanism for providing uninterrupted access to legacy applications while Windows 7 upgrades and transitions are underway.

Med-V consists of several client components that must be installed on Windows 7 client computers. These include the Med-V Management Server that communicates with a central server to obtain information about and access to pre-defined VMs for use with Med-V. Clients also have installed a specific Med-V Client program and a Med-V Management Console to handle and run Med-V VMs.

CERTIFICATION READY
What is Med-V?
3.5

Med-V also works with Windows Virtual PC, and is often used to deploy that software in large organizations. An important advantage of Med-V is that it provides centralized management and uses policies to provide and deliver virtual images to client machines. Med-V also supports Windows XP Mode. In fact, Windows XP Mode lets administrators set up icons for applications inside Windows XP Mode that launch from the Windows 7 desktop just like native application, although they run inside the Windows XP VM.

Users access special pre-defined virtual hard disks (VHDs) to run Med-V VMs. These are made accessible through Med-V Workspaces and specific downloads. The Med-V Management Console is what enables *Quick Start definitions* for Med-V VMs (and the programs they contain), through a special Quick Start Group Policy file.

From an end-user perspective, these elements of Med-V infrastructure are unobtrusive and almost entirely invisible. Though system and desktop administrators have to set up and configure this infrastructure, Med-V creates an end-user experience that is best described as "click and go," even though it uses the basic elements of Windows XP Mode in a centrally controlled and managed fashion.

Understanding VDI and App-V

Microsoft's Virtual Desktop Infrastructure (VDI) depends on a special, licensed access right that permits users to access a virtual machine running a Windows client. This technology permits users to access secure, centrally-managed desktops running in a datacenter.

Microsoft VDI provides unified management of centralized desktops and corporate data using Microsoft System Center server technology. This approach permits IT to extend existing management tools and processes to virtual desktop environments. The goals are to reduce management overhead and enable rapid deployment and quick patching.

This is possible because VDI relies on desktop images that are created, managed, and maintained centrally. System Center Configuration Manager can orchestrate rapid delivery of operating systems and applications as well as driver and software updates for physical and virtual desktop platforms. It even works with self-service applications packaged using Microsoft App-V technologies.

CERTIFICATION READY
What is the purpose of Microsoft VDI and App-V?
3.5

App-V extends virtualized applications from central servers to authorized users on any authorized PCs without requiring application installs. Users simply request access to an application; virtualization technology running in the background brokers a connection to a suitable server and delivers direct access to the application with minimal delay. The environment preserves virtual applications and user settings whether users are active online or inactive and offline. With App-V, users need only to click to launch applications; they don't need to wait for installations or reboots. Updates are automatically applied and immediately available the next time a program is launched.

App-V also helps to minimize conflicts between applications because they run in separate runtime containers that do not interfere with one another. This reduces application compatibility testing requirements and can further speed deployment times. App-V is designed to make applications available anywhere, anytime to users as long as they have Internet access available.

➕ MORE INFORMATION

For more information about desktop virtualization and VDI, visit http://www.microsoft.com/virtualization/en/us/products-desktop.aspx and http://technet.microsoft.com/en-us/edge/microsoft-virtual-desktop-infrastructure-vdi-explained.aspx

SKILL SUMMARY

IN THIS LESSON YOU LEARNED:

- The two primary types of user accounts in Windows 7 are Standard user and Administrator. You generally use a standard account for everyday tasks and an administrative-level account for troubleshooting, installation, and similar tasks that require more rights and permissions.

- User Account Control (UAC) is a security feature in Windows Vista and Windows 7 that helps protect a computer from unauthorized changes. When a user, malicious software, or even an attacker attempts to modify certain system settings, a dialog box displays that requires confirmation or an administrative-level password to continue.

- There are four levels of UAC control, which result in different types of alerts or notifications to the user. Each user can choose the level that works best for them, although the default settings are highly recommended.

- The Control Panel is a utility that allows you to configure operating system features, set up hardware, install and uninstall software, create and modify users, and perform system maintenance.

- The Ease of Access Center provides many accessibility features to help visually and hearing impaired people use Windows more easily and efficiently. The primary tools include Magnifier, Narrator, On-Screen Keyboard, and High Contrast.

- Windows desktop settings is a broad term that refers to many different settings you can configure to personalize Windows, such as the Windows theme, desktop background, mouse click and pointer speed, gadgets, shortcuts, and more. All settings are customizable, and choosing the right mix will make your Windows experience more enjoyable and more productive.

- Windows XP Mode is a free download available to users of Windows 7 Professional, Enterprise, and Ultimate versions. It permits administrators to create and package Windows XP-based VMs, to support legacy applications that don't work on Windows 7. Windows XP Mode programs are available directly through the Windows 7 Start menu, and are easy and convenient for users to launch and run.

- Application Virtualization (App-V) permits users to launch and run applications on their desktops without installing or rebooting their machines. Microsoft's App-V technology makes instant use available through System Center and special centralized configuration and management utilities. A virtual desktop infrastructure (VDI) makes delivery of VMs and virtual applications possible.

- Microsoft Enterprise Desktop-Virtualization (Med-V) provides another way to deliver legacy applications to end users, on centrally configured and managed VMs. This allows for administrators who need only manage master copies in the data center, while users put copies of the master to work on their desktops.

■ Knowledge Assessment

Fill in the Blank

Complete the following sentences by writing the correct word or words in the blanks provided.

1. A _____ is a collection of information that defines the actions you can take on a computer and which files and folders you can access.

2. The _____ account type is best for everyday use.

3. The _____ interface, which is the basis for the default theme in Windows 7, includes translucent borders and animations.

4. To configure accessibility options, open the _____.

5. To minimize all open windows at once, click the _____ button.

6. _____ includes several applets, including System and Security, Programs, and User Accounts and Family Safety.

7. Use _____ to troubleshoot and resolve computer problems, and to keep your system running optimally.

8. The Windows 7 _____ window allows you to configure several display-related settings, such as choice of monitors or content orientation (landscape or portrait).

9. _____ is a free download for Windows 7 Professional, Enterprise, and Ultimate versions that supports legacy applications inside a virtual Windows XP machine running on Windows 7.

10. _____ allows applications to run without being installed on desktop systems.

Multiple Choice

Circle the letter that corresponds to the best answer.

1. Which of the following is *not* an account type in Windows 7?
   a. Guest
   b. Limited user
   c. Standard user
   d. Administrator

2. Which of the following can you perform in the Manage Accounts window? (Choose all that apply.)
   a. Change the account type
   b. Create a password
   c. Delete the account
   d. Set up Parental Controls

3. Which of the following actions is most likely to trigger a User Account Control dialog box?
   a. Uninstalling a program
   b. Creating a shortcut
   c. Changing resolution
   d. Adding a gadget

4. Where can you directly access Event Viewer?
   a. Gadgets window
   b. Programs applet in Control Panel
   c. Administrative Tools
   d. User Account Control dialog box

5. Which of the following is *not* a UAC notification level?
   a. Always notify me
   b. Notify me only when users try to access my files
   c. Notify me only when programs try to make changes to my computer
   d. Never notify me of installations or changes

6. Which Aero feature allows you to quickly minimize all open windows except the active one?
   a. Shake
   b. Snap
   c. Peek
   d. Show Desktop

7. Which of the following settings is *not* configurable from the Screen Resolution window?
   a. Orientation
   b. Font size
   c. Display
   d. Windows theme

8. Which of the following allows you to manage programs that run when Windows starts or when you log on?
   a. Task Scheduler
   b. Performance Monitor
   c. Programs applet in Control Panel
   d. System Configuration

9. Which versions of Windows 7 support Windows XP Mode? (Choose all that apply.)
   a. Starter
   b. Home Premium
   c. Professional
   d. Ultimate
   e. Enterprise

10. Which of the following correctly explains the abbreviation VHD?
    a. Variable Hex Determinant
    b. Virtual Home Directory
    c. Virtual Hard Disk
    d. Virtual Hard Drive

True / False

Circle T if the statement is true or F if the statement is false.

T   F   **1.** A User Account Control dialog box displays when you open your data files.

T   F   **2.** You cannot change the desktop resolution setting because it's a fixed value.

T   F   **3.** Deleting a shortcut does not delete the resource it represents.

T   F   **4.** A user account and a user profile are the same thing.

T   F   **5.** Med-V delivers centrally managed virtual machines to authorized end users.

■ Competency Assessment

Scenario 2-1: Getting Administrative-Level Privileges

As an IT technician, you need to perform some maintenance tasks on an employee's computer that will require elevated privileges. When you go to the Manage Accounts window in Control Panel on that employee's computer, you see only the employee's standard user account. What do you do to be able to log on as a user with administrative-level privileges?

Scenario 2-2: Configuring Accessibility Features

Alexandra, an employee at your company, is visually impaired. Which features can you configure in Windows 7 to help her do her work more efficiently?

■ Proficiency Assessment

Scenario 2-3: Running a Legacy Application

Oscar is the warehouse manager for The OEM Connection, an auto parts business. Although the business standardized on Windows 7 Professional, Oscar needs to run a legacy parts lookup program that does not run in Windows 7. You provide technical support to The OEM Connection. What can you do to help Oscar?

Scenario 2-4: Creating a Better User Experience

Oscar at The OEM Connection asks you to help him speed up his computer, which now runs Windows 7 Professional. He doesn't care about all of the "zippy, new" features in the Windows 7 Aero interface—he just wants the computer to run a bit faster and be more responsive. He would also like to be able to quickly launch Microsoft Excel each time he logs on to his computer, and he does not want the Windows Media Player to be present on the taskbar. How do you meet Oscar's requests?

3 | **LESSON**

Understanding Native Applications, Tools, Mobility, and Remote Management and Assistance

EXAM OBJECTIVE MATRIX

SKILLS/CONCEPTS	EXAM OBJECTIVE DESCRIPTION	EXAM OBJECTIVE NUMBER
Understanding Windows Internet Explorer	Understand native applications and tools.	1.3
Introducing Accessory Programs	Supplemental	
Using the Snipping Tool	Understand native applications and tools.	1.3
Playing Back and Recording to Media	Understand native applications and tools.	1.3
Understanding Sync Center	Understand mobility.	1.4
	Understand libraries.	4.4
Using Windows Mobility Center	Understand mobility.	1.4
Understanding Remote Desktop Services	Understand virtualized clients.	2.4
	Understand mobility.	1.4
Understanding Remote Management and Assistance	Understand remote management and assistance.	1.5

KEY TERMS

ActiveX Filtering

cookies

Computer Management

cross-site scripting attack

cross-site scripting (XSS) filter

domain highlighting

InPrivate Browsing

Internet Explorer 9

62

Microsoft Management Console (MMC)	**SmartScreen filter**
New Tab page	**snap-in**
Notification bar	**Snipping Tool**
offline files	**Sync Center**
One Box	**Tracking Protection**
pinned site	**Windows Media Center**
playlist	**Windows Media Player 12**
Pop-up Blocker	**Windows Mobility Center**
Remote Desktop Connection	**Windows PowerShell**
Remote Desktop Services	**Windows Remote Assistance**
screen shot	

Your IT manager has asked you to find ways to help computer users be more productive and provide support services to them without requiring you to purchase third-party tools and software. You decide to brush up on the native applications in Windows 7, such as Internet Explorer 9, Snipping Tool, Windows Media Player, and Windows Media Center. To help remote users who run into problems with their software or who just need quick tutorials, you'll begin using Windows Remote Assistance. Finally, you plan to show frequent travelers how to use Remote Desktop Connection to access files from their home or work computers.

■ Understanding Windows Internet Explorer

THE BOTTOM LINE

Although Windows 7 usually ships with Internet Explorer 8, the most current Microsoft Web browser as of this writing is Internet Explorer 9, which is also the version that the 98-349 exam focuses on. Microsoft made many improvements to Internet Explorer 9—the Web surfing experience is now much easier, safer, and private than ever before.

Internet Explorer 9 is the latest Web browser from Microsoft. The browser is faster and less cluttered than previous versions, and it includes several privacy, security, and interface features that enhance the user browsing experience with a focus on usability and safety.

CERTIFICATION READY
What are some of the improved features of Internet Explorer 9?
1.3

Microsoft introduced tabbed browsing in Internet Explorer 7 and has improved the feature in Internet Explorer 9. This feature allows you to keep all your favorite Web sites open within one Internet Explorer window. The Internet Explorer 9 interface also includes a large Back button, a consolidated menu, and a combined Address bar and search box (see Figure 3-1).

The *New Tab page* (see Figure 3-2) in Internet Explorer 9 appears when you click the **New Tab** button or press **Ctrl+T**. This page initially provides some thumbnails of Web sites you might

Figure 3-1

The Windows Internet Explorer 9 interface

be interested in visiting. As you use Internet Explorer 9, the sites you visit most often appear on this page, giving you one-click access to frequently visited sites. You can remove sites from the New Tab page by right-clicking a site's thumbnail and selecting **Remove this page** from the shortcut menu.

Figure 3-2

The New Tab page

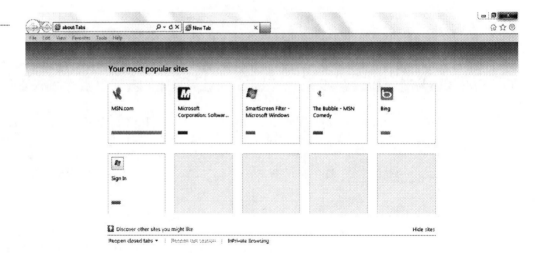

The New Tab page also provides commands for reopening closed tabs and starting InPrivate Browsing, which is explained later in this section.

Internet Explorer 9 introduces **_One Box_**, a feature that combines search functionality into the Address bar. One Box saves you time by using AutoComplete to help you complete Uniform Resource Locators (URLs), and allows you to enter search terms directly in the text box like you would in a search engine. Relevant suggestions for your search appear in a drop-down list (see Figure 3-3) that you can select or you can continue typing and then press Enter to see results in the default search engine.

Figure 3-3

Searching within One Box

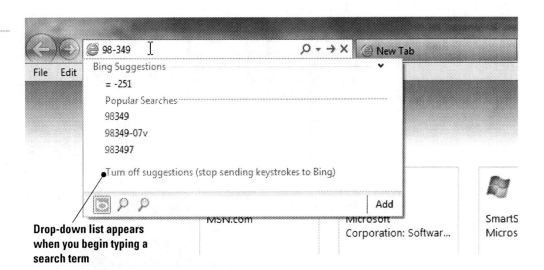

Drop-down list appears when you begin typing a search term

TAKE NOTE* For privacy reasons, search suggestions are turned off by default. To enable search suggestions, select *Turn on suggestions* in the drop-down list.

Another new feature of Internet Explorer 9 is the **Notification bar**, which displays at the bottom of the browser window. All notifications, such as blocked pop-up windows and error messages, display in the Notification bar rather than in pop-up windows. You can click the options in the Notification bar or ignore them, depending on your preference.

+ MORE INFORMATION

For more information about Windows Internet Explorer 9, visit http://windows.microsoft.com/en-US/internet-explorer/products/ie/home

Using Pinned Sites

Pinned sites makes it easy for users to get to frequently visited Web sites.

A **pinned site** is an Internet Explorer 9 Web site you "attach" to the Windows 7 taskbar. A pinned site is simply a quick way to open a Web site, much like you open a program that's pinned to the taskbar. Pinned sites let you access Web sites without having to open and navigate your Favorites list, or even open Internet Explorer first.

 PIN A WEB SITE TO THE WINDOWS 7 TASKBAR

GET READY. To pin a Web site to the Windows 7 taskbar, perform the following steps:

1. Launch Internet Explorer 9 and browse to any Web site.
2. Click the tab for the Web site and drag it to the taskbar (see Figure 3-4). You can also click and drag the Web site's thumbnail that appears on the New Tab page.
   An icon for the pinned site also appears to the left of the Back button in Internet Explorer 9. The site also shows up as a thumbnail on the taskbar (see Figure 3-5). When you hover your mouse pointer over a pinned site, a preview appears if an Aero theme is enabled. If the pinned site is for e-mail, such as Microsoft Hotmail, you may see brief status messages such as the number of new e-mails that have arrived since you last checked your account.

Figure 3-4

Pinning a Web site to the taskbar

Pinned Site icon in Web browser

Figure 3-5

A pinned site appears in Internet Explorer 9 and on the taskbar

To pin additional Web pages to a pinned site so all pages open by clicking a single thumbnail, perform the following steps:

1. Open the pinned Web site.

2. Open the site you want to add, and then click its tab.

3. Right-click the pinned Web site's icon to the left of the Back button, and then click **Add as a home page** (see Figure 3-6).

To unpin a site from the taskbar, right-click the pinned site's icon and select *Unpin this program from taskbar.*

Figure 3-6

Adding a site as a home page

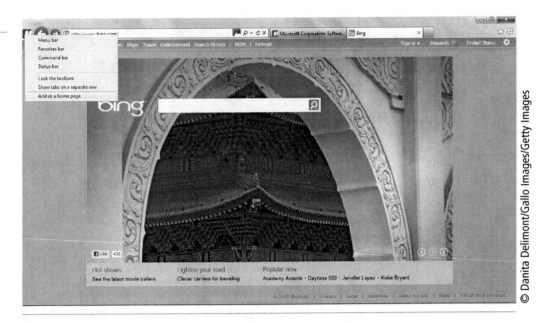

© Danita Delimont/Gallo Images/Getty Images

✚ MORE INFORMATION

To learn more about pinned sites, visit http://windows.microsoft.com/en-US/internet-explorer/products/ie-9/features/pinned-sites

Managing Security Features

The Internet is a great place to find useful information and entertainment, but it's also a vehicle for viruses, worms, and more dangerous attacks on users. Microsoft has included a lot of security and privacy features in Internet Explorer 9 to make Internet browsing a safer experience.

Internet Explorer 9 includes many features that help you protect your computer and privacy while surfing the Web. Some features have been around for a while, such as Pop-up Blocker, while others have been introduced in Internet Explorer 9. With the millions of viruses, worms, and other threats lurking on the Internet, it's highly recommended that you, at minimum, use the default Internet Explorer 9 security settings. You should even choose *more* secure settings for your safety.

You can change a variety of options for safety and security and general default behaviors in Internet Explorer 9 by clicking the Tools icon and then clicking Internet options. The Internet Options dialog box displays; this dialog box features tabs that allow you to customize your Web browsing experience. Let's look at the Security tab and the Privacy tab.

The Security tab (see Figure 3-7) is where you select a security zone, which is a group of security settings for a type of site: Internet, Local intranet, Trusted sites, or Restricted sites. For each zone, you can move the slider up or down to select higher or lower security settings. You can also click the Custom level button to customize individual security settings, such as scripts, ActiveX controls, .NET Framework, and more.

The Privacy tab (see Figure 3-8) also uses a slider to select levels of privacy controls, mainly for blocking or allowing cookies.

The ***Pop-up Blocker*** check box (selected by default) automatically prevents pop-up windows from appearing. Most pop-up windows are created by advertisers and appear when you first open a Web site. However, their content can be malicious, so the Pop-up Blocker feature prevents them from opening.

Figure 3-7

The Security tab

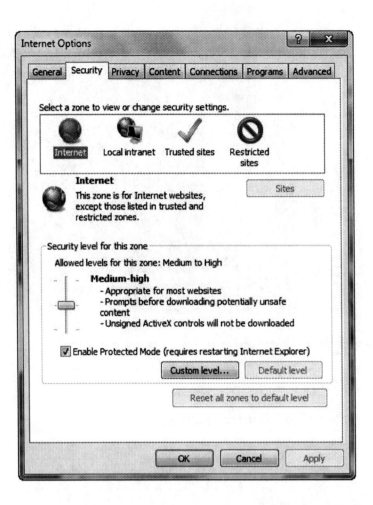

TAKE NOTE*

In Internet terms, "malicious" refers to viruses, worms, spyware, and other content that can harm your computer. Many of the security features in Internet Explorer 9 prevent malicious content from invading your computer.

Many other Internet Explorer 9 security controls are accessible from the Tools menu on the menu bar or the Safety menu on the command bar (if enabled). The first menu item is Delete browsing history, which allows you to erase Temporary Internet files, cookies, history, and many other "trails" of information all from a single dialog box (see Figure 3-9).

When you visit Web sites, your browser might store **cookies** (small text files that Web sites save to a computer's hard disk that contain information about the user and his or her browsing preferences), temporary Internet files, user names, passwords, and other data for your convenience. When you visit the sites again in the future, this information is already available to your browser so you don't have to reenter data. It's also meant to personalize the visit by remembering your information. However, the information can pose a security risk, especially if you share your computer with others, whether at home or work, or if you use a shared computer at the library, for example. **InPrivate Browsing** helps prevent personal information and browsing history from being stored by Internet Explorer 9. When you use InPrivate Browsing, a new tab appears in which you browse the Internet (see Figure 3-10). When you're finished and close the browser window, the session ends and any cookies or temporary files that were used during the session are cleared from your browsing history. A network administrator, however, can view Internet traffic that's generated with InPrivate Browsing.

Figure 3-8

The Privacy tab

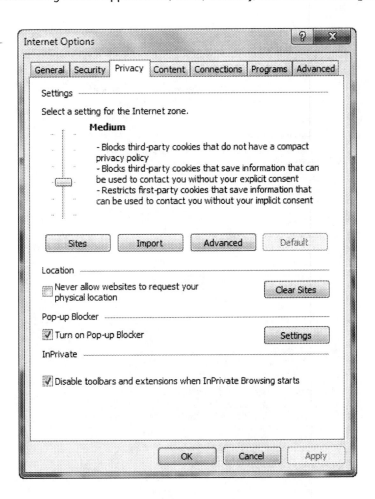

Some Web sites store a lot of information about your browsing sessions in cookies. For example, if you visit a shopping site, one or more cookies on your PC might include information about specific items you viewed or purchased. Advertising networks use cookies to "follow" you on the Web and display targeted advertising. After visiting a social networking site like Facebook, for example, a cookie might contain information related to what you typed on a friend's wall. If, for example, you mentioned you bought a great pair of Nike running shoes, the right side of your Facebook page might display an ad from a sporting goods retailer that sells Nike running shoes or you might even see an ad from Nike.com.

Tracking Protection helps you control which Web sites can track your online browsing activity and receive that information. This is accomplished with a Tracking Protection list. You can create your own Tracking Protection lists or download lists from the Internet Explorer Gallery Tracking Protection Lists Web site at http://iegallery.com/en/trackingprotectionlists/.

ActiveX Filtering blocks ActiveX controls, which are created for interactivity on the Web and commonly used on sites that display animations or offer multimedia such as videos. ActiveX is meant to enhance the user experience on the Web, but it can slow your computer. In addition, some attackers use ActiveX to push harmful content to unsuspecting users. ActiveX Filtering allows you to block ActiveX completely, or to trust certain sites and block all others.

Figure 3-9

The Delete Browsing History
dialog box

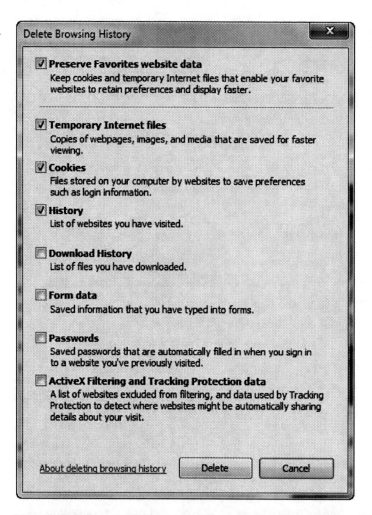

Figure 3-10

InPrivate Browsing runs in a
new browser session

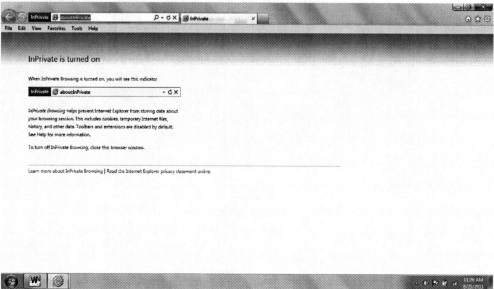

Other important security features include:

- **SmartScreen Filter:** The *SmartScreen Filter* detects threats on Web sites, such as
  phishing attacks and malware downloads, and prevents them from running. When
  Internet Explorer 9 detects a malicious Web site, it blocks the entire site from being

accessed. It can also block malicious portions of legitimate Web sites, allowing the rest of the site to display as normal. SmartScreen Filter is enabled by default.

- **Cross-site scripting (XSS) filter:** A *cross-site scripting attack* occurs when you visit a compromised Web site that runs a script that installs a keylogger program on your computer. The installation occurs without your knowledge. After that, the keylogger records your keystrokes, including when you enter user names and passwords into other sites. The information is usually sent to a third party, who may access your accounts. The *cross-site scripting (XSS) filter* prevents the keylogger script from running.

  - **Domain highlighting:** Some Web sites use deceptive Web addresses, making you think you're visiting a legitimate site when you're actually on a phishing site or another dangerous site. *Domain highlighting* shows you the true Web address of any Web site you visit by highlighting the domain in the Address bar.

Many Internet Explorer 9 security features are available in various forms in third-party Internet security suites.

➕ MORE INFORMATION

To learn more about ActiveX filtering, visit http://windows.microsoft.com/en-US/internet-explorer/products/ie-9/features/activex-filtering. Information on the cross-site scripting filter is available at http://windows.microsoft.com/en-US/internet-explorer/products/ie-9/features/cross-site-scripting-filter. Need extra help understanding InPrivate Browsing? Go to http://windows.microsoft.com/en-US/internet-explorer/products/ie-9/features/in-private. Finally, you can learn more about SmartScreen Filter at http://windows.microsoft.com/en-US/internet-explorer/products/ie-9/features/smartscreen-filter

---

 USE AND CONFIGURE INTERNET EXPLORER 9 SECURITY FEATURES

GET READY. To configure security features in Internet Explorer 9, perform the following steps:

1. Launch Internet Explorer 9.
2. To access Pop-up Blocker settings, click the **Tools** icon in the upper-right corner of the Internet Explorer 9 window, and then click **Internet options**.
3. In the Internet Options dialog box, click the **Privacy** tab, and then click the Pop-up Blocker **Settings** button. To allow pop-ups from a particular trusted Web site, such as your bank, type the URL in the **Address of website to allow** text box and then click **Add**.
4. Click **Close** to close the dialog box.
5. To enable ActiveX Filtering, click the **Tools** icon in Internet Explorer 9, point to **Safety**, and then click **ActiveX Filtering**. A check mark appears next to ActiveX Filtering to indicate the feature is enabled (see Figure 3-11).
6. To use Tracking Protection, click the **Tools** icon, point to **Safety**, and then click **Tracking protection**. In the Manage Add-ons dialog box (see Figure 3-12), click a Tracking Protection list (if available), and then click **Enable**.
7. To download a Tracking Protection list, click the **Get a Tracking Protection List online** link and then follow the prompts.
8. To use InPrivate Browsing, click the **Tools** menu, point to **Safety**, and then click **InPrivate Browsing**. A new browser session opens, which keeps your browsing actions private.
9. When you're finished, just close Internet Explorer to end the InPrivate Browsing session.

Figure 3-11

ActiveX Filtering is enabled

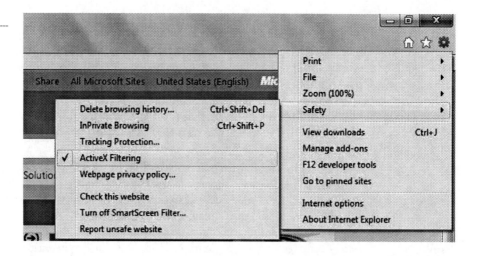

Figure 3-12

The Manage Add-ons dialog box

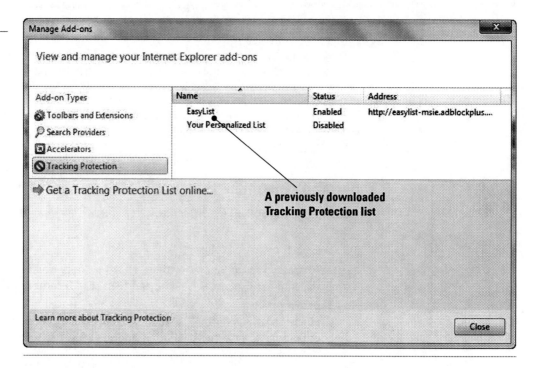

A previously downloaded
Tracking Protection list

Some security features, such as Tracking Protection, might require you to close Internet Explorer 9 and then reopen it to see the features in action.

■ Introducing Accessory Programs

THE BOTTOM LINE

Microsoft provides a wealth of free programs and utilities in Windows to help you be more productive, creative, and efficient. The Accessories folder in the All Programs list is your starting point for lots of handy tools.

Windows 7 comes bundled with many useful accessory programs, such as Calculator, Notepad, Paint, Snipping Tool, Windows Media Player, WordPad, and many more. The programs allow you to be productive in Windows without purchasing third-party programs.

To access these programs, click Start > All Programs > Accessories. Table 3-1 lists the programs in the Windows 7 Accessories folder. Not all programs are available in every edition of Windows 7.

Table 3-1

Window 7 Accessory Programs

Program	Description
Calculator	Performs basic mathematical functions such as addition, subtraction, multiplication, division. Also includes scientific, programmer, and statistics functions, along with unit conversions, date calculations, and worksheets to determine mortgage payments, vehicle lease payments, and fuel economy.
Command Prompt	Opens a window in which you run MS-DOS and other computer commands.
Connect to a Projector Connect to a Network Projector	Allows you to expand your screen to use another monitor or external projector.
Math Input Panel	Allows you to write and correct free-hand math equations using your mouse or other pointing device.
Notepad	Serves as a simple text editor.
Paint	Allows you to perform basic image editing.
Remote Desktop Connection	Connects two computers over a network or the Internet, allowing one computer to see and use the other computer's desktop. Remote Desktop Connection is covered later in this lesson.
Run	Allows you to run commands from the Start menu. Some commands require elevated or administrative privileges; to run these commands, use the *Run as administrator* command.
Snipping Tool	Allows you to capture, annotate, and save screen shots. Snipping Tool is covered later in this lesson.
Sound Recorder	Allows you to record sound from different audio devices, such as a microphone that's plugged into the sound card on your computer.
Sticky Notes	Allows you to keep notes on the desktop to help you remember important items. Available in different colors.
Sync Center	Allows you to sync any folder in your computer with a folder on an external drive connected to your computers or a network drive. Sync Center is covered later in this lesson.
Windows Explorer	Allows you to access files and folders on your computer, copy and move items, search for items, and more. This graphical file management system is built into many versions of Windows.
Windows Mobility Center	Allows you to control many different computer settings, such as screen brightness, volume, power/battery, WiFi, Bluetooth, sound, and so on. Windows Mobility Center is covered later in this lesson.
WordPad	Serves as a word processor, with many more features than Notepad.
Ease of Access	Allows you to open the Ease of Access Center to configure accessibility options, and gives you access to the speech recognition feature. See Lesson 2.

(continued)

Table 3-1

Continued

PROGRAM	DESCRIPTION
System Tools	Gives you access to Control Panel, Disk Cleanup, Disk Defragmenter, Resource Monitor, System Restore, and much more.
Tablet PC	Gives you access to tools to use a tablet PC's input device.
Windows PowerShell	Opens a command window useful for IT professionals. Windows PowerShell is covered later in this lesson.

> **TAKE NOTE***
> This lesson covers Snipping Tool, Sync Center, Windows Mobility Center, and Windows PowerShell in detail because they're listed as measureable skills for the 98-349 exam.

■ Using the Snipping Tool

 THE BOTTOM LINE

Home and business users alike need to capture screen shots occasionally for many different reasons. Windows 7 includes the Snipping Tool, an easy-to-use screen capture program with a few editing features.

A *screen shot*, also referred to as a snip or screen grab, is a snapshot of whatever is displayed on the computer screen. You might take a screen shot of an error message to help trouble-shoot a computer problem, you might capture screen shots of a process in a program to create a how-to guide, or you might capture a screen shot to save as an image to use in a report or other document.

CERTIFICATION READY
What is the Snipping Tool used for?
1.3

The *Snipping Tool* (see Figure 3-13) is an accessory program that comes with Windows 7 that allows you to take screen shots, annotate them, and save them. When using Snipping Tool, you can capture the entire screen, a window, a rectangular portion of the screen, or a free-form image. The free-form capture allows you to use your mouse pointer or other pointing device to draw around a non-rectangular object on the screen.

Figure 3-13

The Snipping Tool window

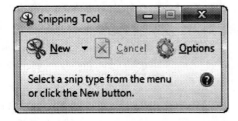

You can save images in GIF, JPG, PNG, or HTML format, then use Snipping Tool to add freehand annotations, highlight or erase part of the image, or send it to a recipient via e-mail. If you select the HTML format, Snipping Tool saves the screen shot as a Web archive file in MHT format, which you can open in a Web browser such as Internet Explorer.

> **TAKE NOTE***
> The Snipping Tool is available in Windows 7 Home Premium, Professional, Ultimate, and Enterprise editions.

USE THE SNIPPING TOOL TO CAPTURE A SCREEN SHOT

GET READY. To capture a screen shot with the Snipping Tool and save it as a graphics file, perform the following steps:

1. Open or display a file, program, window, Web page, or anything that contains an object or picture you want to capture in a screen shot.
2. Click **Start** > **All Programs** > **Accessories** > **Snipping Tool**.
3. Click the **New** drop-down menu and choose **Free-form Snip**, **Rectangular Snip**, **Window Snip**, or **Full-screen Snip** (see Figure 3-14). The default is Rectangular Snip, which is used in this example.

Figure 3-14

Selecting the type of screen shot to capture

4. A white overlay appears on your screen. Click and drag the mouse pointer over the area you want to capture (see Figure 3-15). An editing window appears, displaying the captured image.

> **TAKE NOTE** ✱ You can turn off the Snipping Tool overlay. Just click **Options**, uncheck the **Show screen overlay when Snipping Tool is active** check box, and click **OK**.

Figure 3-15

The captured image

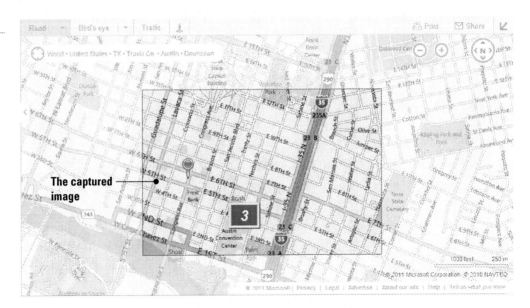

5. To save the image, click the **Save Snip** icon on the toolbar, which looks like a floppy diskette.
6. In the Save As dialog box, navigate to the location where you want to save the screen shot. In the **File name** text box, type a descriptive name for the file.
7. Click the Save as type drop-down menu and select **GIF**, **JPG**, or **PNG**.

TAKE NOTE* GIF files support 256 colors and are used primarily for Web sites. JPG is the most common picture file format, and it supports over 16 million colors. PNG files are an improvement to the GIF format and support "lossless compression," which means you can enlarge a PNG file to a certain extent without losing clarity and crispness.

8. Click **Save**. The screen capture is saved as a graphics file.

USE THE SNIPPING TOOL TO ANNOTATE AN IMAGE

GET READY. To annotate an image using the Snipping Tool, perform the following steps:

1. In the Snipping Tool editing window, click the down arrow to the right of the pen button on the toolbar. Select a pen color from the list.
2. Write or draw on the image (see Figure 3-16).

Figure 3-16

Annotating an image

3. Click the **Save Snip** icon to save the annotated image under the current file name or a new file name.

Remember, you can open an image saved with Snipping Tool in any graphics program (including Paint) to make detailed edits.

＋ MORE INFORMATION

For more information about the Snipping Tool, visit http://windows.microsoft.com/en-US/windows7/products/features/snipping-tool

---

■ Playing Back and Recording to Media

↓
THE BOTTOM LINE

Windows Media Player and Windows Media Center provide a wealth of media playback, ripping, and recording options. No longer relegated only to home use, both programs can be used in the work place for highly appealing presentations, training, and lobby entertainment.

Digital media is popular for both home and business users of Windows 7. Although many media software packages are available on the market, you should check out the latest versions of Windows Media Player and Windows Media Center to see if third-party tools are even needed. Both programs come bundled with most Windows 7, so home and business users have access to these full-featured programs without spending additional money.

Using Windows Media Player

If you need to simply play back almost any type of multimedia file, Windows Media Player should be the program you use. It's built into Windows 7 (so it's free), and its media burning and ripping features, along with the ability to stream multimedia to other networked computers, makes it a great choice at home and work.

CERTIFICATION READY
What is the name of the main window in Windows Media Player?
1.3

TAKE NOTE＊

Windows Media Player 12 supports the 3GP, AAC, AVCHD, MPEG-4, WMV, and WMA audio and video formats. It also supports most AVI, DivX, MOV, and Xvid files.

Windows Media Player 12 is a program that allows you to play back music and video files and view photos. Files stored in your Music, Pictures, Videos, and Recorded TV libraries appear in the Windows Media Player file list by default. If you're connected to a network, you can stream digital media files—audio, video, or photos—for playback or viewing from another computer or a server that hosts Windows media files. The main window in Windows Media Player is called the Player Library (see Figure 3-17).

Whether playing digital files on your computer, or from a CD or DVD, Windows Media Player includes common playback controls, such as Play, Shuffle, Repeat, Stop, Next, Previous, and a volume slider. You can switch to a smaller window, referred to as Now Playing mode, by clicking the *Switch to Now Playing* button in the lower-right corner. The Now Playing mode window appears (see Figure 3-18). To return to your library, click the *Switch to Library* button.

With Windows Media Player, you can do the following as well:

- **Create playlists:** Organize your music files into *playlists*, which are simply lists of music composed of songs from different albums, and may even be located on different areas of your computer or attached devices. Whatever appears in the library may be included in a playlist.

Figure 3-17

Windows Media Player main
window—the Player Library

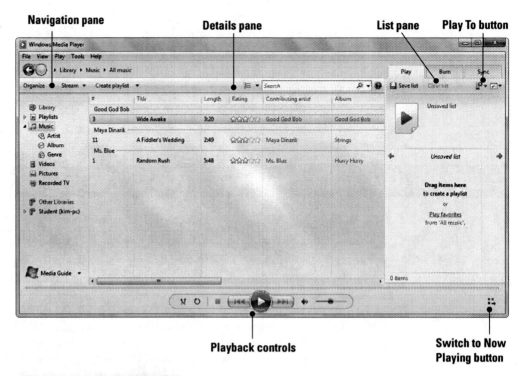

Navigation pane   Details pane   List pane   Play To button

Playback controls

Switch to Now
Playing button

Figure 3-18

Windows Media Player Now
Playing mode

Switch to
Library button

- **Rip music from CDs to your computer:** Insert a CD and, when a list of its tracks appears in the Windows Media Player window, click the Rip CD button. Windows Media Player rips the tracks on the CD to your Music library.

- **Burn CDs:** If you have a recordable optical drive on your computer, you can use Windows Media Player to burn a collection of your favorite songs to a CD.

- **Create slide shows:** Use Windows Media Player to create slide shows with playback controls in just a few clicks.

- **Share media across a network:** You can use the *Play to* command to share multimedia files across a network with a homegroup (a personal network, usually set up at home) or across the Internet.

If you pin Windows Media Player 12 to the Windows 7 taskbar, you can take advantage of Jump Lists for previously accessed files. The Jump List also includes playback controls at the bottom of the Jump List window to play music, a video, or view photos without having to open Windows Media Player first.

TAKE NOTE*

Microsoft has made Windows Media Player available in most editions of Windows 7: Starter, Home Premium, Professional, Ultimate, and Enterprise.

➕ MORE INFORMATION

For more information about Windows Media Player in Windows 7, visit http://windows.microsoft.com/en-US/windows7/products/features/windows-media-player-12 and http://windows.microsoft.com/en-US/windows7/Getting-started-with-Windows-Media-Player

PLAY BACK MEDIA FILES

GET READY. To listen to music files, watch videos, or view photos in Windows Media Player, perform the steps in this section.

To listen to music files in Windows Media player, perform the following steps:

1. Open Windows Media Player by clicking **Start**, selecting **All Programs**, and then selecting **Windows Media Player** near the top of the programs list. You can also click its icon in the taskbar if it appears there.

2. Click the **Music** library in the navigation pane, click the file you want to hear in the file list, and click the **Play** button along the bottom of the window.

   Another option is to click the **Play** tab in the upper-right corner of the Windows Media Player window, drag the songs you want to hear to the **Play** tab, and then click the **Play** button.

3. After the file has finished playing, Windows Media Player automatically plays the next file in the list.

To watch a video in Windows Media Player, perform the following steps:

1. Click the **Videos** library in the navigation pane, and then double-click the file you want to view in the file list. Windows Media Player launches a special viewing window and plays back the video.

2. Place your mouse pointer over the window to display playback controls (see Figure 3-19).

Figure 3-19

Playback controls appear in the video viewing window when you hover your mouse pointer over the window

Playback controls

To view photos in Windows Media Player, perform the following steps:

1. Click the **Pictures** library in the navigation pane. Thumbnails of the photos in your Pictures library appear.

2. To view all of the photos as a slide show, click the **Play** button. Windows starts the slide show in its own window (see Figure 3-20).

Figure 3-20

A slide show in Windows Media Player

Courtesy of Marion Post Wolcott, Farm Security Administration/Office of War Information

To stop any playback feature, click the Stop button in the playback controls, and then click Go To Library.

⊕ CREATE A PLAYLIST

GET READY. To create a playlist of music, perform the following steps:

1. In Windows Media Player, in the Player Library, click the **Create playlist** button on the toolbar.

2. Type a name for the new playlist that appears in the Navigation pane (see Figure 3-21).

3. Drag and drop songs from the file list to the new playlist in the Navigation pane.

An auto playlist gives you more control and options. To create an autoplaylist, click the down arrow on the *Create playlist* button, select *Create auto playlist*, and follow the prompts.

⊕ BURN A MUSIC CD

GET READY. To burn a music CD, perform the following steps:

1. Insert a blank CD or DVD into your computer's recordable media drive.

2. In Windows Media Player, in the Player Library, click the **Music** library to display the file list.

3. Click the **Burn** tab.

4. Drag individual songs, playlists, or entire albums to the burn list on the right (see Figure 3-22).

5. Click **Start burn**.

Figure 3-21

Creating a playlist in Windows Media Player

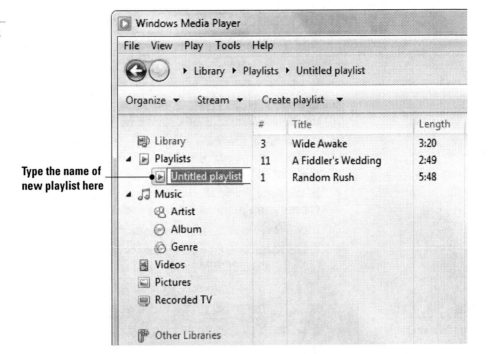

Type the name of new playlist here

Figure 3-22

Creating a list of files to burn to media

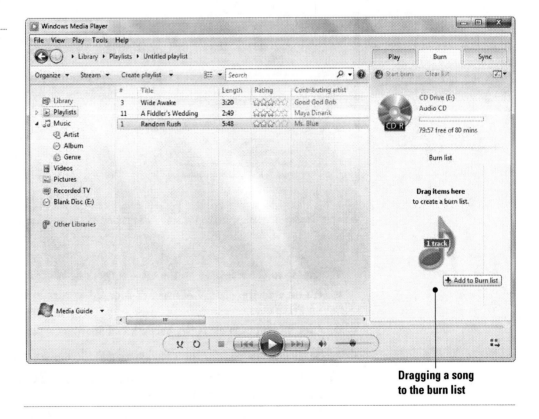

Dragging a song to the burn list

The CD ejects when the burning process completes. The burn process works similarly for other types of media files.

PREPARE YOUR COMPUTER TO STREAM MEDIA FILES

GET READY. To stream media from your home computer, perform the following steps:

1. Ensure your computer is connected to your local network and that you are connected to a homegroup. For information on homegroups, see Lesson 6.

2. In Windows Media Player, in the Player Library, click **Stream** on the menu bar and then select **Turn on media streaming with HomeGroup**.

3. On the Media streaming options page, click **Turn on media streaming**. If you're prompted for an administrator password or confirmation, type the password or provide confirmation and then click **OK**.

4. In the Network and Sharing Center window, click **Advanced sharing settings** (or click **Choose homegroup and sharing options**).

5. Click **Choose media streaming options**.

6. Type a name for your media library in the text box at the top (see Figure 3-23).

Figure 3-23

Configuring streaming media options

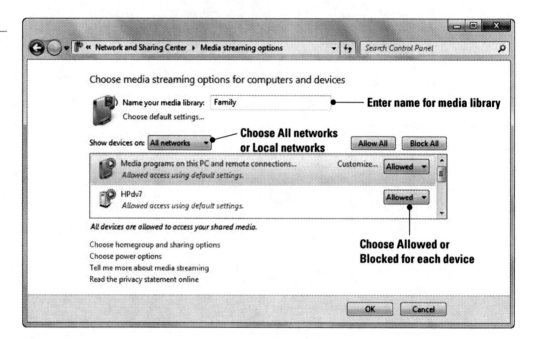

7. Choose to show devices on the local network or on all networks.

8. For each device, choose **Allowed** or **Blocked** to control whether others can see files on those devices.

9. Click **OK** and then close the Network and Sharing Center window.

To stream media files over the Internet, perform the following steps:

1. In Windows Media Player, in the Player Library, click **Stream** and then click **Allow Internet access to my home media**.

2. In the Internet Home Media Access dialog box, click **Link an online ID**.

3. Follow the prompts to link your user account with an online ID, such as your Windows Live ID. When you return to the Internet Home Media Access dialog box, click **Allow Internet access to my home media** again (see Figure 3-24). Click **Yes** in the dialog box that appears, and then click **OK**.

Figure 3-24

The Internet Home Media Access dialog box

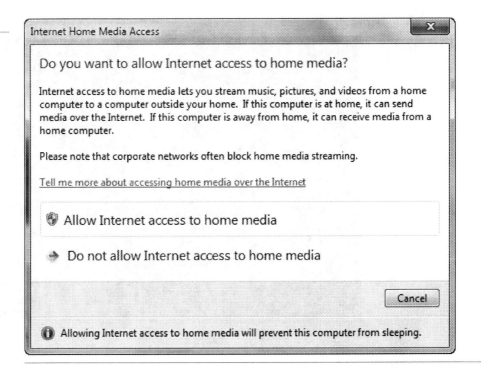

The Play To feature in Windows Media Player allows you to select multimedia you would like to play on a connected device, such as a stereo system at home. Just select the media you want to stream in Windows Media Player, click the Play tab, click the *Play to* button near the upper-right corner of the window, and then select the device on your network that will play back the media. You can use the controls in the Play To dialog box to control playback volume and other settings.

Using Windows Media Center

Windows Media Center is a cut above Windows Media Player, incorporating many of the same types of features but with digital video recorder functionality and built-in access to online entertainment content.

Windows Media Center (see Figure 3-25) is a multi-faceted program that provides a complete entertainment system for your computer. Similar to Windows Media Player, you use Windows Media Center to play music, create playlists, watch videos, play recorded TV programs, and display pictures and slide shows. However, Media Center offers much more. For example, you can watch, pause, and record HDTV, watch live TV and online programming, and listen to radio stations.

CERTIFICATION READY
What Windows 7 program is used to play recorded TV programs?
1.3

Watching TV programming requires a TV tuner and a subscription to a cable service or a similar service. You don't need a digital video recorder (DVR)—your computer acts like a DVR, enabling you to record shows and even schedule shows in advance. If you don't have a TV tuner but do have Internet access, you can still use Internet TV in the latest version of Windows Media Center. Internet TV is a service that allows you to watch some TV shows, movies, and clips streamed from the Internet.

Windows Media Center supports the same audio and video formats as Windows Media Player: 3GP, AAC, AVCHD, MPEG-4, WMV, and WMA, and most AVI, DivX, MOV, and Xvid files.

Figure 3-25

The Windows Media Center
main window

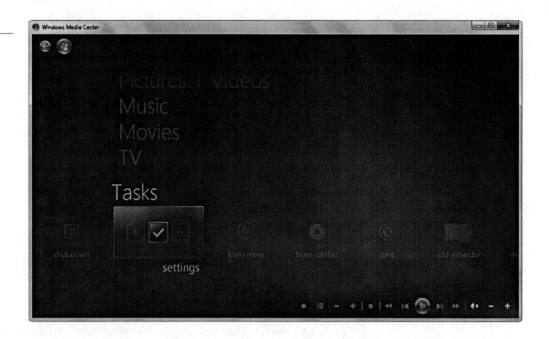

You can also share media over a network from Windows Media Center with the use of a
Windows Media Center Extender. You can buy an actual Extender device or use an Xbox
360 as an Extender. Each device you want to stream media to, such as an HDTV, needs
an Extender. You can stream to up to five Extenders from a single computer running
Windows 7.

 PLAY BACK OR VIEW MULTIMEDIA

GET READY. To use Windows Media Center for multimedia playback and viewing, perform
the following steps:

1. Click the **Start > All Programs > Windows Media Center**.
2. To view photos or videos, click **Pictures + Videos**, and then click **Picture Library** or **Video Library**. Just double-click any pictures or videos you want to view.
3. Click the green Windows Media Center button in the upper-left corner of the Windows Media Center to return to the main menu.
4. To listen to music, click **Music Library**. Select music you want to listen to, and then click **Add to now playing**.

Use the playback controls at the bottom of the window to stop, pause, play, rewind, and forward the multimedia file that's playing.

 CONFIGURE SETTINGS

GET READY. To configure settings in Windows Media Center, perform the following steps:

1. In the Windows Media Center main window, hover your mouse pointer over the last menu item at the bottom. A down arrow displays. Scroll down to the Tasks menu and click **Settings**. The Settings window displays (see Figure 3-26).

Figure 3-26

The Windows Media Center
Settings window

To add an Extender:

1. Click **Extender**, click **add extender**, and then follow the prompts.

   To add libraries of content to Windows Media Center, return to the Settings window and then perform the following steps:

2. Return to the Settings window and click **Media Libraries.**

3. In the Media Library window, select the type of media you want to add (see Figure 3-27) and then click **Next.**

4. Click **Add folders to the library** and click **Next.**

5. Choose **On this computer** or **On another computer** and then click **Next.**

6. Select the folders to add to the library (see Figure 3-27) and then click **Next.**

Figure 3-27

Adding media to Windows
Media Center

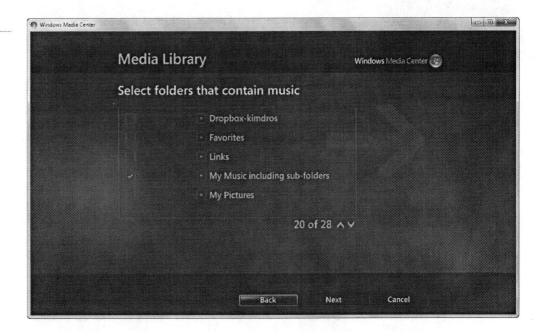

7. Select **Yes, use these locations** and then click **Finish**. Windows Media Center adds the content of the folders to your library.

There are many more settings to be familiar with in Windows Media Center. Take some time to browse all of the options in the Settings window.

> **+ MORE INFORMATION**
>
> To get details about Windows Media Center, visit http://windows.microsoft.com/en-US/windows/products/windows-media-center

■ Understanding Sync Center

> ↓
> **THE BOTTOM LINE**
>
> If you need to frequently switch between network folders and the files on your laptop hard drive, use Sync Center to ensure that you always have the latest files.

CERTIFICATION READY
What Windows 7 feature allows you to sync files between your computer and mobile devices?
1.4

CERTIFICATION READY
What term best describes the type of files you can access without being connected to the resource from which you synchronized?
4.4

Sync Center (see Figure 3-28) is a feature in Windows 7 that allows you to sync files between your computer and a network location or with some mobile devices. Syncing allows you to keep two or more versions of the same file, stored on your computer and on a network folder, identical to the other. For example, if you add, delete, or modify a file in one location, the synchronization process ensures the files match each other.

After syncing is complete, you can access network files without being connected to the resource. These files are referred to as *offline files*. You can also use Sync Center to check the results of a recent sync to ensure the files were synced successfully, or to re-sync if errors occurred.

To get started with Sync Center, you must first set up a sync partnership with the network or external drive you want to use. Then, anytime you want to ensure your files are synced, right-click the network drive and select Always available offline. Once your files are done syncing, a symbol appears next to the network drive so you can see at a glance that the files are synchronized.

The Sync Center allows you to schedule synchronization, resolve errors that occurred during synchronization, change the amount of disk space allocated to offline files, and encrypt your offline files for security.

> **TAKE NOTE***
>
> Although you can use Sync Center to sync a mobile device with your computer, Sync Center doesn't work with all devices. Instead, try Device Stage in Windows 7 or use the sync software provided by the mobile device manufacturer.

> **+ MORE INFORMATION**
>
> For more information about Sync Center, visit http://windows.microsoft.com/en-US/windows7/What-is-Sync-Center

Figure 3-28

The Sync Center main window

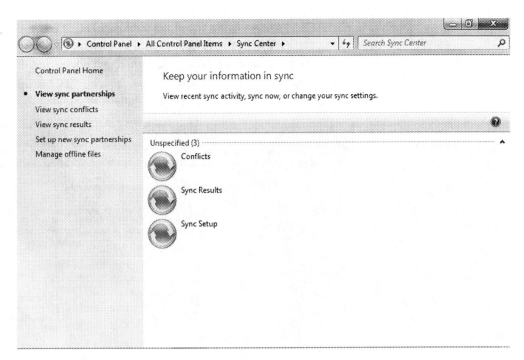

SET UP A SYNCHRONIZATION PARTNERSHIP

GET READY. To set up a synchronization partnership, perform the following steps:

1. Open Sync Center by clicking **Start > Control Panel > Sync Center.** (Alternately, click **Start**, and in the **Search programs and files** search box, type **sync.** In the results list that displays, select **Sync Center.**)

2. In Sync Center, in the left pane, click **Manage offline files.** The Offline Files dialog box displays (see Figure 3-29).

Figure 3-29

The Offline Files dialog box

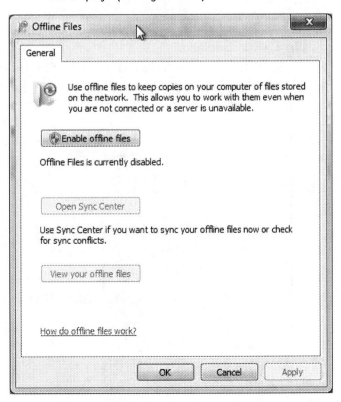

3. Click **Enable offline files**, and then click **OK**. If you're prompted for an administrator password or confirmation, type the password or provide confirmation.

4. Close any open windows, shut down all programs, and then restart your computer.

5. Return to Sync Center and, in the left pane, click **Set up new sync partnerships**. The Sync Setup screen displays (see Figure 3-30).

Figure 3-30

The Sync Setup screen

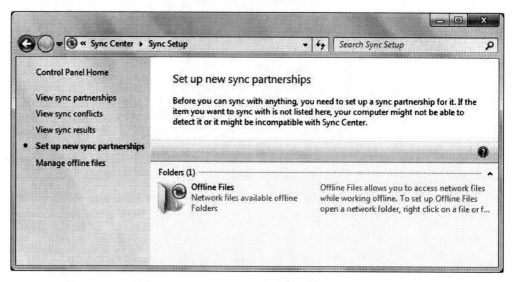

6. Click the name of the drive in the list of available sync partnerships.

7. On the toolbar, click **Set up**.

8. Select the settings and schedule to determine how and when you want to sync your device with your computer.

SYNCHRONIZE FILES

GET READY. To sync files on your computer with a network location, perform the following steps:

1. Click **Start > Computer**.

2. Browse to the drive or folder that contains the files you want to keep synchronized.

3. Right-click the name of the drive or folder, and then click **Always available offline** (see Figure 3-31).

Figure 3-31

Synchronizing files

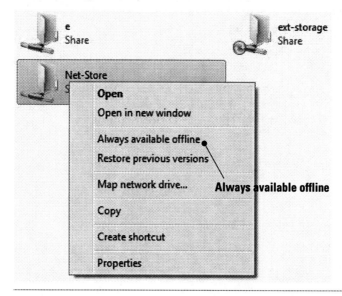

Once the synchronization process is complete, a symbol displays next to the network drive or folder indicating that the files are synchronized.

■ Using Windows Mobility Center

Rather than using different tools to adjust your laptop's screen brightness, wireless settings, and more, just open the Windows Mobility Center, which displays groups of settings all in one interface.

Windows Mobility Center is a control panel of sorts that gives you access to several laptop settings, from volume to screen brightness to power options to WiFi and Bluetooth settings—all in one place. Although the settings can be accessed from various icons and commands within Windows, you can make adjustments from a single window in Windows Mobility Center. Figure 3-32 shows the Windows Mobility Center window.

 TAKE NOTE*

Windows Mobility Center is included on laptops running the Windows 7 Home Premium, Professional, Ultimate, and Enterprise editions. Presentation settings, however, are not available in Windows 7 Home Premium.

Figure 3-32

The Windows Mobility Center window

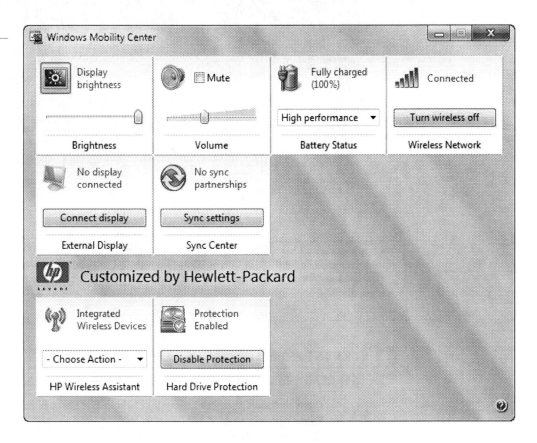

Windows Mobility Center displays settings in boxes, or tiles. The tiles that are displayed depend on your hardware and laptop manufacturer. In addition, a setting that is turned off or disabled might not display, or display with a red X, such as if you turn off your WiFi antenna by pressing the F key.

CERTIFICATION READY
Which settings can be adjusted by using the Mobility Center?
1.4

Table 3-2 describes common Windows Mobility Center settings. Not all settings are available on all laptops, so a few settings in the table are not displayed in Figure 3-32.

Table 3-2

Typical Window Mobility Center Settings

SETTING	DESCRIPTION
Brightness	Allows you to adjust the brightness of your laptop display. Move the slider to the left to decrease brightness, and to the right to increase brightness. Display brightness is related to the power plan for your laptop; those settings are adjusted in the Battery Status tile.
Volume	Allows you to increase or decrease speaker volume, or check the Mute check box to temporarily disable audio.
Battery Status	Allows you to see how much battery charge remains and adjust the power plan for your laptop. Power plans vary but offer two at a minimum: one for running on battery power and another for running on AC power.
Wireless Network	Allows you to turn your wireless network adapter on or off and see the status of your wireless network connection.
Screen Rotation	For tablet PCs, this feature allows you to change the orientation of your screen (portrait or landscape).
External Display	Allows you to connect an external monitor to your laptop.
Sync Center	Allows you to access settings to sync files with a network location, or with a mobile device. Sync Center is covered in more detail in this lesson.
Presentation Settings	Provides you with access to settings for connecting your laptop to a projector for presentations.

✛ MORE INFORMATION

For more information about settings in Windows Mobility Center, visit http://windows.microsoft.com/en-US/windows7/products/features/windows-mobility-center

CHANGE MOBILITY CENTER SETTINGS

GET READY. To adjust settings in Windows Mobility Center, perform the following steps:

1. Open Windows Mobility Center by clicking the **Start** button, typing **mobility** in the **Search programs and files** search box, and then selecting **Windows Mobility Center** from the results list.
2. Adjust the screen brightness by moving the **Brightness** slider left or right.
3. Click the **Battery Status** drop-down list (see Figure 3-33) and then select another power plan, such as **Power saver**. Notice how the screen brightness changes again.
4. Click the drop-down list again and select the original power plan.

Figure 3-33

Selecting a different power plan in the Battery Status drop-down list

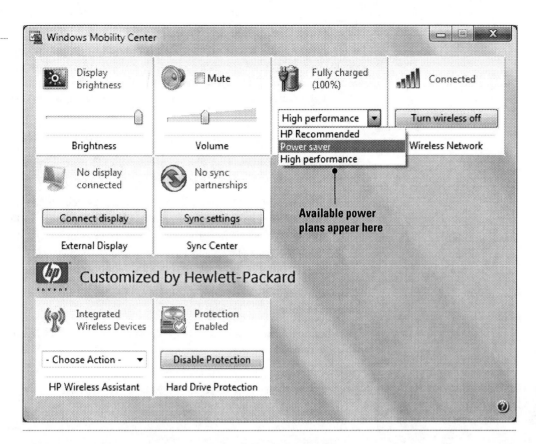

Click the drop-down lists in other tiles of Windows Mobility Center to see which options are available.

■ Understanding Remote Desktop Services

THE BOTTOM LINE

Remote Desktop Services, formerly known as Terminal Services, enables computers to act like mainframe terminals. The processing required to run applications and even use the desktop is performed by the server rather than the client computer.

CERTIFICATION READY
What term best describes the Windows 7 technology that allows a computer to connect to a remote server and then run applications from that server?
2.4

TAKE NOTE*

The Remote Desktop Services server must run Windows Server 2008 R2, Windows Server 2008, Windows Server 2003, or Windows 2000 Server.

Windows 7 **Remote Desktop Services** is the technology that allows a computer (the client) to connect to a remote server (also called a host computer) and run applications from the server. Although the client computer may be running Windows 7, it doesn't run the actual application—the server handles all processing. This is the opposite of a typical Windows 7 computer with applications such as Microsoft Office installed on the hard disk. Remote Desktop Services can also provide a virtual user desktop for remote users. When a user accesses the server, the user is provided a virtual desktop interface that looks and responds similarly to the client computer's actual desktop.

A major benefit of Remote Desktop Services is that administrators can manage user desktops and applications from a central place—at the server—rather than at the physical client computer.

A few of the services provided by Remote Desktop Services include the following:

- **RemoteApp:** Enables a remote user to log on to a Remote Desktop Services server via a Web browser and run a single application.
- **Remote Desktop Web Access:** Enables a remote user to log on and run programs and virtual desktops. This feature lets users create a RemoteApp and Desktop Connection using the Start menu on a computer running Windows 7 or via a Web browser.

In a Remote Desktop Services environment, a network administrator must first set up resources for a remote user to connect to. This is referred to as "publishing the resources." The administrator must also send the user a setup file or Web address. The user either runs the setup file or enters the Web address in a Web browser to make the connection to the server. Once a user accesses the remote server, the resources will be available in a folder on the user's computer.

 CONNECT TO A SERVER USING REMOTE DESKTOP WEB ACCESS

GET READY. To connect to a remote server using Remote Desktop Web Access in a Web browser, perform the following steps:

1. In a Web browser, type the Web address provided by the network administrator. The Web address is in the **https://computer name/rdweb** format or the **https://ipaddress/rdweb** format.
2. Type the **User Name** and **Password**, and then click **OK**.

When the user is finished with the session, she should log off and close the Web browser to ensure the connection is closed.

The client application for Remote Desktop Services is called Remote Desktop Connection, which is covered next.

Understanding Remote Desktop Connection

Anyone who's on the go often needs to access a computer at home or at work. Remote Desktop Connection allows you to set up a computer for remote access, and then connect to that computer wherever you may be. All you need is an Internet connection.

Windows 7 *Remote Desktop Connection* allows you to access another computer on a network or over the Internet, and use the computer as if you were sitting in front of it. This feature is handy for people who want to access files on their home computer while at work, for example. Remote Desktop Services is the technology that allows Remote Desktop Connection to work.

When setting up Remote Desktop Connection, you must allow remote connections to the computer you want to access remotely. The remote computer may run any of these operating systems:

- Windows XP Professional edition
- Windows Vista Business, Ultimate, or Enterprise edition
- Windows 7 Professional, Ultimate, or Enterprise edition

Setting up Remote Desktop Connection can take some effort if the remote computer is outside of your network. You might need to configure your firewall to allow Remote Desktop connections. You must also determine the IP address of the remote computer (such as the home computer you want to connect to), and configure the remote computer's router to forward TCP port 3389 to the destination computer's IP address.

CERTIFICATION READY
Which Windows 7 feature allows you to set up a computer for remote access and then connect to that computer regardless of where you might be located?
1.4

CERTIFICATION READY
What does Remote Desktop Connection allow you to do?
2.4

TAKE NOTE★
Remote Desktop comes with all editions of Windows 7; however, you can only connect to computers running the Professional, Ultimate, or Enterprise editions.

TAKE NOTE★
Allowing remote connections between your computer and a remote computer outside your network presents a security risk. The session can be hijacked by a malicious user. Whenever possible, be sure both computers use strong encryption, complex passwords, and strong authentication to minimize the possibility of attack.

To learn how to set up a Remote Desktop connection with a computer outside of your network, visit the Allow Remote Desktop connections from outside your home network Web page at http://windows.microsoft.com/en-US/windows7/allow-remote-desktop-connections-from-outside-your-home-network.

➕ MORE INFORMATION

For more information about how to use Remote Desktop Connection, visit http://windows.microsoft.com/en-US/windows7/products/features/remote-desktop-connection. You can learn about Remote Desktop Services at http://windows.microsoft.com/en-US/windows7/What-is-Remote-Desktop-Services

---

⊘ SET UP REMOTE DESKTOP CONNECTION

GET READY. To set up Remote Desktop Connection, perform the following steps:

1. Click **Start**, right-click **Computer**, and then click **Properties**. The System window displays.

2. In the left pane, click **Remote settings.** If you're prompted for an administrator password or confirmation, type the password or provide confirmation. The System dialog box displays with the Remote tab displayed (see Figure 3-34).

Figure 3-34

The Remote tab

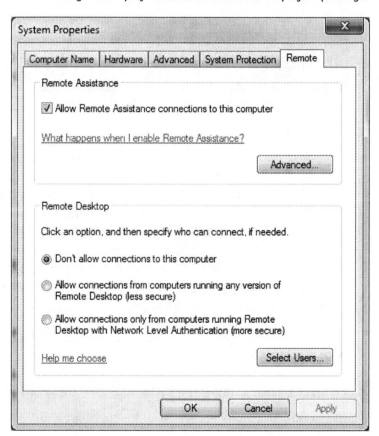

3. In the **Remote Desktop** section, select one of the options to allow connections:

   - **Don't allow connections to this computer:** Selecting this option prevents anyone from connecting to your computer using Remote Desktop or RemoteApp.

   - **Allow connections from computers running any version of Remote Desktop:** This option allows users running Windows XP, Windows Vista, or Windows 7 to connect to your computer using Remote Desktop or RemoteApp. If you aren't sure which operating system is running on the remote computer, use this option.

- **Select Allow connections only from computers running Remote Desktop with Network Level Authentication:** This option allows Windows 7 users to connect to your computer if they're running Remote Desktop or RemoteApp with Network Level Authentication. This option offers the most security.

4. Click **Select Users.**

5. In the Remote Desktop Users dialog box, click **Add.** The Select Users dialog box displays (which might be named Select Users or Groups). See Figure 3-35.

Figure 3-35

The Select Users dialog box

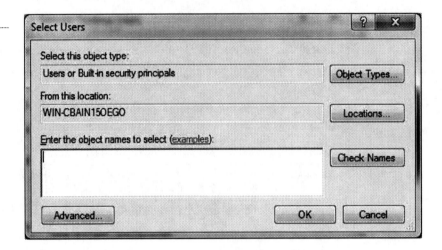

6. Perform one of the following steps:

- To find users, specify the types of user names (objects) you want to search for by clicking the **Object Types** button.
- To specify the search location, click the **Locations** button.
- In the Enter the object names to select box, type the user name that you want to search for, and then click **Check Names.** If the user name isn't found, click **Advanced** to run an advanced search.

7. When you find the user name you want to add, click **OK.** The name will be displayed in the list of users in the Remote Desktop Users dialog box.

8. Click **OK,** and then click **OK** again.

Once the remote computer is set up to accept connections, leave the computer running in order to connect to it at a later time.

 CONNECT TO A COMPUTER WITH REMOTE DESKTOP CONNECTION

GET READY. To connect to a remote computer, perform the following steps:

1. Click **Start** and in the **Search programs and files** search box, type **remote connect.** In the results list that displays, select **Remote Desktop Connection.** The Remote Desktop Connection window displays (see Figure 3-36).

2. In the **Computer** field, type the IP address or name of the remote computer if both computers are on the same private network. If the remote computer is on a different network, type the router's public IP address followed by a colon and the port number (for example, **XXX.XXX.XX.XXX:3389**). Replace the Xs with your actual public IP address.

3. Log on to the remote computer.

Figure 3-36

The Remote Desktop Connection window

Once you connect, you can access resources on the remote computer as if you were sitting in front of it.

+ MORE INFORMATION

For more information about Remote Desktop Connection, visit http://windows.microsoft.com/en-US/windows7/products/features/remote-desktop-connection

■ Understanding Remote Management and Assistance

THE BOTTOM LINE

When you're asked to help a friend or co-worker with a computer problem, being able to see the person's computer can make all the difference in resolving the problem. Windows Remote Assistance allows you to see the desktop of another user even though that user (and his computer) is located remotely. You can even take control of the remote computer if necessary.

Windows Remote Assistance is similar to Remote Desktop Connection, but the purpose of Remote Assistance is to allow one person to connect to another user's computer to provide "hands-on" help. For example, Albert is a traveling salesperson who is having trouble formatting a document in Microsoft Word. Maria, a technical support specialist at the main office, can set up a Remote Assistance connection with Albert's laptop, and then take control of his computer and show him how to fix the formatting issues.

Windows Remote Assistance sessions are encrypted for safety. They're also password protected, so only a person who is invited to the Remote Assistance session can connect to the computer.

To request remote help and initiate a Remote Assistance session, you send an invitation to the person who will be assisting you. That person accepts the invitation and connects to your computer.

+ MORE INFORMATION

For more information about Windows Remote Assistance, visit http://windows.microsoft.com/en-US/windows7/What-is-Windows-Remote-Assistance

⊖ SET UP A WINDOWS REMOTE ASSISTANCE SESSION

GET READY. To set up a Windows Remote Assistance session, perform the following steps:

1. Click **Start** and in the **Search programs and files** search box, type **remote assist**. In the results list that displays, select **Windows Remote Assistance**. The Windows Remote Assistance window displays.

2. Click **Invite someone you trust to help you.**

If an error message appears stating that your computer is not set up to send invitations, click Repair. The problem may be related to your firewall, which needs to be disabled temporarily. Start Windows Remote Assistance again after the problem is resolved.

3. In the screen that displays (see Figure 3-37), either create an invitation as a file and send it via e-mail automatically (if the option is available) or click **Save this invitation as a file**. If you chose to save the file, the file is named Invitation.msrc. Send it via e-mail to the support person.

Figure 3-37

The Windows Remote Assistance window

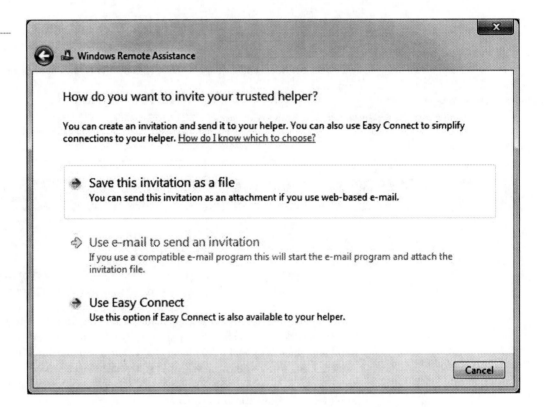

4. A dialog box displays with a password (see Figure 3-38). Give this password to the support person over the phone.

Figure 3-38

The Windows Remote Assistance password dialog box

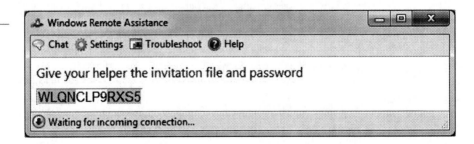

5. Leave the session open and wait for the support person to connect to your computer.
6. The support person receives the invitation and opens it. A Remote Assistance dialog box displays, prompting for the password (see Figure 3-39).

Figure 3-39

The Remote Assistance dialog box appears on the support person's desktop

7. After typing the password, Windows Remote Assistance attempts to connect to the client's computer.

8. The client must click **OK** in the dialog box that displays, asking if it is OK for the support person to connect.

9. The Windows Remote Assistance window displays on both the client's desktop (see Figure 3-40) and the support person's desktop.

Figure 3-40

The Windows Remote Assistance window on the client's computer

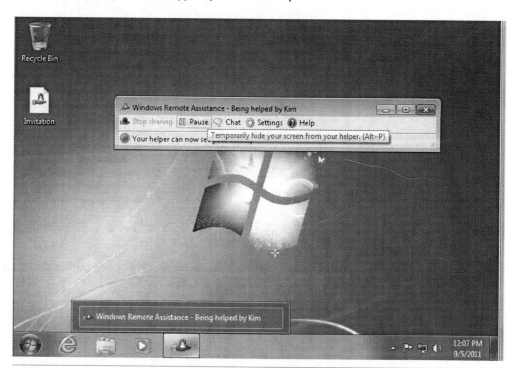

Any actions the client performs are displayed to the support person. The support person can click *Request control* to take control of the client's desktop through the Windows Remote Assistance window. For security purposes, a dialog box is displayed on the client's desktop, prompting for permission. At any time, either user can click *Stop sharing* to prevent the support person from controlling the client's desktop. While a Remote Assistance session is live, both the support person and the client can open a chat window to communicate rather than communicate using a telephone. To end the session, simply close the Windows Remote Assistance window.

Using the MMC

When assisting users with computer problems or maintaining systems, a support person often needs to check computer events, look at computer resource usage, or examine a disk's partition, among other tasks. You may use Microsoft Management Console (MMC) tools and utilities for this purpose.

Lesson 2 introduced the *Microsoft Management Console (MMC)*, a collection of administrative tools called *snap-ins*. An MMC snap-in is a utility provided by Microsoft or a third party that's accessible through a common interface. Administrators use MMC tools for managing hardware, software, and network components on a computer.

Administrative Tools is a popular collection of tools that use the MMC. You can access Administrative Tools by typing **admin tools** in the *Search programs and files* search box and selecting Administrative Tools from the results list. The Administrative Tools window (see Figure 3-41) lists several tools.

CERTIFICATION READY
What is an MMC snap-in?
1.5

Figure 3-41

The Administrative Tools window

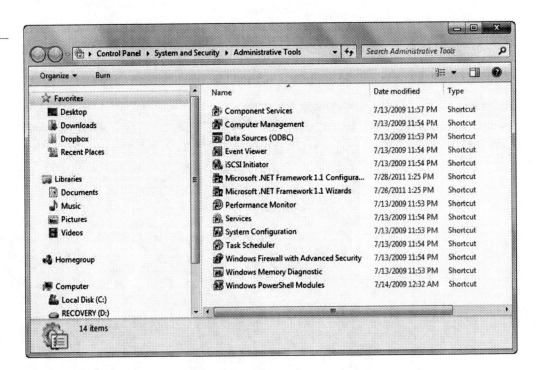

TAKE NOTE✱ To show Administrative Tools in the Start menu, right-click Start, click Properties, and then click Customize. Scroll down to the System administrative tools heading, select *Display on the All Programs menu*, and then click OK.

Computer Management is a popular snap-in that includes several tools such as Disk Management for configuring hard disks and their partitions and Event Viewer, which allows you to view computer event information such as program starting and stopping (including program crashes) and security problems. (See Figure 3-42.) You can manage system performance and resources using Performance Monitor, which is under Performance > Monitoring Tools.

Some administrators and power users create a custom MMC that includes only the tools they use regularly, creating a toolkit of sorts.

Figure 3-42

The Computer Management window

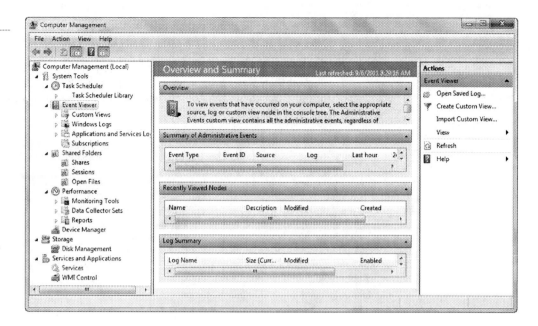

CREATE A CUSTOM MMC

GET READY. To create a custom MMC, perform the following steps:

1. Click **Start**, type **MMC** in the Start menu and in the **Search programs and files** search box, type **mmc**. In the results list that displays, select **mmc.exe**.

2. In the MMC Console window that displays, click **File > Add/Remove Snap-in**. The Add or Remove Snap-ins dialog box displays.

3. In the Available snap-ins on the left, select a snap-in of your choice, such as **Computer Management** (see Figure 3-43). In the middle of the dialog box, click the **Add** button.

Figure 3-43

Selecting snap-ins for a custom MMC

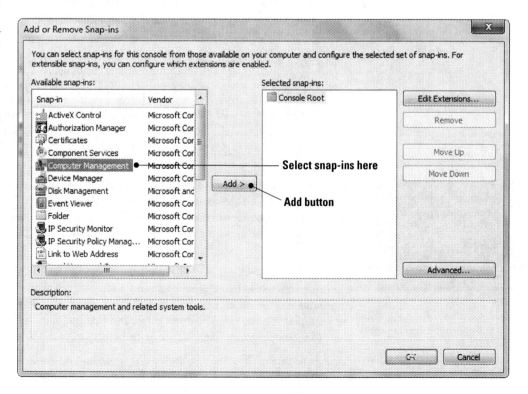

In the dialog box that displays, leave **Local computer** selected (unless the computer you want to manage is one other than the current computer).

4. Click **Finish**. The snap-in is added to the Selected snap-ins pane on the right.

5. Repeat Step 3 and Step 4 for each snap-in you want to include in the custom MMC. Figure 3-44 shows the Console window with a few snap-ins added.

Figure 3-44

A custom MMC

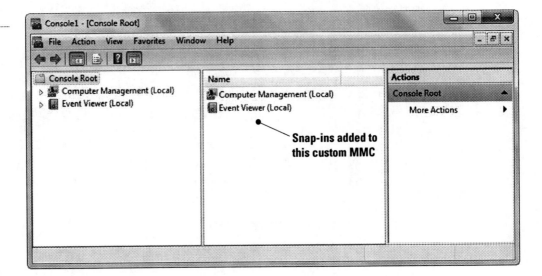

6. Click **OK**.

7. Click **File > Save As**. In the **File name** text box, type a name for the custom MMC and then click **Save**.

To avoid exposing a computer to malicious attacks, Microsoft recommends that you use MMC snap-ins when you are not logged on as Administrator.

Using Windows PowerShell

The MS-DOS command window—accessed by clicking Start and typing **cmd** in the *Search programs and files* search box and selecting cmd.exe in the resulting list—doesn't provide all of the commands you might need. For scripting and other administrative tasks, you must use Windows PowerShell.

CERTIFICATION READY
What term describes the command-line interface used mainly by IT professionals to run scripts?
1.5

Windows PowerShell is a command-line interface used mainly by IT professionals to run cmdlets (pronounced *command-lets*), complete background jobs (processes or programs that run in the background without a user interface), and run scripts to perform administrative tasks. If you're familiar with the UNIX shell, Windows PowerShell commands should seem highly familiar.

The Windows PowerShell environment is built on the .NET Framework, which allows administrators to use many more tools and commands than the MS-DOS command window environment. PowerShell and the MS-DOS command environment are compatible, however. For example, you can run Windows command-line programs in Windows PowerShell and also start Windows programs like Calculator and Notepad at the Windows PowerShell prompt.

Another feature of Windows PowerShell is remoting. Administrators can use cmdlets to access remote computers or use the Windows PowerShell Remoting service to run commands on remote computers or even many remote machines. Windows PowerShell Remoting can require substantial setup, which is not within the scope of this book.

 MORE INFORMATION

For more information about Windows PowerShell, visit the Windows PowerShell Getting Started Guide at http://msdn.microsoft.com/en-us/library/aa973757%28v=vs.85%29.aspx. Windows PowerShell Remoting commands can be found at http://msdn.microsoft.com/en-us/library/ee706585(v=vs.85).aspx

RUN A CMDLET IN WINDOWS POWERSHELL

GET READY. To run a cmdlet in Windows PowerShell, perform the following steps:

1. Click **Start > All Programs > Accessories**, click the **Windows PowerShell** folder, and then click **Windows PowerShell**. (Alternately, click **Start**, and in the **Search programs and files** search box, type **powershell**. In the results list that displays, select Windows PowerShell. The **Windows PowerShell** window displays.

2. A commonly used command is ps (or get-process). The ps command lists the currently running processes and their details, such as the process ID, process name, and percentage of processor usage (CPU). Type **ps** and press Enter. (See Figure 3-45.)

Figure 3-45

Running the ps command in Windows PowerShell

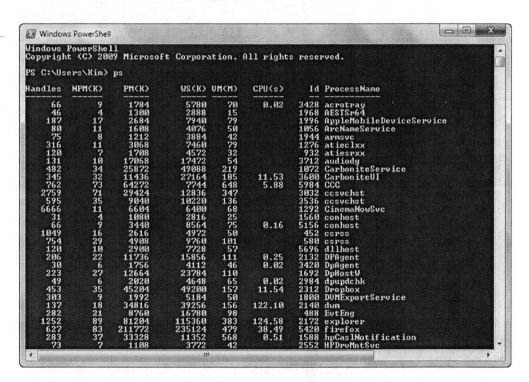

3. To get help with the ps command, type **get-help ps** and press **Enter**.

4. To view running services, type **get-service** and then press **Enter**. A list of services displays, along with their status (Running or Stopped).

TAKE NOTE*

You'll learn about managing services in Lesson 4 using the MMC; for now, know that you can use the PowerShell commands Stop-Service *servicename* and Start-Service *servicename* to accomplish the same tasks.

5. To exit the Window PowerShell window, type **exit** and then press **Enter**.

SKILL SUMMARY

IN THIS LESSON YOU LEARNED:

- Internet Explorer 9 is the latest Web browser from Microsoft. The Internet Explorer 9 interface includes enhanced user features, such as a large Back button, a combined Address bar and search box, One Box, the New Page tab, and the ability to pin sites to the Windows 7 taskbar.

- Internet Explorer 9 security and privacy features include ActiveX Filtering, SmartScreen Filter, a Cross-Site Scripting (XSS) Filter, InPrivate Browsing, Tracking Protection, and domain highlighting.

- Windows 7 native applications include accessory programs such as Calculator, Notepad, and Paint, plus much more. The Snipping Tool allows you to capture, save, an annotate screen shots. Windows Media Player is a versatile music and video player, with the ability to view slide shows of photos, share media across a network, and burn and rip CDs.

- Windows Media Center turns your computer into a digital video recorder, allowing you to record and play back TV programs, including HDTV. You need a TV tuner and a subscription to a TV programming service (such as cable).

- Sync Center is a feature in Windows 7 that allows you to sync files between a computer and a network location, and between a computer and some mobile devices.

- Windows Mobility Center is a control panel of sorts that gives you access to several laptop settings, from volume to screen brightness to power options to WiFi and Bluetooth settings—all in one place.

- Windows 7 Remote Desktop Connection allows you to access another computer on a network or over the Internet and use the computer as if you were sitting in front of it.

- Windows Remote Assistance is similar to Remote Desktop Connection. Remote Assistance allows one person to connect to another user's computer to provide "hands-on" help.

- You can access Administrative Tools from the Microsoft Management Console (MMC) and even create your own custom MMCs.

- Windows PowerShell is a command-line utility that enables administrators to perform many administrative tasks, similar to MS-DOS and UNIX commands.

■ Knowledge Assessment

Fill in the Blank

Complete the following sentences by writing the correct word or words in the blanks provided.

1. _____ is a feature in Internet Explorer 9 that incorporates search functionality into the Address bar.

2. A _____ is an Internet Explorer 9 Web site you "attach" to the Windows 7 taskbar.

3. _____ helps prevent personal information and browsing history from being stored by Internet Explorer 9.

4. The _____ detects threats on Web sites, such as phishing attacks and malware downloads, and prevents them from running.

5. _____ is an accessory program that comes with Windows 7 that allows you to take screen shots, annotate them, and save them.

6. _____ is a feature of Internet Explorer 9 that helps you control which Web sites can track your online browsing activity and receive that information.

7. After you synchronize files between your computer and a network location, the files you use on your computer are referred to as _____.

8. _____ allows you to set up a computer for remote access and then connect to that computer wherever you may be.

9. An MMC _____ is a utility provided by Microsoft or a third party that's accessible through a common interface, such as Administrative Tools.

10. _____ is a command-line interface used mainly by IT professionals to run cmdlets, background jobs, and scripts to perform administrative tasks.

Multiple Choice

Circle the letter that corresponds to the best answer.

1. Which of the following is not a security or privacy feature of Internet Explorer 9?
   a. InPrivate Browsing
   b. Pinned site
   c. ActiveX Filtering
   d. Domain highlighting

2. Which of the following can you do with the Snipping Tool?
   a. Annotate an image with the pen tool
   b. Change the color of a captured image
   c. Add typed callouts
   d. Save in PDF format

3. You want to use the Run command, however, the program requires elevated or administrative privileges. When you right-click the program to run it, which command do you select from the shortcut menu?
   a. Run elevated
   b. Run protected
   c. Run with permission
   d. Run as administrator

4. Which of the following can you do with Windows Media Player 12? (Choose all that apply.)
   a. Stream video files over the Internet
   b. Rip music from a CD
   c. Play a slide show
   d. Create playlists

5. Where do you configure security zones in Internet Explorer 9?
   a. Internet Options Security tab
   b. Internet Options Privacy tab
   c. Safety menu
   d. Tracking Protection window

6. You want to run the ps cmdlet. Which utility do you use?
   a. MS-DOS command window
   b. Windows Remote Assistance
   c. Windows PowerShell
   d. Computer Management

7. Which of the following are accessible from the Computer Management window? (Choose all that apply.)
   a. Event Viewer
   b. Performance Monitor
   c. Remote Desktop Connection
   d. Disk Management

8. You want to access your home computer from work to get a file you worked on last night. Which program can you use?
   a. Disk Management
   b. Remote Desktop Connection
   c. Windows Remote Assistance
   d. Sync Center

9. Which of the following is an option in Windows Media Center but not in Windows Media Player?
   a. Record TV programming
   b. Watch recorded TV
   c. Share files over a network
   d. Create playlists

10. Where can you find the program to help you use a projector connected to your computer?
    a. The All Programs Accessories folder
    b. Computer Management console
    c. Administrative Tools folder
    d. Windows Media Player

True / False

Circle T if the statement is true or F if the statement is false.

T | F 1. You can click and drag a Web site's thumbnail that appears on the Internet Explorer 9 New Tab page to the taskbar to pin it.

T | F 2. Remote Desktop Connection and Windows Remote Assistance are the same program used in different ways.

T | F 3. Windows Remote Assistance sessions are encrypted for safety.

T | F 4. Remote Desktop comes with all editions of Windows 7; however, you can only connect to computers running the Professional, Ultimate, or Enterprise editions.

T | F 5. Windows Mobility Center includes access to power plans and screen brightness.

■ Competency Assessment

Scenario 3-1: Securing Internet Explorer 9

Your co-worker Preena is finalizing a big project for a medical client and has many sensitive client files on her computer. She asks you to help her make her computer as safe as possible while accessing the Internet. What do you do?

Scenario 3-2: Offering Remote Assistance

Your sales people travel extensively and often need technical assistance with configuration settings on their laptops running Windows 7. Which feature or program do you use to provide remote support for these employees?

■ Proficiency Assessment

Scenario 3-3: Pinning Multiple Web Sites

Roberta is a high-tech researcher who uses the Bing search site and the Microsoft Web site daily. She wants to access the sites quickly whenever she uses Internet Explorer. How do you advise her on how she can access sites quickly?

Scenario 3-4: Creating a Playlist

You provide technical support to a small dental practice. The office manager, Shanice, hands you several company-owned music CDs. She wants the music piped to the lobby area where patients wait to be seen for their appointments. The computer used at the reception-ist's desk is running Windows 7 and has wireless speakers that can be set up in the waiting area. What is one method of providing the requested music without spending additional money?

MODULE 3: Linux Operating System

Selecting an Operating System

The fact that you're reading this book means you want to learn about the Linux operating system (OS). To begin this journey, you must first understand what Linux is and what an OS is. This chapter is therefore devoted to these basic issues. I describe what an OS is, how users interact with an OS, how Linux compares to other OSs with which you may be familiar, and how specific Linux implementations vary. Understanding these issues will help you make your way as you learn about Linux and switch between Linux-based systems and other computers.

▶ **What is an OS?**

▶ **Investigating user interfaces**

▶ **Where does Linux fit in the OS world?**

▶ **What is a distribution?**

What Is an OS?

An OS provides all the most fundamental features of a computer, at least from a software point of view. An OS enables you to use the computer's hardware devices, it defines the user interface standards, and it provides basic tools that begin to make the computer useful. Ultimately, many of these features trace their way back to the OS's *kernel*, which is described in more detail next. Other OS features are owed to additional programs that run atop the kernel, as described later in this chapter.

What Is a Kernel?

An OS kernel is a software component that's responsible for managing various low-level features of the computer, including:

> ▶ Interfacing with hardware devices (network adapters, hard disks, and so on)

▶ Allocating memory to individual programs

▶ Allocating CPU time to individual programs

▶ Enabling programs to interact with each other

When you use a program (say, a Web browser), it relies on the kernel for many of its basic functions. The Web browser can only communicate with the outside world by using network functions provided by the kernel. The kernel allocates memory and CPU time to the Web browser, without which it couldn't run. The Web browser may rely on plug-ins to display multimedia content; such programs are launched and interact with the Web browser through kernel services. Similar comments apply to any program you run on a computer, although the details vary from one OS to another and from one program to another.

In sum, the kernel is the software "glue" that holds the computer together. Without a kernel, a modern computer can do very little.

Kernels are not interchangeable; the Linux kernel is different from the Mac OS X kernel or the Windows kernel. Each of these kernels uses a different internal design and provides different software interfaces for programs to use. Thus, each OS is built from the kernel up and uses its own set of programs that further define each OS's features.

Linux uses a kernel called *Linux*—in fact, technically speaking, the word *Linux* refers *only* to the kernel. Other features that you might associate with Linux are provided by non-kernel programs, most of which are available on other platforms, as described shortly, in "What Else Identifies an OS."

A student named Linus Torvalds created the Linux kernel in 1991. Linux has evolved considerably since that time. Today, it runs on a wide variety of CPUs and other hardware. The easiest way to learn about Linux is to use it on a desktop or laptop PC, so that's the type of configuration that's emphasized in this book. The Linux kernel, however, runs on everything from tiny cell phones to powerful supercomputers.

Many programs run on multiple kernels, but most need OS-specific tweaks. Programmers create *binaries*—the program files for a particular processor and kernel—for each OS.

What Else Identifies an OS?

The kernel is at the core of any OS, but it's a component that most users don't directly manipulate. Instead, most users interact with a number of other software components, many of which are closely associated with particular OSs. Such programs include the following:

Certification Objective

Command-line shells   Years ago, users interacted with computers exclusively by typing commands in a program (known as a *shell*) that accepted such commands. The commands would rename files, launch programs, and so on. Although many computer users today don't use text-mode shells, they're still important for intermediate and advanced Linux users, so I describe them in more detail in Chapter 6, "Getting to Know the Command Line," and subsequent chapters rely heavily on your ability to use a text-mode shell. Many different shells are available, and which shells are available and popular differ from one OS to another. In Linux, a shell known as the Bourne Again Shell (bash or Bash) is popular.

Graphical user interfaces   A graphical user interface (GUI) is an improvement on a text-mode shell, at least from the perspective of a beginning user. Instead of using typed commands, GUIs rely on icons, menus, and a mouse pointer. Windows and Mac OS both have their own OS-specific GUIs. Linux relies on a GUI known as the X Window System, or X for short. X is a very basic GUI, so Linux also uses *desktop environment* program suites, such as the GNU Object Model Environment (GNOME) or the K Desktop Environment (KDE), to provide a more complete user experience. It's the differences between a Linux desktop environment and the GUIs in Windows or OS X that will probably strike you most when you first begin using Linux.

Certification Objective

Utility programs   Modern OSs invariably ship with a wide variety of simple utility programs—calculators, calendars, text editors, disk maintenance tools, and so on. These programs differ from one OS to another. Indeed, even the names and methods of launching these programs can differ between OSs. Fortunately, you can usually find the programs you want by perusing menus in the main desktop environment.

Libraries   Unless you're a programmer, you're unlikely to need to work with libraries directly; nonetheless, I include them in this list because they provide critical services to programs. Libraries are collections of programming functions that can be used by a variety of programs. For instance, in Linux most programs rely on a library called libc. Other libraries provide features associated with the GUI or that help programs parse options passed to them on the command line. Many libraries exist for Linux, which helps enrich the Linux software landscape.

You can search for Linux equivalents to popular Mac OS X or Windows programs on Web sites such as http:// www.linuxrsp .ru/win-lin- soft/table-eng or http://www .linuxalt.com.

Productivity programs   Major productivity programs—Web browsers, word processors, graphics editors, and so on—are the usual reason for using a computer. Although such programs are often technically separate from the OS, they are sometimes associated with certain OSs. Even when a program is available on many OSs, it may have a different "feel" on each OS because of the different GUIs and other OS-specific features.

In addition to software that runs on an OS, several other features can distinguish between OSs, such as the details of user accounts, rules for naming disk files, and technical details of how the computer starts up. These features are all controlled by software that's part of the OS, of course—sometimes by the kernel and sometimes by non-kernel software.

Investigating User Interfaces

Earlier, I noted the distinction between text-mode and graphical user interfaces. Although most end users favor GUIs because of their ease of use, Linux retains a strong text-mode tradition. Chapter 6 describes Linux's text-mode tools in more detail, and Chapter 4, "Using Common Linux Programs," covers basic principles of Linux GUI operations. It's important that you have some grounding in the basic principles of both text-mode and graphical user interfaces now, since user interface issues crop up from time to time in intervening chapters.

Using a Text-Mode User Interface

Certification Objective

In the past, and even sometimes today, Linux computers booted in text mode. Once the system had completely booted, the screen would display a simple text-mode login prompt, which might resemble this:

```
Debian GNU/Linux 6.0 essentials tty1

essentials login:
```

The details of such a login prompt vary from one system to another. This example includes several pieces of information:

- ▶ The OS name and version—Debian GNU/Linux 6.0
- ▶ The computer's name—`essentials`
- ▶ The name of the hardware device being used for the login—`tty1`
- ▶ The login prompt itself—`login:`

To log in to such a system, you must type your username at the `login:` prompt. The system then prompts you for a password, which you must also type. If you entered a valid username and password, the computer is likely to display a login message, followed by a shell prompt:

```
rodsmith@essentials:~$
```

> To try a text-mode login, you must first install Linux on a computer. Neither the Linux Essentials exam nor this book covers Linux installation; consult your distribution's documentation to learn more.

> If you see a GUI login prompt, you can obtain a text-mode prompt by pressing Ctrl+Alt+F1 or Ctrl+Alt+F2. To return to the GUI login prompt, press Alt+F1 or Alt+F7.

In this book, I omit most of the prompt from example commands when they appear on their own lines. I keep the dollar sign ($) prompt, though, for ordinary user commands. Some commands must be entered as root, which is the Linux administrative user. I change the prompt to a hash mark (#) for such commands, since most Linux distributions make a similar change to their prompts for the root user.

The details of this shell prompt vary from one installation to another, but you can type text-mode commands at the shell prompt. For instance, you could type **ls** (short for *list*) to see a list of files in the current directory. The most basic commands are shortened by removing vowels, and sometimes consonants, in order to minimize the amount of typing required to execute a command. This has the unfortunate effect of making many commands rather obscure.

Some commands display no information, but most produce some type of output. For instance, the ls command produces a list of files:

```
$ ls
106792c01.doc   f0101.tif
```

This example shows two files in the current directory: 106792c01.doc and f0101.tif. You can use additional commands to manipulate these files, such as cp to copy them or rm to remove (delete) them. Chapter 6 ("Getting to Know the Command Line") and Chapter 7 ("Managing Files") describe some common file manipulation commands.

Some text-mode programs take over the display in order to provide constant updates or to enable you to interact with data in a flexible manner. Figure 1.1, for instance, shows the nano text editor, which is described in more detail in Chapter 11, "Editing Files." Once nano is working, you can use your keyboard's arrow keys to move the cursor around, add text by typing, and so on.

Chapter 13, "Understanding Users and Groups," describes Linux accounts, including the root account, in more detail.

```
  GNU nano 2.2.4              File: parts.txt

# partition table of /dev/sdb
unit: sectors

/dev/sdb1 : start=          63, size=257447873, Id= 7_
/dev/sdb2 : start=348336128, size=140060672, Id=83
/dev/sdb3 : start=272781310, size= 75554818, Id= f
/dev/sdb4 : start=257447936, size= 15331328, Id=83, bootable
/dev/sdb5 : start=272781312, size= 16224256, Id=83
/dev/sdb6 : start=289007616, size=  9764864, Id=82
/dev/sdb7 : start=298774528, size= 17745920, Id=83




                    [ Read 10 lines ]
^G Get Help  ^O WriteOut  ^R Read File ^Y Prev Page ^K Cut Text  ^C Cur Pos
^X Exit      ^J Justify   ^W Where Is  ^V Next Page ^U UnCut Text^T To Spell
```

F I G U R E   1 . 1   Some text-mode programs take over the entire display.

Even if you use a graphical login, you can use a text-mode shell inside a window, known as a *terminal*. Common Linux GUIs provide the ability to launch a terminal program, which provides a shell prompt and the means to run text-mode programs.

Using a Graphical User Interface

Most users are more comfortable with GUIs than with text-mode commands. Thus, many modern Linux systems start up in GUI mode by default, presenting a login screen similar to the one shown in Figure 1.2. You can select your username from a list or type it, followed by typing your password, to log in.

> **Some Linux GUI login screens don't prompt you for a password until after you've entered a valid username.**

FIGURE 1.2 Graphical login screens on Linux are similar to those for Windows or Mac OS X.

Unlike Windows and Mac OS X, Linux provides a number of desktop environments. Which one you use depends on the specific variety of Linux you're using, what software options you selected at installation time, and your own personal preferences. Common choices include GNOME, KDE, Xfce, and Unity. Many other options are available as well. In Figure 1.2, you can see a selection option for the desktop environment in the lower-left corner of the central dialog box. It reads GNOME in Figure 1.2, meaning that if the item is left unchanged, the computer will launch GNOME when the user logs in.

Linux desktop environments can look quite different from one another, but they all provide similar functionality. Figure 1.3 shows the default KDE on an openSUSE 12.1 installation, with a couple of programs running. Chapter 4 describes common desktop environments and their features in more detail, but for now, you should know that they all provide features such as:

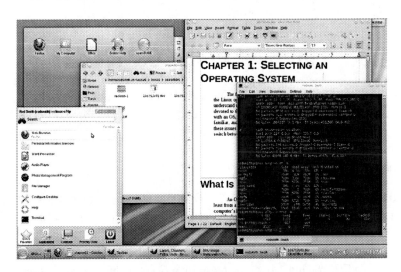

FIGURE 1.3 Linux desktop environments provide the types of GUI controls that most users expect.

Program launchers   You can launch programs by selecting them from menus or lists. Typically, one or more menus exist along the top, bottom, or side of the screen. In Figure 1.3, you can click the openSUSE gecko icon in the bottom-left corner of the screen to produce the menu that appears in that figure.

File managers   Linux provides GUI file managers similar to those in Windows or Mac OS X. A window for one of these is open in the center of Figure 1.3.

Window controls   You can move windows by clicking and dragging their title bars, resize them by clicking and dragging their edges, and so on.

Multiple desktops   Most Linux desktop environments enable you to keep multiple virtual desktops active, each with its own set of programs. This feature is very handy to keep the screen uncluttered while you run many programs simultaneously. Typically, an icon in one of the menus enables you to switch between virtual desktops.

Logout options   You can log out of your Linux session, which enables you to shut down the computer or let another user log in.

Logging out is very important in public computing environments. If you fail to log out, a stranger might come along and use your account for malicious purposes.

You may need to install extra desktop environments to use them. This topic is not covered in this book.

As you learn more about Linux, you'll discover that its GUI environments are quite flexible. If you find you don't like the environment that's the default for your distribution, you can change it. Although they all provide similar features, some people have strong preferences about desktop environments. Linux gives you a choice in the matter that's not available in Windows or Mac OS X, so feel free to try multiple desktop environments.

Where Does Linux Fit in the OS World?

As described later, in "What Is a Distribution?," Linux can be considered a family of OSs. Thus, you can compare one Linux version to another one.

This chapter's title implies a comparison, and as this book is about Linux, the comparison must be to non-Linux OSs. Thus, I compare Linux to three other OSs or OS families: Unix, Mac OS X, and Microsoft Windows.

Comparing Linux to Unix

Certification Objective

If you were to attempt to draw a "family tree" of OSs, you would end up scratching your head a lot. This is because OS designers often mimic each other's features, and sometimes even incorporate each other's code into their OSs' workings. The result can be a tangled mess of similarities between OSs, with causes ranging from coincidence to code "borrowing." Attempting to map these influences can be difficult. In the case of Linux and Unix, though, a broad statement is possible: Linux is modeled after Unix.

Open source software is software that you can not only run, but modify and redistribute yourself. Chapter 2, "Investigating Linux's Principles and Philosophy," covers the philosophy and legal issues concerning open source software.

Unix was created in 1969 at AT&T's Bell Labs. Unix's history is complex and involves multiple *forks* (that is, splitting of the code into two or more independent projects) and even entirely separate code rewrites. Modern Linux systems are, by and large, the product of open source projects that clone Unix programs, or of original open source code projects for Unix generally. These projects include:

The Linux kernel   Linus Torvalds created the Linux kernel as a hobby programming project in 1991, but it soon grew to be much more than that. The Linux kernel was designed to be compatible with other Unix kernels, in the sense that it used the same software interfaces in source code. This made using open source programs for other Unix versions with the Linux kernel easy.

The GNU project   The GNU's Not Unix (GNU) project is an effort by the Free Software Foundation (FSF) to develop open source replacements for all the core elements of a Unix OS. In 1991, the FSF had already released the most important such tools, with the notable exception of the kernel. (The GNU HURD kernel is now available but is not as popular as the Linux kernel.) Alternatives to the GNU tools include proprietary commercial tools and open source tools developed for the BSD Unix variants. The tools used on a Unix-like OS can influence its overall "flavor," but all of these tool sets are similar enough to give any Unix variety a similar feel compared to a non-Unix OS.

Xorg-X11   The X Window System is the GUI environment for most Unix OSs. Most Linux distributions today use the Xorg-X11 variety of X. As with the basic text-mode tools provided by the GNU project, choice of an X server can affect some features of a Unix-like OS, such as the types of fonts it supports.

Desktop environments   GNOME, KDE, Xfce, and other popular open source desktop environments have largely displaced commercial desktop environments even on commercial versions of Unix. Thus, you won't find big differences between Linux and Unix in this area.

Server programs   Historically, Unix and Linux have been popular as server OSs—organizations use them to run Web servers, e-mail servers, file servers, and so on. Linux runs the same popular server programs as do commercial Unix versions and the open source BSDs.

User productivity programs   In this realm, as in server programs, Linux runs the same software as do other Unix-like OSs. In a few cases, Linux runs more programs, or runs them better. This is mostly because of Linux's popularity and the vast array of hardware drivers that Linux offers. If a program needs advanced video card support, for example, it's more likely to find that support on Linux than on a less popular Unix-like OS.

On the whole, Linux can be thought of as a member of the family of Unix-like OSs. Although Linux is technically *not* a Unix OS, it's similar enough that the differences are unimportant compared to the differences between this family as a whole and other OSs, such as Windows. Because of its popularity, Linux offers better hardware support, at least on commodity PC hardware. Some Unix varieties offer specific features that Linux lacks, though. For instance, the Zettabyte File System (ZFS), available on Solaris, FreeBSD, and some other OSs, provides advanced filesystem features that aren't yet fully implemented in Linux.

GNU is an example of a recursive acronym—an acronym whose expansion includes the acronym itself. This is an example of geek humor.

Mac OS X, described shortly, is a commercial Unix that eschews both X and the desktop environments that run on it in favor of Apple's own GUI.

A ZFS add-on for Linux is available, but it's not fully integrated into the OS. A Linux filesystem known as Btrfs offers many ZFS features, but Btrfs isn't yet complete.

CODE TYPES

Human beings write programs in a form known as *source code*. Although source code can seem arcane to the uninitiated, it's crystal clear compared to the form a program must take for a computer to run it: *binary code*. A program known as a *compiler* translates source code to binary code. (Alternatively, some programming languages rely on an *interpreter*, which converts source code to binary code "on the fly," eliminating the need to compile source code.)

(Continues)

CODE TYPES *(Continued)*

The term *open source* refers to the availability of source code, which is generally withheld from the public in the case of commercial programs and OSs. A programmer with access to a program's source code can fix bugs, add features, and otherwise alter how the program operates.

Comparing Linux to Mac OS X

Certification Objective

Mac OS X is a commercial Unix-based OS that borrows heavily from the BSDs and discards the usual Unix GUI (namely X) in favor of its own user interface. This makes OS X both very similar to Linux and quite different from it.

You can open an OS X Terminal window and type many of the same commands described in this book to achieve similar ends. If a command described in this book isn't present, you may be able to install it in one way or another. OS X ships with some popular Unix server programs, so you can configure it to work much like Linux or another Unix-like OS as a network server computer.

OS X differs from Linux in its user interface, though. The OS X user interface is known as *Cocoa* from a programming perspective, or *Aqua* from a user's point of view. It includes elements that are roughly equivalent to both X and a desktop environment in Linux. Because Cocoa isn't compatible with X from a programming perspective, applications developed for OS X can't be run directly on Linux (or on other Unix-like OSs), and porting them (that is, modifying the source code and recompiling them) for Linux is a non-trivial undertaking. Thus, native OS X applications seldom make the transition to Linux.

OS X includes an implementation of X that runs under Aqua. This makes the transfer of GUI Linux and Unix programs to OS X relatively straightforward. The resulting programs don't entirely conform to the Aqua user interface, though. They may have buttons, menus, and other features that look out of place compared to the usual appearance of OS X equivalents.

> The X in X server is a letter X, but the X in OS X is a Roman numeral (10), denoting the tenth version of Mac OS.

Apple makes OS X available for its own computers. Its license terms forbid installation on non-Apple hardware, and even aside from licensing issues, installing OS X on non-Apple hardware is a non-trivial undertaking. A variant of OS X, known as iOS, runs on Apple's iPad and iPhone devices, and is equally non-portable to other devices. Thus, OS X is largely limited to Apple hardware. Linux, by contrast, runs on a wide variety of hardware, including most PCs. You can even install Linux on Macintosh computers.

Comparing Linux to Windows

Most desktop and laptop computers today run Microsoft Windows. Thus, if you're considering running Linux, the most likely comparison is to Windows. Broadly speaking, Linux and Windows have similar capabilities; however, there are significant differences in details. These include the following:

Certification
Objective

Licensing Linux is an open source OS whereas Windows is a proprietary commercial OS. Chapter 2 covers open source issues in greater detail, but for now you should know that open source software gives you greater control over your computer than does proprietary software—at least in theory. In practice, you may need a great deal of expertise to take advantage of open source's benefits. Proprietary software may be preferable if you work for an organization that's only comfortable with the idea of software that's sold in a more traditional way. (Some Linux variants, though, are sold in a similar way, along with service contracts.)

Costs Many Linux varieties are available free of charge, and so are appealing if you're trying to cut costs. On the other hand, the expertise needed to install and maintain a Linux installation is likely to be greater, and therefore more expensive, than the expertise needed to install and maintain a Windows installation. Different studies on the issue of total cost of ownership of Linux vs. Windows have gone both ways, but most tend to favor Linux.

Hardware compatibility Most hardware components require OS support, usually in the form of drivers. Most hardware manufacturers provide Windows drivers for their devices, or work with Microsoft to ensure that Windows includes appropriate drivers. Although some manufacturers provide Linux drivers, too, for the most part the Linux community as a whole must supply the necessary drivers. This means that Linux drivers may take a few weeks or even months to appear after a device becomes available. On the other hand, Linux developers tend to maintain drivers for old hardware for much longer than manufacturers continue to support their own old hardware. Thus, a modern Linux may run better than a recent version of Windows on old hardware. Linux also tends to be less resource-intensive, so you can be productive on older hardware when using Linux.

Software availability Some popular desktop applications, such as Microsoft Office, are available on Windows but not on Linux. Although Linux alternatives, such as OpenOffice.org or LibreOffice, are available, they haven't caught on in the public's mind. In other realms, the situation is reversed. Popular server programs, such as the Apache Web server, were developed first for Linux or Unix.

Although many such servers are available for Windows, they run more efficiently on Linux. If you have a specific program you must run, you may want to research its availability and practicality on any platforms you're considering.

User interfaces   Like Mac OS X, Windows uses its own unique user interface. This fact contributes to poor inter-OS portability. (Tools exist to help bridge the gap, though; X Window System implementations for Windows are available, as are tools for running Windows programs in Linux.) Some users prefer the Windows user interface to any Linux desktop environment, but others prefer a Linux desktop environment.

▶ Microsoft is making major changes to its user interface with Windows 8. The new user interface, Metro, works the same on everything from cell phones to desktop computers.

Configurability   Linux is a much more configurable OS than is Windows. Although both OSs provide means to run specific programs at startup, change user interface themes, and so on, Linux's open source nature means you can tweak any detail you want. Furthermore, you can pick any Linux variant you like to get a head start on setting up the system as you see fit.

Security   Advocates of each OS claim it's more secure than the other. They can do this because they focus on different security issues. Many of the threats to Windows come from viruses, which by and large target Windows and its huge installed user base. Viruses are essentially a non-issue for Linux; in Linux, security threats come mostly from break-ins involving misconfigured servers or untrustworthy local users.

For over a decade, Windows has dominated the desktop arena. In both homes and offices, users have become familiar with Windows and are used to popular Windows applications, such as Microsoft Office. Although Linux *can* be used in such environments, it's a less popular choice for a variety of reasons—its unfamiliarity, the fact that Windows comes pre-installed on most PCs, and the lack of any compelling Linux-only applications for most users.

Unix generally, and Linux in particular, on the other hand, have come to dominate the server market. Linux powers the Web servers, email servers, file servers, and so on that make up the Internet and that many businesses rely on to provide local network services. Thus, most people use Linux daily even if they don't realize it.

In most cases, it's possible to use either Linux or Windows on a computer and have it do an acceptable job. Sometimes, though, specific needs dictate use of one OS or another. You might need to run a particular exotic program, for instance, or your hardware might be too old for a modern Windows or too new for Linux. In other cases, your own or your users' familiarity with one OS or the other may favor its use.

What Is a Distribution?

Up until now, I've described Linux as if it were a single OS, but this isn't really the case. Many different Linux *distributions* are available, each consisting of a Linux kernel along with a set of utilities and configuration files. The result is a complete OS, and two Linux distributions can differ from each other as much as either differs from OS X or even Windows. I therefore describe in more detail what a distribution is, what distributions are popular, and the ways in which distribution maintainers keep their offerings up to date.

Creating a Complete Linux-Based OS

I've already described some of what makes up a Linux OS, but some details need reiteration or elaboration:

Certification
Objective

A Linux kernel   A Linux kernel is at the core of any Linux OS, of course. I've written this item as *a* Linux kernel because the Linux kernel is constantly evolving. Two distributions are likely to use slightly different kernels. Distribution maintainers also often *patch* kernels—that is, they make small changes to fix bugs or add features.

Core Unix tools   Tools such as the GNU tool set, the X Window System, and the utilities used to manage disks are critical to the normal functioning of a Linux system. Most Linux distributions include more or less the same set of such tools, but as with the kernel, they can vary in versions and patches.

Supplemental software   Additional software, such as major server programs, desktop environments, and productivity tools, ships with most Linux distributions. As with core Unix software, most Linux distributions provide similar options for such software. Distributions sometimes provide their own "branding," though, particularly in desktop environment graphics.

Startup scripts   Much of a Linux distribution's "personality" comes from the way it manages its startup process. Linux uses scripts and utilities to launch the dozens of programs that link the computer to a network, present a login prompt, and so on. These scripts and utilities vary between distributions, which means that they have different features and may be configured in different ways.

An installer   Software must be installed to be used, and most Linux distributions provide unique installation software to help you manage this important task. Thus, two distributions may install in very different ways, giving you different options for key features such as disk layouts and initial user account creation.

> ▶
>
> **The UNetbootin tool**
> (http://unetbootin
> .sourceforge.net)
> **can copy the files
> from a Linux installa-
> tion disc image file to
> a USB flash drive.**

Typically, Linux distributions are available for download from their Web sites. You can usually download a CD-R or DVD image file that you can then burn to an optical disc. When you boot the resulting disc, the installer runs and you can install the OS. You can sometimes download an image that can be copied to a USB flash drive if your computer lacks an optical drive.

Some Linux installers come complete with all the software you're likely to install. Others come with only minimal software and expect you to have a working Internet connection so that the installer can download additional software. If your computer isn't connected to the Internet, be sure to get the right type of installer.

A Summary of Common Linux Distributions

Certification
Objective

Depending on how you count, there are about a dozen major Linux distributions for desktop, laptop, and small server computers, and hundreds more that serve specialized purposes. Table 1.1 summarizes the features of the most important distributions.

TABLE 1.1 Features of major Linux distributions

Distribution	Availability	Package format	Release cycle	Administrator skill requirements
Arch	Free	pacman	Rolling	Expert
CentOS	Free	RPM	approximately 2-year	Intermediate
Debian	Free	Debian	2-year	Intermediate to Expert
Fedora	Free	RPM	approximately 6-month	Intermediate
Gentoo	Free	ebuild	Rolling	Expert
Mandriva	Free	RPM	1-year	Intermediate
openSUSE	Free	RPM	8-month	Intermediate
Red Hat Enterprise	Commercial	RPM	approximately 2-year	Intermediate

(Continues)

TABLE 1.1 *(Continued)*

Distribution	Availability	Package format	Release cycle	Administrator skill requirements
Slackware	Free	tarballs	Irregular	Expert
SUSE Enterprise	Commercial	RPM	2–3 years	Intermediate
Ubuntu	Free	Debian	6-month	Novice to Intermediate

These features require explanation:

Availability Most Linux distributions are entirely open source or free software; however, some include proprietary components and are sold for money, typically with a support contract. Red Hat Enterprise Linux (RHEL) and SUSE Enterprise Linux are the two most prominent examples of this type of distribution. Both have completely free cousins. For RHEL, CentOS is a near-clone that omits the proprietary components, and Fedora is an open version that serves as a testbed for technologies that may eventually be included in CentOS. For SUSE Enterprise, openSUSE is a free alternative.

Package format Most Linux distributions distribute software in *packages*, which are collections of many files in one. Package software maintains a local database of installed files, making upgrades and uninstallations easy. The RPM Package Manager (RPM) system is the most popular one in the Linux world, but Debian packages are very common, too. Other packaging systems work fine but are distribution-specific. Slackware is unusual in that it uses *tarballs* for its packages. These are package files created by the standard tar utility, which is used for backing up computers and for distributing source code, among other things. The tarballs that Slackware uses for its packages contain Slackware-specific information to help with package management. Gentoo is unusual because its package system is based on compiling most software from source code. This is time-consuming but enables experienced administrators to tweak compilation options to optimize the packages for their own hardware and software environments.

Tarballs are similar to the zip files that are common on Windows. Chapter 10, "Searching, Extracting, and Archiving Data," describes how to create and use tarballs.

Release cycle I describe release cycles in more detail shortly, in "Understanding Release Cycles." As a general rule, distributions with short release cycles aim to provide the latest software possible, whereas those with longer release cycles strive to provide the most stable environments possible. Some try to have it both ways; for instance, Ubuntu releases long-term support (LTS) versions in April of even-numbered years. Its other releases aim to provide the latest software.

Administrator skill requirements   The final column in Table 1.1 provides my personal estimation of the skill level required to administer a distribution. As you can see, I've described most Linux distributions as requiring "intermediate" skill to administer. Some, however, provide less in the way of user-friendly GUI administrative tools, and so require more skill. Ubuntu aims to be particularly easy to use and administer.

> Don't be scared off by the "intermediate" classification of most distributions. This book's purpose is to help you manage the essential features of such distributions.

Most Linux distributions are available for at least two platforms—that is, CPU types: $x86$ (also known as IA32, i386, and several variants) and $x86$-64 (also known as AMD64, EM64T, and $x64$). Until about 2007, $x86$ computers were the most common variety, but more recently, $x86$-64 computers have become the standard. If you have an $x86$-64 computer, you can run either an $x86$ or an $x86$-64 distribution on it, although the latter provides a small speed improvement. More exotic platforms, such as PowerPC, Alpha, and SPARC, are available. Such platforms are mostly restricted to servers and to specialized devices (described shortly).

In addition to the mainstream PC distributions, several others are available that serve more specialized purposes. Some of these run on regular PCs, but others run on their own specialized hardware:

Android   Many cell phones today use a Linux-based OS known as *Android*. Its user interface is similar to that of other smart phones, but underneath lies a Linux kernel and a significant amount of the same Linux infrastructure you'll find on a PC. Such phones don't use X or typical desktop applications, though; instead, they run specialized applications for cell phones.

> Android is best known as a cell phone OS, but it can be used on other devices. Some e-book readers, for instance, run Android.

Network appliances   Many broadband routers, print servers, and other devices you plug into a local network to perform specialized tasks run Linux. You can sometimes replace the standard OS with a customized one if you want to add features to the device. Tomato (`http://www.polarcloud.com/tomato`) and OpenWrt (`https://openwrt.org`) are two examples of such customized Linux distributions. Don't install such software on a whim, though; if done improperly, or on the wrong device, they can render the device useless!

> I recommend you download Parted Magic, or a similar tool, to have on hand in case you run into problems with your main Linux installation.

TiVo   This popular digital video recorder (DVR) uses a Linux kernel and a significant number of standard support programs, along with proprietary drivers and DVR software. Although many people who use them don't realize it, they are Linux-based computers under the surface.

Parted Magic   This distribution, based at `http://partedmagic.com`, is a Linux distribution for PCs that's intended for emergency recovery operations. It runs from a single CD-R and you can use it to access a Linux or Windows hard disk if the main installation won't boot.

Android, Linux-based network appliances, and TiVo are examples of *embedded systems* that use Linux. Such devices typically require little or no administrative work from users, at least not in the way such tasks are described in this book. Instead, these devices have fixed basic configurations and guided setup tools to help inexperienced users set critical basic options, such as network settings and your time zone.

Certification
Objective

Understanding Release Cycles

Table 1.1 summarized the release cycles employed by a number of common Linux distributions. The values cited in that table are the time between releases. For instance, new versions of Ubuntu come out every six months, like clockwork. Most other distributions' release schedules provide some "wiggle room"; if a release date slides a month, that may be acceptable.

Certification
Objective

After its release, a distribution is typically supported until sometime *after* the next version's release—typically a few months to a year or more. During this support period, the distribution's maintainers provide software updates to fix bugs and security problems. Once the support period has passed, you can continue to use a distribution, but you're on your own—if you need updated software, you'll have to compile it from source code yourself or hope that you can find a compatible binary package from some other source. As a practical matter, therefore, it's generally a good idea to upgrade to the latest version before the support period ends. This fact makes distributions with longer release cycles appealing to businesses, since a longer time between installations minimizes disruptions and costs associated with upgrades.

Two of the distributions in Table 1.1 (Arch and Gentoo) have *rolling* release cycles. Such distributions have no version numbers in the usual sense; instead, upgrades occur in an ongoing manner. Using such a distribution makes it unnecessary to ever do a full upgrade, with all the hassles that creates; however, you'll occasionally have to do a disruptive upgrade of one particular subsystem, such as a major upgrade in your desktop environment.

Prior to the release of a new version, most distributions make pre-release versions available. *Alpha software* is extremely new and very likely to contain serious bugs, while *beta software* is more stable but nonetheless more likely to contain bugs than is the final release software. As a general rule, you should avoid using such software unless you want to contribute to the development effort by reporting bugs or unless you're desperate to have a new feature.

Certification
Objective

THE ESSENTIALS AND BEYOND

Linux is a powerful OS that you can use on everything from a cell phone to a supercomputer. At Linux's core is its *kernel*, which manages the computer's hardware. Built atop that are various utilities (many from the GNU project) and user applications. Linux is a clone of the Unix OS, with which it shares many programs. Mac OS X is another Unix OS, although one with a unique user interface. Although Windows shares many features with Unix, it's an entirely different OS, so software compatibility between Linux and Windows is limited. Linux comes in many varieties, known as distributions, each of which has its own unique "flavor." Because of this variety, you can pick a Linux version that best suits your needs, based on its ease of use, release cycle, and other unique features.

SUGGESTED EXERCISES

▶ Make a list of the programs you run as an ordinary user, including everything from a calculator applet to a major office suite. Look for equivalents at http://www .linuxrsp.ru/win-lin-soft/table-eng or http://www.linuxalt.com. Is there anything you can't find? If so, try a Web search to find an equivalent.

▶ Read more about two or three Linux distributions by perusing their Web pages. Which distribution would you select for running a major Web server? Which distribution sounds most appealing for use by office workers who do word processing and email?

REVIEW QUESTIONS

1. Which of the following is *not* a function of the Linux kernel?

    A. Allocating memory for use by programs

    B. Allocating CPU time for use by programs

    C. Creating menus in GUI programs

    D. Controlling access to the hard disk

    E. Enabling programs to use a network

2. Which of the following is an example of an embedded Linux OS?

    A. Android   D. Debian

    B. SUSE   E. Fedora

    C. CentOS

(Continues)

THE ESSENTIALS AND BEYOND *(Continued)*

3. Which of the following is a notable difference between Linux and Mac OS X?

    A. Linux can run common GNU programs, whereas OS X cannot.

    B. Linux's GUI is based on the X Window System, whereas OS X's is not.

    C. Linux cannot run on Apple Macintosh hardware, whereas OS X can run only on Apple hardware.

    D. Linux relies heavily on BSD software, whereas OS X uses no BSD software.

    E. Linux supports text-mode commands, but OS X is a GUI-only OS.

4. True or false: The Linux kernel is derived from the BSD kernel.

5. True or false: If you log into a Linux system in graphical mode, you cannot use text-mode commands in that session.

6. True or false: CentOS is a Linux distribution with a long release cycle.

7. A Linux text-mode login prompt reads _____ (one word).

8. A common security problem with Windows that's essentially nonexistent on Linux is _____.

9. Pre-release software that's likely to contain bugs is known as _____ and _____.

CHAPTER 2

Investigating Linux's Principles and Philosophy

You can frequently select a product or technology on purely pragmatic grounds—what OS works well for a given task, which software suite is the least expensive, and so on. Sometimes, though, understanding the principles and philosophy that underlie a technology can be useful, and might even guide your choice. This is true of some Linux users; the open source model of Linux, which I introduced in Chapter 1, "Selecting an Operating System," has implications that can affect how Linux works. Furthermore, some people in the Linux world can become quite passionate about these principles. Whether or not you agree with these people, understanding their point of view can help you appreciate the Linux culture that you'll find in the workplace, online, at conferences, and so on.

This chapter covers these issues, beginning with information on Linux's origins and development over time up to the present. I then describe open source principles and how they can affect the way an open source OS works in the real world. Finally, I describe some of the roles in which Linux can work—as an embedded OS, as a desktop or laptop OS, and as a server OS.

▶ **Linux through the ages**

▶ **Using open source software**

▶ **Understanding OS roles**

Linux through the Ages

Although Linux's birth date of 1991 is recent by most historical standards, in the computer world 20 years is an eternity. Nonetheless, the software and culture in the early 1990s, and even before then, has had quite a legacy on today's software world. After all, what we use today is built atop the foundation created in the past. Thus, looking at how Linux originated will help you to understand Linux as it exists today.

Understanding Linux's Origins

Computers today can be classified in much the same way as was done in 1991, although some details have changed. A notable addition is embedded computers, as in cell phones.

In 1991, as today, computers were classified by their sizes and capabilities. Computers could belong to any of a handful of categories, ranging from desktop personal computers (PCs) to supercomputers. The PC marketplace of 1991 was dominated by *x*86-based computers that are the direct ancestors of today's PCs; however, other types of PCs were available, such as Macintoshes. Such computers generally used different CPUs and ran their own custom OSs.

In 1991, most PCs ran Microsoft's Disk Operating System (MS-DOS, PC-DOS, or DOS). DOS was extremely limited by today's standards; it was a single-tasking OS that didn't take full advantage of the memory or CPUs available at the time. The versions of Microsoft Windows available in 1991 ran on top of DOS. Although Windows helped work around some of DOS's limitations, it didn't fundamentally fix any of them. These early versions of Windows employed *cooperative multitasking*, for instance, in which programs could voluntarily give up CPU time to other processes. The DOS kernel could not wrest control from a program that hogged CPU time.

Unix was not the only multi-user, multitasking OS in 1991. Others, such as Virtual Memory System (VMS), were available. Unix is most relevant to Linux's history, though.

Above the PC level, Unix was a common OS in 1991. Compared to DOS and the Windows of that time, Unix was a sophisticated OS. Unix supported multiple accounts and provided true *preemptive multitasking*, in which the kernel could schedule CPU time for programs, even if the programs didn't voluntarily give up control. These features were practical necessities for many servers and for multi-user computers such as minicomputers and mainframes.

As time has progressed, the capabilities of each class of computer have grown. By most measures, today's PCs have the power of the minicomputers or even the mainframes of 1991. The OSs used on the PCs of 1991 don't scale well to more powerful hardware, and today's PCs are now powerful enough to run the more sophisticated OSs of 1991. For this reason, DOS and its small-computer contemporaries have been largely abandoned in favor of Unix and other alternatives.

Today's versions of Windows are not derived from DOS. Instead, they use a new kernel that shares many design features with VMS.

In 1991, Linus Torvalds was a student at the University of Helsinki, studying computer science. He was interested in learning about both Unix and the capabilities of the new *x*86 computer he'd just purchased. Torvalds began the program that would become the Linux kernel as a low-level terminal emulator—a program to connect to his university's larger computers. As his program grew, he began adding features that turned his terminal program into something that could be better described as an OS kernel. Eventually, he began writing with the goal of creating a Unix-compatible kernel—that is, a kernel that could run the wide range of Unix software that was available at the time.

Unix's history, in turn, stretched back two more decades, to its origin at AT&T in 1969. Because AT&T was at that time a telephone monopoly in the United

States, it was legally forbidden from selling software. Therefore, when its employees created Unix, AT&T basically gave the OS away. Universities were particularly enthusiastic about adopting Unix, and some began modifying it, since AT&T made the source code available. Thus, Unix had a two-decade history of open software development. Most Unix programs were distributed as source code, since Unix ran on a wide variety of hardware platforms—binary programs made for one machine would seldom run on a different machine.

Early on, Linux began to tap into this reservoir of available software. As noted in Chapter 1, early Linux developers were particularly keen on the GNU's Not Unix (GNU) project's software, so Linux quickly accumulated a collection of GNU utilities. Much of this software had been written with workstations and more powerful computers in mind, but because computer hardware kept improving, it ran fine on the *x*86 PCs of the early 1990s.

Linux quickly acquired a devoted following of developers who saw its potential to bring workstation-class software to the PC. These people worked to improve the Linux kernel, to make the necessary changes in existing Unix programs so that they would work on Linux, and to write Linux-specific support programs. By the mid-1990s, several Linux distributions existed, including some that survive today. (Slackware was released in 1993, and Red Hat in 1995, for example.)

The 386BSD OS was a competing Unix-like OS in the early 1990s. Today it has forked into several related OSs: FreeBSD, NetBSD, OpenBSD, Dragonfly BSD, and PC-BSD.

THE MICROKERNEL DEBATE

Linux is an example of a monolithic kernel, which is a kernel that does everything a kernel is supposed to do in one big process. In 1991, a competing kernel design, known as a microkernel, was all the rage. Microkernels are much smaller than monolithic kernels; they move as many tasks as they can into non-kernel processes and then manage the communications between processes.

Soon after Linux's release, Linus Torvalds engaged in a public debate with Andrew Tanenbaum, the creator of the Minix OS that Torvalds used as an early development platform for Linux. Minix uses a microkernel design, and Tanenbaum considered Linux's monolithic design to be backward.

As a practical matter for an end user, either design works. Linux and the BSD-derived kernels use monolithic designs, whereas modern versions of Windows, the GNU HURD, and Minix are examples of microkernels. Some people still get worked up over this distinction, though.

Seeing Today's Linux World

By the mid-1990s, the most important features of Linux as it exists today had been established. Changes since then have included:

Improvements in the kernel   The Linux kernel has seen massive changes since 1991, when it lacked many of the features we rely on today. Improvements include the addition of networking features, innumerable hardware drivers, support for power management features, and support for many non-x86 CPUs.

Improvements in support tools   Just as work has progressed on the Linux kernel, improvements have also been made to the support programs on which it relies—the compilers, shells, GUIs, and so on.

Creation of new support tools   New support tools have emerged over the years. These range from simple and small utilities to big desktop environments. In fact, some of these tools, such as modern desktop environments, are far more obvious to the end user than is the kernel itself.

Creation of new distributions   As noted earlier, Slackware dates to 1993 and Red Hat (the predecessor to Red Hat Enterprise Linux, CentOS, and Fedora) originated in 1995. Other distributions have emerged in the intervening years, and some have been quite important. The Android OS used on smart phones and tablets, for instance, is becoming influential in the early 2010s.

Linux's roots remain very much in the open source software of the 1980s and 1990s. Although a typical desktop or embedded OS user is likely to perceive the OS through the lens of the GUI, much of what happens under the surface happens because of the Linux kernel and open source tools, many of which have existed for decades.

Using Open Source Software

The philosophies that underlie much software development for Linux are different from those that drive most software development for Windows. These differing philosophies affect how you obtain the software, what you can do with it, and how it changes over time. Thus, I describe these principles. I also describe how Linux functions as a sort of "magnet," integrating software from many sources in one place.

Understanding Basic Open Source Principles

Broadly speaking, software can be described as coming in several different forms, each with different expectations about payment, redistribution, and users' rights.

The number of categories varies depending on the depth of analysis and the prejudices of the person doing the categorization, but as a starting point, four categories will do:

Commercial software   Individuals or companies develop commercial software with the intent to sell it for a profit. Developers generally keep the source code for commercial source software secret, which means that users can't normally make changes to the software except to alter configuration settings the software supports. In the past, commercial software was sold in stores or by mail order, but today it's often sold via downloads from the Internet. Redistributing commercial software is generally illegal. Microsoft Windows and Microsoft Office are both common examples of commercial software.

Shareware software   From a legal perspective, *shareware* software is similar to commercial software in that it's copyrighted and the author asks for payment. The difference is that shareware is distributed on the Internet or in other ways and "sold" on an honor system—if you use the software beyond a trial period, you're expected to pay the author. Shareware was common in 1991 and is still available today, but it's much rarer.

Freeware   Freeware, like shareware, is available for free. Unlike shareware authors, though, the authors of freeware don't ask for payment. Sometimes, freeware is a stripped-down version of a more complete shareware or commercial program. Other times, the authors make it available for free to promote another product. Examples include Windows drivers for many hardware devices or the Adobe Reader program for reading Portable Document Format (PDF) files. As with commercial and shareware programs, freeware generally comes without source code.

Freeware should not be confused with *free software*, which is closely related to open source software. Chapter 3, "Understanding Software Licensing," describes free software in more detail.

Open source software   Open source software is defined by a set of ten principles, available at http://www.opensource.org/docs/osd. The most important of these principles are the right of the user to redistribute the program, the availability of source code, and the right of the user to make and distribute changed versions of the program. These principles mean that users can alter open source programs to suit their own needs, even in ways or for purposes the original author doesn't support.

Certification
Objective

Variants within each of these categories exist, as well as hybrids that don't quite fit in any category. For instance, the Open Source Initiative maintains a list of licenses it has approved as fulfilling its criteria (http://www.opensource.org/licenses); however, developers sometimes release software using obscure licenses or using licenses that impose conditions that run afoul of one of the more obscure Open Source Initiative rules. Such software is technically not open source, but it might be closer to open source than to another category.

Chapter 3 covers specific open source licenses in greater detail.

The basic idea behind open source software is that software developed in a transparent manner is likely to be superior to software developed in a closed manner. This superiority (and arguments against it) comes in several ways:

▶

This principle is sometimes referred to as "Linus's Law," which was stated by Eric S. Raymond in "The Cathedral and the Bazaar": "Given enough eyeballs, all bugs are shallow."

Better code   Exposing source code to the community at large means that it can be reviewed, judged, and improved upon by any interested party. Otherwise obscure bugs might be found and squashed when they might linger and cause problems in a closed-source product. On the other hand, the validity of this claim is not well supported by research, and smaller projects might not gain much in the way of interest from other programmers, so they might not benefit from outside code review.

More flexibility   By providing users with the source code, an open source project gives users the ability to customize the software for their own needs. If users submit changes back to the maintainer, or release them as a new branch of the project, then everybody can benefit from such changes. Of course, critics would argue that this flexibility is only a benefit to those with the necessary skill and time to make such changes, or to those with the money to hire somebody to do it.

Lower cost   Although the open source definition does not forbid sale of software, the redistribution requirements mean that open source software ends up being available free of charge. On the other hand, if you want support you may need to purchase a support contract, which can reduce or eliminate the cost benefits.

Lack of vendor lock-in   The developers of some proprietary products, and particularly very popular ones, can make it difficult for competing products by using proprietary file formats or standards and by not supporting more open standards. Open source tools are less subject to such problems, since they can be modified to support open standards even if they initially don't do so. As a practical matter, though, even proprietary file formats and protocols are usually reverse-engineered, so vendor lock-in usually ends up being a temporary problem rather than a permanent one.

Of course, within the Linux community the general consensus is that each of these factors is a real point in favor of Linux, and of open source software generally; the downsides noted are generally regarded as minor compared to the advantages. In the end, you'll need to make up your own mind on these matters after using different types of software.

Linux as a Software Integrator

Since soon after Unix was created, the OS fragmented into a set of loosely affiliated OSs. These OSs were incompatible on the binary level but more or less compatible on the source code level. This is still true today. You can take the same program and compile it for FreeBSD, OS X, and Linux, and it will work the same on all three platforms—but the compiled binaries made for one platform won't work on the others.

There are exceptions to this rule, though. Some programs rely on features that are available on just some Unix-like OSs. Others have quirks that make it impossible to compile them on some OSs. If a program falls into disuse, it may become unusable on newer OSs because it relies on compiler or OS features that have changed. Such problems tend to be ironed out over time, but they do crop up periodically.

Because of Linux's popularity, most open source Unix programs compile and work fine on Linux. Commercial programs for Linux also exist, although most of these are obscure or specialized. In any event, Linux has become an OS that most open source Unix programs must support. This effect is so strong that many projects now target Linux as the primary platform.

Understanding OS Roles

Computers fill many roles in the world, and as computers have become more common and less expensive, those roles have multiplied. Linux can serve as the OS for most of these roles, each of which draws on its own subset of support utilities. Some of these roles also require tweaking the kernel itself. I briefly describe three of these roles: embedded computers, desktop and laptop computers, and server computers.

Understanding Embedded Computers

As noted in Chapter 1, embedded computers are specialized devices that fulfill a specific purpose. Examples include:

Cell phones   Modern cell phones use computers with OSs that range from simple to complex. Linux powers some of these cell phones, usually in the form of Android.

Certification
Objective

Apple, Microsoft, and other vendors provide their own OSs for cell phones.

e-book readers   These devices, like cell phones, are specialized computers and so use an OS to power them. For many current e-book readers, that OS is Linux—either a custom Linux version or Android.

DVRs   Digital video recorders (DVRs), which record TV shows for later viewing, are computers with specialized software. Some of these, including the popular TiVo models, run Linux.

> The MythTV package (http://www.mythtv.org) can turn an ordinary PC into a Linux-based DVR, although you'll need a TV tuner and other specific hardware to make it work.

Car computers   Automobiles have included computers for years. These have mostly been tucked out of the way to monitor and control the engine; however, modern cars increasingly come with computers that users more readily identify as being computers. They manage global positioning system (GPS) navigation systems, control the radio, and even provide Internet access.

Appliances   Televisions, refrigerators, and other appliances are increasingly using computers to monitor energy use and for other purposes.

You might also think of tablet computers as falling in this category as well, although they can more closely resemble desktop or laptop computers. The distinction is mainly one of how much control the user has over the OS; embedded devices are designed to be used, but not maintained, by end users. The system administration tasks described in this book are done at the factory or using much simpler and more specialized user interfaces.

Understanding Desktop and Laptop Computers

> Certification
> Objective

Linux began life on a desktop computer, and although Linux doesn't come close to dominating that market, desktop computers are a good way to begin learning about Linux. Laptop computers are similar to desktop computers from a system administration perspective; both types of computers are often used by a small number of people for productivity tasks, such as word processing, Web browsing, and managing digital photos. For brevity, I'll use the term *desktop* to refer to both types of computer from here on.

> Desktop computers are similar to another class of computer, known as *workstations*. Workstations tend to be more powerful and specialized, and they often run Unix or Linux.

Linux software for such tasks is widely available and is quite good, although some people prefer commercial counterparts, such as Microsoft Office or Adobe Photoshop, that aren't available for Linux. This preference for a few specific commercial products is part of why Microsoft Windows continues to dominate the desktop market. Some people have speculated that the open source development model doesn't lend itself to the creation of popular GUI applications because software developers tend to be too technically oriented to fully appreciate the needs of less technically capable users. Without an explicit way to require developers to fulfill these needs, which for-profit companies create, open source software projects lag behind their commercial counterparts in usability. This view is not universally held, though, and at worst, open source projects lag behind their commercial counterparts just a bit.

Specific software that's required on most Linux-based desktop computers includes:

▶ The X Window System GUI (X for short)

▶ A popular desktop environment, such as GNOME, KDE, Xfce, or Unity

▶ A Web browser, such as Mozilla Firefox

▶ An email client, such as Mozilla Thunderbird or Evolution

▶ A graphics editor, such as the GIMP

▶ An office suite, such as OpenOffice.org or the similar LibreOffice

Additional requirements vary depending on the user's needs. For instance, one user might need multimedia editing tools, whereas another might need scientific data analysis software.

Linux distributions such as Fedora and Ubuntu typically install these popular desktop tools by default, or as a group by selecting a single install-time option. These distributions are also designed for relatively easy maintenance, so that users with only modest skill can install the OS and keep it running over time.

Understanding Server Computers

Server computers can be almost identical to desktop computers in terms of their hardware, although servers sometimes require bigger hard disks or better network connections, depending on how they're used. Many popular network server programs were written for Unix or Linux first, making these platforms the best choice for running them. Examples include:

Certification Objective

▶ Web servers, such as Apache

▶ Email servers, such as sendmail and Postfix

▶ Databases, such as MySQL

▶ File servers, such as the Network File System (NFS) or Samba

▶ Print servers, such as the Common Unix Printing System (CUPS) or Samba

▶ Domain Name System (DNS) servers, such as the Berkeley Internet Name Domain (BIND)

▶ Dynamic Host Configuration Protocol (DHCP) servers, such as the Internet Software Consortium's (ISC's) dhcpd

▶ Time servers, such as the Network Time Protocol (NTP)

▶ Remote login servers, such as Secure Shell (SSH) or Virtual Network Computing (VNC)

> **Remote login servers enable users to run desktop-style programs on a computer remotely. Therefore, they're sometimes found even on desktop systems.**

In a large organization, each of these services may have a distinct associated server computer. It's possible, though, for one computer to run many of these server programs simultaneously.

Most of these servers do not require a GUI, so server computers can do without X, desktop environments, or the typical desktop programs you'll find on a desktop computer. One of Linux's advantages over Windows is that you can run the computer without these elements, and even uninstall them completely. Doing so means that the GUI won't be needlessly consuming system resources such as RAM. Furthermore, if an item such as X isn't running, any security bugs it might harbor become unimportant. Some distributions, such as Debian, Arch, and Gentoo, eschew GUI configuration utilities. This makes these distributions unfriendly to new users, but the reliance on text-mode configuration tools is not a problem to experienced administrators of server computers.

The people who maintain large server computers are generally technically quite proficient and can often contribute directly to the open source server projects they use. This close association between users and programmers can help keep server projects on the cutting edge of what's required in the real world.

Note that the distinction between desktop and server computers is not absolute; a computer can run a mixture of both types of software. For instance, you might configure desktop computers in an office environment to run file server software. This configuration enables users to more easily share their work with others in the office. In a home or small office setting, running other servers on desktop computers can obviate the need to buy specialized hardware to fulfill those roles.

THE ESSENTIALS AND BEYOND

Linux's development history is tied to that of Unix and to open source development generally. Open source software is provided with source code and with the right to modify and redistribute the source code. This guarantees your ability to use the software even in ways the original author did not anticipate or support, provided you have the knowledge and time to alter it, or the resources to hire somebody else to do so. These open source principles have led to a great deal of popular software, particularly in the server arena; however, open source developers have been less able to capture the general public's excitement with applications designed for desktop computers.

(Continues)

THE ESSENTIALS AND BEYOND (Continued)

SUGGESTED EXERCISES

▶ Read the Features Web page on FreeBSD, `http://www.freebsd.org/features` `.html`, a competitor to Linux. How would you say it differs from Linux?

▶ Research the features of two or three open source programs that interest you, such as Apache, LibreOffice, and Mozilla Firefox. Do the feature lists seem complete? Are there features missing that are present in commercial counterparts?

REVIEW QUESTIONS

1. What type of multitasking does Linux use?

    A. Preemptive

    B. Multi-user

    C. Co-operative

    D. Single-tasking

    E. Single-user

2. Which of the following is a characteristic of all open source software?

    A. The software cannot be sold for a profit; it must be distributed free of charge.

    B. It must be distributed with both source code and binaries.

    C. Users are permitted to redistribute altered versions of the original software.

    D. The software was originally written at a college or university.

    E. The software must be written in an interpreted language that requires no compilation.

3. Which of the following programs is *most* likely to be installed and regularly used on a desktop computer that runs Linux?

    A. Apache

    B. Postfix

    C. Android

    D. Evolution

    E. BIND

4. True or false: VMS was a common OS on *x86* PCs at the time Linux was created.

5. True or false: Some DVRs run Linux.

6. True or false: A Linux computer being used as a server generally does not require X.

7. Linux uses a _____ kernel design, as contrasted with a microkernel design.

8. A type of software that's distributed for free but that requires payment on the "honor system" if a person uses it is called _____.

9. A _____ computer is likely to run a word processor and Web browser.

The black banner at top right contains:

CHAPTER 3

Understanding Software Licensing

Software is a type of intellectual property (IP), which is governed by copyright laws and, in some countries, patent laws. As a general rule, this makes it illegal to copy software unless you're the software's author. Open source software, however, relies on licenses, which are documents that alter the terms under which the software is released. As described in this chapter, open source licenses grant additional rights to software's users.

Open source software in general owes a great deal to three organizations: the Free Software Foundation (FSF), the Open Source Initiative (OSI), and the Creative Commons. Each organization has a distinct philosophy and role to play in the open source world. There are also numerous specific open source licenses, which I summarize at the end of this chapter, along with ways that businesses can use them.

▶ **Investigating software licenses**

▶ **The Free Software Foundation**

▶ **The Open Source Initiative**

▶ **The Creative Commons**

▶ **Using open source licenses**

Investigating Software Licenses

Copyright law has existed for centuries, and as such, it wasn't designed with software in mind. Nonetheless, copyright law does apply to software, and licenses that software authors apply to their software interact with copyright law to create the specific rights that you have—and *don't* have—to use, modify, and redistribute software. I therefore describe these basic principles, as well as the differences, in broad strokes, between proprietary and open source license terms.

Copyright and Software

Certification
Objective

A copyright is, as the name implies, a legally recognized right to create a copy of something. In most countries, if you write a book, take a photograph, or create a computer program, you and you alone have a right to make copies of that book, photograph, or computer program. You can give others a right to make such copies, or even relinquish control of the copyright to somebody else.

Copyright laws vary from one country to another, but most countries are signatories to the Berne Convention, an international treaty that requires countries to recognize each other's copyrights. That is, if Fred writes a book (or opera, or computer program) in the United States, that work will be copyrighted not only in the United States, but also in Iceland, Kenya, the United Kingdom, and other countries that have ratified the treaty.

Because most copyright laws were written long before computers came into being, they frequently don't mesh well with the needs of computers. For instance, copyright laws forbid copying of a work, but a computer program is useless without such copies. Examples of copies that must necessarily be made to run a program, or that are advisable for safety, include:

- ▶ A copy of the program from an installation medium to a hard disk

- ▶ A copy of the program from the hard disk to the computer's random access memory (RAM)

- ▶ A copy of the RAM into swap space

- ▶ A copy of the RAM into various smaller caches on the motherboard or CPU used to improve performance

- ▶ One or more backups of the hard disk, to protect against disk failures

Swap space is disk space that serves as an adjunct to RAM. For instance, if RAM fills up, the OS begins to use swap space as if it were RAM.

In the past, such copies were generally ignored, on the principle of *fair use*—that is, exceptions to the otherwise exclusive right to copy a work given to copyright holders. Other examples of fair use include quotes used in reviews or news reports and excerpts used in research or teaching. Today, copyright law explicitly recognizes the need to copy software to use it, at least in the United States.

PATENTS, TRADEMARKS, AND SOFTWARE

Copyright is one example of IP, but there are others. One of these is patents. A copyright protects a single creative work, which can be considered an expression of an idea, but a patent protects the *idea* itself. Patents typically apply to inventions, such as the proverbial "better mousetrap."

In the United States, software patents are legal. Although you can't patent an entire program, you can patent the algorithms that the program uses. Such patents are both common and controversial. Some open source programs don't use certain file formats because the algorithms required to use them are patented and the patent-holders have threatened to sue unauthorized users. Critics of software patents contend that most such patents are trivial or obvious—two things that a patented invention must not be. Companies sometimes use software patents as a way to block another company from selling a product, or to demand payment from a company that sells a product. Many companies selling Android-based cell phones have paid fees to patent-holders who have made software patent claims against their products.

In many other countries, software algorithms cannot be patented. Efforts are underway to change the relationships between software and patents—both to make software patentable in countries where it is not and to restrict or eliminate software patents in countries where software can currently be patented.

Trademarks are another type of IP. These are names, logos, and similar identifiers of a specific company or product. Software and the companies that produce it often use trademarks, as do hardware companies. The name *Linux* was trademarked in 1994 by an individual with little real involvement in the Linux community who attempted to charge royalties on the name. After a lawsuit, the trademark was transferred to the Linux Mark Institute (LMI; http://www.linuxfoundation.org/programs/legal/trademark).

As an end user, you're unlikely to need to deal explicitly with software patents or trademarks. The software patent and trademark games are played at the level of corporations. This contrasts with copyright issues, which can affect individuals who violate copyright law. If you work for a company that releases software, though, patent and trademark law could affect you if your software runs afoul of somebody's software patent or trademark. You should consult an attorney if you believe this might be the case.

Using Licenses to Modify Copyright Terms

Although software is subject to copyright law, most software is released with a *license*, which is a document written in legalese that claims to modify the rights granted by copyright law. In most cases, you don't sign such a license, although in some cases you must click a button to accept the license terms. In the past, licenses were sometimes printed on the boxes in which software was distributed. Such licenses are often called *end-user license agreements (EULAs)*, *click-through licenses*, *shrink-wrap licenses*, or *click-wrap licenses*. Open source software generally comes with a license in a file, often called COPYING.

Software licenses can modify copyright terms by making the terms either more or less restrictive. For example:

▶ The license to Microsoft Windows 7 Home Basic ties the software to a single computer; once you use the software, you cannot move the software to another computer without violating the license terms. This clause represents a restriction compared to copyright law, which applies to the software without explicit reference to the machine on which it's run.

▶ The General Public License (GPL), which is the license used by the Linux kernel, grants you the right to redistribute the software, including both the source code and binaries. This represents a loosening of the restrictions provided by copyright law.

As a general rule, licenses for proprietary software provide restrictions on what would otherwise be your rights under copyright law, whereas open source licenses grant you additional rights. There can be exceptions to this rule, though; for instance, a *site license* is a license for a proprietary program that grants an organization a right to make a certain number of copies of the program—say, 100 copies of a word processor for all the company's computers.

The Free Software Foundation

The Free Software Foundation (FSF) is a critical force in the open source world. Founded in 1985 by Richard Stallman, the FSF is the driving force behind the GNU's Not Unix (GNU) project described in the previous two chapters. The FSF has a certain philosophy, which I describe next. This philosophy manifests itself in the GPL, which is the FSF's favored software license.

Understanding the FSF Philosophy

The FSF advocates what it calls *free software*, which it defines in terms of freedom to do things you want to do with the software, not the price of the software. A common phrase to make this distinction clear is "free as in speech, not free as in beer." The FSF defines four specific software freedoms:

Certification Objective

> Free software, as the FSF defines it, is different from *freeware*. This term generally refers to software that's free of charge, but not necessarily free as in speech.

> ► Freedom to use the software for any purpose

> ► Freedom to examine the source code and modify it as you see fit

> ► Freedom to redistribute the software

> ► Freedom to redistribute your modified software

These freedoms are similar to the principles espoused by the OSI, described shortly; however, there are some important differences in interpretation, also as described shortly. The FSF elaborates on the implications of each of its principles, and their interactions, at http://www.gnu.org/philosophy/free-sw.html.

In an ideal world, by the FSF's standards, all software would be free—distributed with source code and all the freedoms just outlined. Some Linux distributions meet this ideal in isolation; however, some distributions include proprietary software. Sometimes this software is freeware, but other times it's a bit of proprietary code that enables the vendor to restrict redistribution and charge money to sell the software. Since free software is not necessarily free of charge, selling it is not a problem from the FSF's point of view, but given the other freedoms, free software's price tends toward zero as it gets passed around.

The point of all this talk of freedom is to empower users—not just developers or companies. If you can modify a program that does *almost* what you want it to do so that it does *exactly* what you want it to do, that fact is a big advantage compared to a proprietary program. If you can then redistribute your modified version of the program, you can help others (assuming they want similar functionality). Thus, the FSF philosophy, when applied, can create a benefit to the wider community.

The FSF philosophy and the licenses it inspires are often referred to as *copyleft*. This is a play on the word *copyright*, reflecting the fact that copyright provisions are used to ensure freedoms that are, in some respects, the exact opposite of what copyright was created to do—that is, to guarantee a freedom of users to copy software, rather than to restrict that right.

Free Software and the GPL

The legal expression of the FSF's principles comes in the form of the GPL (sometimes called the *GNU GPL*). Two versions of the GPL are common, version 2 and version 3. (The older version 1 is seldom used anymore.) Both versions of the GPL apply the four freedoms of the FSF philosophy to the licensed software. They also make explicit an implication of those four freedoms, by stating that derivative works must also be released under the GPL. This clause prevents a company from wholly appropriating an open source program. For instance, many companies make Linux distributions, and some use Linux kernels that incorporate bug-fix "patches." These kernels, like the mainstream Linux kernel, are all available under the GPL. No company could legally release a distribution based on a patched Linux kernel and then refuse to make its kernel patches available.

> A Linux distribution is a collection of many programs, which may use different individual licenses. No one license takes priority over the others.

The GPL version 2 (or GPLv2 for short) was released in 1991, and held sway for many years. In 2007, GPLv3 appeared, with the intention of closing what the FSF viewed as loopholes in the GPLv2, particularly with respect to changes in laws and practices since 1991. Specifically, the GPLv3 contains clauses that are intended to combat use of hardware restrictions that limit the FSF's four freedoms and to address issues related to software patents. Many new programs are now being released under the terms of the GPLv3, and many older programs now use the GPLv3 rather than the GPLv2. Some programs have not changed, though. Notable among these is the Linux kernel itself, which still uses the GPLv2. This is an important choice because it means that the Linux kernel can still be used at the heart of devices that are otherwise fairly closed, such as TiVos and Android-based phones. Many such devices use restrictive boot processes to prevent unauthorized kernels from booting—a process that the GPLv3 would forbid.

A variant of the GPL is the Lesser GPL, or LGPL. Developers often use the LGPL with *libraries*, which are collections of code that can be used by other programs. For instance, in Linux libraries implement the features that create dialog boxes and menus. Many GUI programs use these features, and placing them in libraries helps programmers and reduces the size of the programs that use them. The wording of the GPL, however, would require that all the programs that use a GPLed library also be released under the terms of the GPL. This strong requirement motivated the creation of the LGPL, which is similar to the GPL but enables programs that use a library to be released under another license—even a commercial license.

> The acronym LGPL used to expand to *Library GPL*, but this was changed in 1999.

Another related license is the GNU Free Documentation License (FDL), which is intended to be used by documentation rather than by programs. The GPL, being written for software, doesn't apply perfectly to static documents, so the FSF created the GNU FDL to fill the gap. A notable user of the FDL is Wikipedia (http://www.wikipedia.org); all of its content is available under the terms of the GNU FDL.

The Open Source Initiative

The OSI was founded in 1998 by Bruce Perens and Eric S. Raymond as an umbrella organization for open source software generally. Its philosophy, described in more detail shortly, is similar to that of the FSF but differs in some important details. As a general rule, more software qualifies as open source than qualifies as free (in the way the FSF means), but precisely what qualifies depends on the open source definition and, in a strict sense, on what the OSI has approved in terms of its licenses.

Understanding the Open Source Philosophy

In the 1980s and 1990s, the free software movement gathered momentum in certain circles, including academia and among hobbyists. Businesses, however, were slow to adopt free software. Many who did adopt it did so reluctantly or even unwittingly—system administrators, pressed to perform their duties with minuscule budgets, would quietly install Linux, Apache, Samba, and other free software as a way to avoid having to buy expensive commercial alternatives.

The FSF's advocacy efforts were (and are) based on a strong moral imperative—software *should be free*, in the FSF's view, with "free" defined as described earlier. This approach appeals to some people, but others—particularly businesses that want to make money off of software—find this type of advocacy strange at best and threatening at worst.

For these reasons, the OSI's creators designed their organization as a way to advocate free software. By using a new term—*open source*—and by softening some of the FSF's moral imperatives, the OSI aims to promote open source software in the business world. The difference in tone from the FSF's moral imperative can be seen in the opening statement on the OSI's Web site (http://www.opensource.org):

> *Open source is a development method for software that harnesses the power of distributed peer review and transparency of process. The promise of open source is better quality, higher reliability, more flexibility, lower cost, and an end to predatory vendor lock-in.*

 Certification Objective

The biggest philosophical difference between the FSF and the OSI is reflected in a requirement of the GPL: that derived works also be distributed under the GPL. The OSI has certified many licenses as being open source, including the GPL;

however, many of these licenses lack similar restrictions. Software released under such licenses has, in the past, found its way into closed-source products. The OSI does not object to such a path, provided the software was licensed in a way that permits it. The FSF, on the other hand, explicitly forbade such appropriation for proprietary uses in its GPL.

As a general rule, free software in the FSF's sense is also open source software, although some licenses the FSF recognizes as being free have not been approved by the OSI. Many open source licenses do not qualify as free by the FSF's definition, though. Figure 3.1 illustrates this relationship.

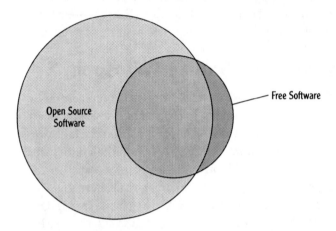

Open Source
Software

Free Software

FIGURE 3.1 Most free software is open source, but a significant amount of open source software is not free.

 Certification Objective

Today, there is some tension between free software purists in the FSF's sense and the more pragmatic open source community. For the most part, though, the two share goals that are similar enough that their differences are minor. In fact, two terms, *free and open source software (FOSS)* and *free/libre open source software (FLOSS)*, are sometimes used as umbrella terms to explicitly refer to both types of software and development.

Defining Open Source Software

 Certification Objective

The open source definition appears at http://www.opensource.org/docs/osd. It consists of ten principles, which are (paraphrased):

Free redistribution   The license must permit redistribution, including redistribution as part of a larger work.

▶

The OSI's ten principles were derived from those expressed by the Debian GNU/Linux developers.

Source code availability   The author must make source code available and permit redistribution of both source code and (if applicable) binary code.

Permission to derive works   The license must permit others to modify the software and to distribute such modifications under the same license as the original.

Respect for source code integrity   The license may restrict redistribution of modified source code, but only if patch files may be distributed along with the original source code. The license may require that derived works change the software's name or version number.

No discrimination against persons or groups   The license must not discriminate against any person or group of people.

No discrimination against fields of endeavor   The license must not forbid use of the program in any field, such as in business or by genetics researchers.

Automatic license distribution   The license must apply to anybody who receives the program without needing a separate agreement.

Lack of product specificity   The license must not require that the program be used or distributed as part of a larger program—that is, you may extract a single program from a larger collection and redistribute it alone.

Lack of restrictions on other software   The license must not impose restrictions on other software that's distributed along with the licensed software.

Technology neutrality   The license must not be restricted based on specific technologies or interfaces.

Note that the open source definition permits, but does not require, that the license require redistribution under the original license.

The first three of these principles are the most important, at least in understanding the point of open source technology. The collection as a whole bears a strong resemblance to the FSF's four principles and the extended description of its implications on the FSF's Web page (http://www.gnu.org/philosophy/free-sw.html). As already described, however, there are some differences, particularly with respect to licensing requirements for derived works.

The Creative Commons

The Creative Commons, headquartered at http://creativecommons.org, was founded by Lawrence Lessig. Its goal is to combat what its creators and supporters view as a creative culture that is increasingly tied to permissions granted

Certification
Objective

(or *not* granted) by those who hold copyrights on earlier works. Much of our current culture is derived from earlier cultural works—for instance, *Star Wars* is inspired, in part, by common myths and legends. *Star Wars* itself is copyrighted, however, which limits the rights of current artists to distribute works that are derivative of it, at least without permission.

The Creative Commons promotes its aims by providing six licenses that are designed for various purposes. You can select a license by answering a few questions on the Creative Commons Web site (at `http://creativecommons.org/choose/`), such as whether you want to permit commercial use of your work.

The FSF and the OSI are dedicated to promoting software freedoms. The Creative Commons' goals are broader, though; their licenses are aimed at audio recordings, video recordings, textual works, and so on, not just computer programs. Nonetheless, the Creative Commons as an organization helps promote the types of freedoms that also concern the FSF and the OSI.

Using Open Source Licenses

As an individual user, you might not need to delve too deeply into open source license details. The principles behind the OSI guidelines guarantee that you have the right to use open source programs as you see fit, and even to redistribute those programs. If you're building a business, though, and particularly a business that creates or distributes open source software, you may need to better understand these licenses. Thus, I describe a few of them in more detail and I also describe some of the ways that companies have found to use open source licenses as parts of their business models.

Understanding Open Source Licenses

Every open source license has its own unique characteristics. These are mostly of interest to developers who might want to contribute to a software project, but on occasion they may be important to a system administrator. The major open source licenses include the following:

GNU GPL and LGPL　As noted earlier, the Linux kernel uses the GPLv2, and many other Linux tools use the GPL (either version 2 or version 3). Many Linux libraries use the LGPL.

BSD　The BSD license is used by the open source BSD OSs, and by various software components developed for them. Unlike the GPL, the BSD license allows modifications to be distributed under other licenses. The latest versions of this license are very similar to the MIT license.

Two BSD licenses are common: an older 3-clause and a newer 2-clause. (The 3-clause version is sometimes called the "new" or "revised" license, in reference to a still older version.)

Certification
Objective

MIT   The Massachusetts Institute of Technology (MIT) was the original moving force behind the X Window System (X for short), and the MIT license (sometimes called the X11 license) continues to be used for Xorg-X11—the implementation of X included with all major Linux distributions. The MIT license is unusually short.

Apache   Like the BSD and MIT licenses, the Apache license is an open source license that permits redistribution under the same or another license. If a text file called NOTICE comes with the original work, it must be included in any derived work. This enables the original developer to provide contact or other information, even to users of heavily modified versions of the program.

Certification
Objective

◀ As the name implies, the Apache license originated with the Apache Web browser; however, it's used by many other projects, as well.

Artistic   The Artistic license was originally developed for the Perl programming language, but it has been used with other programs. It's filled with requirements and loopholes for those requirements. Most software that uses the Artistic license is shipped with the stipulation that this license is optional; the user may elect to follow the terms of some other license (usually the GPL) instead.

NPL and MPL   The Netscape Public License (NPL) and Mozilla Public License (MPL) were developed by Netscape when they brought their Netscape Web browser (the parent of the Firefox Web browser) into the open source field. The NPL reserves some rights for the copyright holder, but the MPL is more open.

Certification
Objective

Many additional licenses meet the OSI's requirements. You can find a complete list on the Open Source Initiative Web site, http://www.opensource.org/licenses/.

The details of the various open source licenses are probably not important to most system administrators. You may use and redistribute any open source program as you like. If you modify a program, though, you should be aware of redistribution requirements, particularly if you want to merge two or more programs or distribute a program under a modified license. You should also be aware that some Linux distributions may include software that doesn't qualify as open source. Some of this is commercial software, and some of it falls into some variant category.

◀ Some combinations of open source licenses are *incompatible* with each other, meaning that you can't legally combine the code and release the modified version.

One final concern when describing software licenses is the license for Linux as a whole. When you download a CD-ROM image file or buy a Linux package, the software you obtain uses many different licenses—the GPL, the BSD license, the MIT license, and so on. Most of these licenses are open source, but some aren't. Many distributions ship with a few shareware or not-quite-open-source packages, such as the shareware XV graphics program. Retail packages sometimes include outright commercial software. For this reason, you shouldn't copy a retail Linux package's disc unless you've researched the issue and found that copying is OK. If the distribution vendor provides free-as-in-beer download links, copying is probably OK.

Linux distributions include installation programs, configuration programs, and the like. These tools are usually all that a distribution packager can lay claim to, in terms of copyright. Most distribution maintainers have made their installation and configuration routines available under the GPL or some other open source license, but this isn't always the case. Such details can turn what might seem like an open source OS into something that's not quite fully open source. Debian maintains a policy of using only open source software in its main package set, although it lets freely redistributable but non-open source programs into its "non-free" package set.

Because a complete Linux distribution is composed of components using many different licenses, it's not very useful to speak of a single copyright or license applying to the entire OS. Instead, you should think of a Linux distribution as being a collection of different products that comes with a unifying installation utility. The vast majority of all the programs use one open source license or another, though.

Understanding Open Source Business Models

 Certification Objective

Some Linux distributions, such as Debian, are maintained by volunteers or by not-for-profit organizations. Others, such as Red Hat Enterprise Linux, are maintained by a company that expects to make a profit. How, though, can a company make a profit if its core product is available for free on the Internet? Several approaches exist to making money from open source software, including:

Services and support   The product itself can be open source, and even given away for free, while the company sells services and support, such as training and a technical support phone line. For instance, a game might be open source but require a subscription to an online service to provide a full set of features.

Dual licensing   A company can create two versions of the product: One version is completely open source and another adds features that are not available in the open source version. The open source version is then akin to the free samples that supermarkets often provide—it's a way to draw in paying customers.

Multiple products   The open source product may be just one offering from the company, with revenue being generated by other product lines. These other product lines could be other software or some other product, such as manuals.

Open source drivers   A special case of the preceding one is that of hardware vendors, who make money by selling hardware. They might opt to release drivers, or perhaps even hardware-specific applications, as open source as a way to promote their hardware.

> Some hardware vendors are reluctant to release open source drivers because doing so necessarily reveals programming information about their hardware, which some vendors are reluctant to do.

Bounties   Users can drive open source creation by offering to pay for new software or new features in existing software. Sites such as FOSSFactory (http://www.fossfactory.org) can help bring together users, each of whom as an individual might not be able to offer enough money to motivate development, to entice programmers to write the desired code.

Donations   Many open source projects accept donations to help fund development. Although this isn't a commercial funding model in the usual sense, it does help fund the operations of organizations such as the FSF.

Beyond these commercial opportunities, of course, a great deal of open source software is developed in academia, by governments, by non-profit organizations, by hobbyists, and so on. Even companies can be motivated to give back changes they make for themselves because hoarding their changes will create more work—if an internal change is not given back to the original author, the change will have to be re-applied with each new release.

THE ESSENTIALS AND BEYOND

Software licensing can be complex, and it's a topic that seldom interests technical people. Nonetheless, license terms can affect how the software community as a whole functions and therefore how software evolves over time. Linux is dominated by a handful of open source licenses, which permit (and sometimes require) that changes remain free. Such licenses typically impose few or no restrictions on how you can use the software. This contrasts with proprietary licenses, which are often loaded with restrictions. Organizations such as the FSF, the OSI, and the Creative Commons promote open source licenses. The OSI in particular tries to convince businesses to adopt open source licenses, advocating business models that employ open source as a way to generate revenue.

SUGGESTED EXERCISES

▶ Look up the GPLv2, GPLv3, and BSD 2-clause licenses. (http://www.opensource.org/licenses/ is a good place to find them all.) Read them and compare them. Which would you use if you were to write an open source program?

▶ Read the OSI mission statement (three paragraphs at the top of its main Web page at http://www.opensource.org) and the "Our Core Work" section of the FSF's "About" page (http://www.fsf.org/about/).

(Continues)

THE ESSENTIALS AND BEYOND *(Continued)*

REVIEW QUESTIONS

1. Which of the following is *not* required in order for software to be certified as open source?

   A. The license must not discriminate against people or groups of people.

   B. The license must not require that the software be distributed as part of a specific product.

   C. The license must require that changes be distributed under the same license.

   D. The program must come with source code, or the author must make it readily available on the Internet.

   E. The license must automatically apply to anybody who acquires the software.

2. Which is true of Linux distributions as a whole?

   A. They're covered by the GPL or the BSD license, depending on the distribution.

   B. Sometimes, they may not be copied because of non-open source software they may contain.

   C. They may be copied only after software using the MIT license is removed.

   D. They all completely conform to the principles of the open source movement.

   E. They all qualify as free software, as the FSF uses the term.

3. Which of the following is a key part of the FSF's philosophy?

   A. Developers should use the latest version of the FSF's GPL.

   B. Users should have the right to modify free software and distribute it under a commercial license.

   C. Developers should write software only for free operating systems such as GNU/Linux.

   D. Users should engage in civil disobedience by copying proprietary software.

   E. Users must have the right to use software as they see fit.

4. True or false: Copyright law governs the distribution of software in most countries.

(Continues)

THE ESSENTIALS AND BEYOND *(Continued)*

5. True or false: The FSF's free software definition and the OSI's ten principles of open source software both require that users have the ability to examine a program's workings—that is, its source code.

6. True or false: Because their hardware designs are proprietary, hardware vendors cannot release open source drivers for their products.

7. A license created by the FSF and often used for libraries is the _____.

8. An organization devoted to promoting open source-like principles in fields such as video and audio recordings is the _____.

9. The FSF's general principles are summarized by the term _____, which refers to using copyright laws for purposes that are in some ways contrary to copyright's original intent.

CHAPTER 4

Using Common Linux Programs

This chapter begins a more hands-on look at Linux, as opposed to the more abstract information presented in the previous chapters. This chapter begins with a look at Linux desktop environments, including information on the most common desktop environments and basic use information. If you're using a desktop environment, chances are good that you're doing so in order to run productivity software, so I describe some common productivity packages for Linux. Another major use of a Linux system is as a network server, so I also describe some of the most common server programs you may encounter. Although you might not need to write programs yourself, you may need to compile programs from source code, so you should be familiar with some common Linux programming tools, and I describe these.

▷ **Using a Linux desktop environment**

▷ **Working with productivity software**

▷ **Using server programs**

▷ **Managing programming languages**

Using a Linux Desktop Environment

Chances are your first experience with a working Linux system will involve a *desktop environment*, which is a set of programs that control the screen and provide small utility programs to perform tasks such as manage files. Linux provides several desktop environment options, so if you don't like one you can choose another. In addition to presenting information on available desktop environments, I describe some of the tools you can use to launch programs and manage files.

Choosing a Desktop Environment

Depending on your Linux distribution and installation options, chances are good your system has more than one desktop environment available. The most common desktop environments are:

> A *widget set* is a library that handles GUI features such as menus and dialog boxes. Qt and GTK+ are the two most common widget sets on Linux today.

KDE   The K Desktop Environment (KDE; http://www.kde.org) is one of the most popular desktop environments for Linux. It's the default desktop environment for Mandriva and SUSE. It includes many powerful tools that integrate together very well. It's built using the Qt widget set.

GNOME   The GNU Network Object Model Environment (GNOME; http://www.gnome.org) is KDE's primary rival in the Linux desktop environment arena. Fedora and Debian use it as a default desktop environment. GNOME is built atop the GIMP Tool Kit (GTK+) widget set. Like KDE, GNOME includes many powerful tools that work together. GNOME aims to provide a very easy-to-use desktop environment, and so it provides fewer options than KDE.

LXDE   The Lightweight X11 Desktop Environment (LXDE; http://lxde.org) is, as its full name suggests, intended to consume few resources and therefore work well on old or modest computers.

Unity   Canonical, the publisher of the Ubuntu distribution, released the Unity desktop environment in 2010. Like GNOME, it aims for simplicity as a way of helping users who are inexperienced or who don't want a lot of clutter.

Xfce   This desktop environment, headquartered at http://www.xfce.org, was originally modeled on a commercial desktop environment known as CDE, but it is built using the GTK+ widget set. Xfce provides more configurability than GNOME or Unity, and it aims to consume fewer system resources than most other desktop environments.

Roll-Your-Own   It's possible to build a desktop environment of your own from components you like. At a minimum, you need a window manager (dozens are available; see http://xwinman.org for a partial list), but for the configuration to truly be a desktop environment, you'll need other components, such as a file manager and small productivity tools. All of the components need to be accessible from some sort of menu system.

Unfortunately, it's impossible to give a simple set of rules for when one desktop environment works better than another, although some generalities do apply.

New users who are accustomed to Windows or Mac OS will probably be happiest with KDE; this environment is most like these traditional desktop operating systems' environments. Although they deviate more from the model used by other OSs, GNOME and Unity aim for ease of use and so can be good choices for the inexperienced. Users who are familiar with commercial Unix OSs might give Xfce a try. Xfce and LXDE are good choices on systems that have less than copious RAM or less than blazing CPUs. People who like to customize everything or who have less-capable computers should investigate the roll-your-own approach.

You may want to give two or three desktop environments a try. In most cases, you can install multiple environments using a package manager, as described in Chapter 9, "Using Programs and Processes." Thereafter, you'll see an option to select your desktop environment when you log into the computer, as shown in Figure 4.1, which shows a login screen for a Fedora system. Note the button in the lower-left corner of the login dialog box. It reads GNOME in Figure 4.1, but by clicking it, you can select another desktop environment before you type your password. The details of how you select a desktop environment vary from one system to another, though, so you may need to peruse options on your login screen to find the one you want.

Password selection is extremely important. Chapter 14, "Creating Users and Groups," covers this topic.

FIGURE 4.1 GUI login managers usually provide a selection of environments from which you can choose what to run.

Launching Programs

Certification
Objective

Most desktop environments provide several ways to launch programs. Details vary considerably from one environment to another, but examples include the following:

Desktop menus   Many desktop environments provide menus along a top, bottom, or side edge of the screen. One or more items in these menus can give you access to a preselected set of applications.

Desktop icons   Some desktop environments enable you to place icons in the main area of the desktop. Clicking or double-clicking these icons then launches the applications they represent. This approach generally requires customization, though; few default configurations place applications in the main desktop area.

Panels   Some desktop environments provide panels, typically located on the sides of the screen, in which icons for common applications appear. Unity uses such a configuration by default, as does GNOME 3—although in the case of GNOME 3, the panel appears only when you click the Activities item in the upper-left corner of the screen.

Context menus   You can sometimes right-click in an unused part of the screen to obtain a context menu with a variety of options, which may include the option to run programs.

Searching for programs   Some desktop environments, such as GNOME 3, provide a prominent search feature that you can use to find a program by name. Typically, you type part of a program's name and programs whose names match appear in a list. You can then select the program you want to run from that list.

Certification
Objective
Terminals   You can launch a program called a *terminal*, which provides a text-mode user interface inside a window. You can then run either text-mode or GUI programs by typing their filenames in this window. This approach is covered in more detail in Chapter 6, "Getting to Know the Command Line."

To help clarify some of these methods, a couple of examples are in order. First, consider launching the Firefox Web browser in Fedora 16 using GNOME 3. To do so, you would follow these steps:

1. Click the Activities item in the upper-left corner of the screen. The result is a panel (called Favorites) on the left side of the screen, as shown in Figure 4.2.

▶

The procedure described here requires that you have a modern video card. If you lack such hardware, GNOME 3 falls back on an older menu-based system for launching programs.

FIGURE 4.2 Panels enable you to launch popular programs in GNOME, Unity, and some other desktop environments.

2. Move the mouse over the Firefox icon, which is the topmost icon in Figure 4.2.

3. Click the Firefox icon. After a brief delay, a Firefox window should open.

Several other ways to do this also exist, such as typing the program's name in the search field (visible near the upper-right corner of Figure 4.2) or finding the program in an applications list (accessible by clicking Applications near the top middle-left of Figure 4.2). Because only a handful of programs appear in the GNOME 3 panel, you must either add programs to it or launch programs that the Fedora developers did not include by default in some other way.

For comparison, KDE under openSUSE 12.1 provides several obvious ways to launch Firefox:

▶ By clicking its icon in the Desktop Folder window (visible in the upper-left corner of Figure 4.3).

▶ By clicking its icon near the left side of the panel on the bottom of the screen (again, see Figure 4.3).

▶ By finding it in the Applications list. You can open this list by starting with the Kicker (accessible via the SUSE chameleon icon in the lower-left corner of the screen) and selecting Applications ➢ Internet ➢ Web Browser ➢ Web Browser (Firefox). Figure 4.3 shows the beginning of this selection in progress.

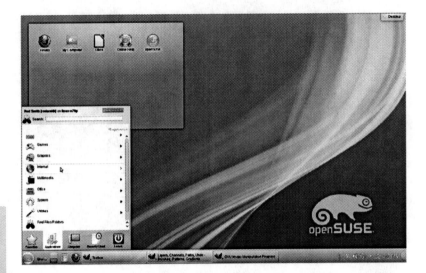

FIGURE 4.3 KDE's desktop interface provides launch methods similar to those available in Windows.

Each distribution sets up its defaults in its own way. Thus, your own GNOME or KDE configuration might not resemble the ones shown here.

As with GNOME, the widest range of launch options are available for a handful of popular applications such as Firefox. You may need to use the more complex methods, such as locating the program in the Applications list, for less popular programs. You can, however, reconfigure the desktop environment to add programs you use frequently.

Using a File Manager

Besides GNOME's Nautilus, other file managers include Thunar (Xfce's file manager) and Konqueror (KDE's file manager). Konqueror doubles as a Web browser.

If you're used to Windows or Mac OS X, you've almost certainly used a *file manager* to manipulate your files. Linux, of course, provides a file manager for this purpose, too—in fact, you have a choice of several, although most of them operate in a similar way. As an example, consider Nautilus, which is GNOME's default file manager. If you were running GNOME 3 on Fedora, the Nautilus icon resembles a filing cabinet in the Favorites panel, as shown in Figure 4.2. Your desktop environment may also launch a file manager when you insert a removable disk, such as a USB flash drive or a CD-ROM or DVD-ROM disc. Figure 4.4 shows Nautilus running on a fresh installation.

Because Nautilus is similar to the file managers in other OSs, chances are you'll be able to use its main features quite easily. A few items do deserve mention:

If you double-click a location, Nautilus will attempt to access it.

Locations Along the left side of the window, you'll see a series of locations. In Figure 4.4, these fall into three categories:

> ▶ The Devices category includes disk partitions that aren't part of your standard installation, including removable disks.

▶ The Computer category is mostly common folders in your own home directory, although File System refers to the entire Linux installation.

▶ The Network category provides access to network resources; however, this may require extra configuration before it works correctly.

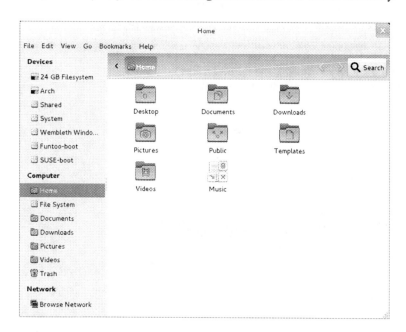

FIGURE 4.4 Nautilus provides a view of your files similar to that in other OSs' file managers.

Home The Home location refers to your *home directory*—that is, the directory where you store your own user files. Ordinarily, you'll create all of your personal files in your home directory. The default view of Nautilus when you launch it manually is of your home directory, as shown in Figure 4.4, so the right pane shows the files and subdirectories of this directory.

Bookmarks If you want to change the list of default locations, you can select Edit ➤ Bookmarks from the main menu. The resulting dialog box resembles Figure 4.5. You can remove existing bookmarks or create new ones by entering the path to the directory, giving it a name, and clicking Close. If you add bookmarks, they'll appear in a new section titled Bookmarks.

Document Properties You can right-click a file and select Properties from the resulting dialog box. This produces a Properties dialog box, as shown in Figure 4.6. The Open With tab enables you to associate a document type with an application.

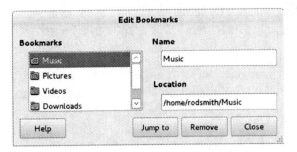

FIGURE 4.5 You can manage bookmarks to enable quick access to directories that interest you.

FIGURE 4.6 Nautilus enables you to associate document types with applications.

Working with Productivity Software

The area of productivity software is extremely broad; hundreds, if not thousands, of productivity applications exist, and entire books have been written about many of them. Therefore, in this chapter I can only provide names and brief descriptions of a few of the most important such tools. I begin by providing some tips on how to find a program to perform a task in Linux. I then describe some of the tools in a few common categories, including Web browsers, email clients, office tools, multimedia applications, cloud computing, and mobile applications.

Finding the Right Tool for the Job

Linux provides productivity applications in many broad categories, but if you're not already familiar with the field, you might have a hard time tracking them down. This is particularly true because applications' names don't always clearly identify their purpose.

A few techniques can help you to find suitable applications:

Using desktop menus   You can use the menus or other application display tools on your desktop environment to locate productivity applications. Such tools often categorize applications in helpful ways. For example, the KDE Kicker (shown in Figure 4.3) breaks applications down into categories (Edutainment, Games, Graphics, and so on) and subcategories (Photography and Scanning in the Graphics category, for instance). This can help you track down an application, but only if it's already installed.

Using search features   You may be able to use a search feature, either in a desktop environment or in a Web browser, to locate a suitable application. Typing in a critical word or phrase, such as *office* (in conjunction with *Linux* if you're doing a Web search) may help you locate office applications (word processors, spreadsheets, and so on).

Using tables of equivalents   If you normally use a particular Windows application, you may be able to find a Linux substitute by consulting a table of equivalent applications, such as the ones at `http://www.linuxrsp.ru/win-lin-soft/table-eng` or `http://www.linuxalt.com`.

Using others' expertise   You can ask other people—co-workers, friends, or people in online forums—for help in finding a suitable application. This technique is particularly helpful if you've performed a basic search yourself but found nothing that meets your specific criteria.

Some of these methods, such as using desktop menus, can only find software that's already installed. Other techniques, such as Web searches, can find programs that you don't have installed. You can usually install software with the help of your distribution's packaging system, as described in Chapter 9.

Using a Web Browser

Linux supports a variety of Web browsers, including the following:

Chrome   Google's Chrome browser (http://www.google.com/chrome) aims to be fast and easy to use. Since its introduction in 2008, it's gained rapidly in popularity. Although Chrome is technically a commercial project, it's available free of charge. An open source variant, known as Chromium, is also available.

Firefox   This program, headquartered at http://www.mozilla.org, is the most popular browser for Linux, and is also quite popular on Windows and Mac OS X. It's a very complete browser, but it can consume a lot of memory, so it may not be the best choice on an older or weaker computer.

Galeon   This program, headquartered at http://galeon.sourceforge.net, is a browser that's officially part of the GNOME Office suite. It's designed as a lightweight GUI Web browser.

Konqueror   This KDE program serves a dual function: It's both a Web browser and a file manager. Konqueror does a good job with most Web pages. It's fairly lightweight, and so is well worth trying, particularly if you use KDE. You can read more at http://www.konqueror.org.

Lynx   Most Web browsers are GUI programs that display text in multiple fonts, show graphics inline, and so on. Lynx (http://lynx.browser.org) is unusual in that it's a text-based Web browser. As such, it's a useful choice if you run Linux in text mode or if you don't want to be bothered with graphics. Lynx is also useful as a test browser when you develop your own Web pages—if a page is readable in Lynx, chances are visually impaired people who browse the Web with speech synthesizers will be able to use your page.

Opera   An unusual commercial entrant in the Linux Web browser sweepstakes, Opera (http://www.opera.com) claims to be unusually fast. Although Opera is commercial, you can download it at no charge.

Notably absent from this list is Microsoft's Internet Explorer, which is extremely popular on Windows. Unfortunately, some Web sites just won't work with anything but Internet Explorer. Other sites are somewhat picky, but they can work with at least one Linux browser. Thus, you should probably install at least two Linux Web browsers.

Web browsers give users easy access to a world of information—literally! Unfortunately, the Web has a dark side, too. Problems include:

▶   Web sites can log user access data, which can be used in marketing or in other ways you might not like.

▶ Much Web-based content is dynamic, meaning that Web sites download small programs (often written in Java) that your Web browser runs. This content might be harmless, but it's increasingly being used to deliver malware.

▶ Malicious Web sites can trick users into giving up sensitive data, such as financial information, by pretending to be a trusted site. This technique is known as *phishing*.

▶ Most Web sites are not secure—data transferred can be read on intervening computers. Most sensitive sites, such as Internet banking sites and online retailers, now encrypt their sensitive data, but you should be cautious when sending such data.

▶ Because of security concerns, passwords used on most Web sites are subject to theft. This can pose a dilemma because it can be hard to remember all your Web site passwords. Many browsers can do this for you, but that stores your passwords on your hard disk, which makes them vulnerable to theft or loss.

> ◀
>
> Chapter 14, "Creating Users and Groups," describes how to create passwords that are both memorable and hard to guess.

Some of these problems aren't unique to the Web, of course. For instance, most email transfers are insecure, so you shouldn't send sensitive data via email.

Using Email Clients

Email client programs enable you to read and write email messages. Such programs can either access a mailbox on your own computer or, using email network protocols described later, send and receive email with the help of network mail server computers. Common Linux email clients include the following:

Evolution   This program, based at `http://projects.gnome.org/evolution/`, is a powerful GUI email client. It also includes groupware and scheduling features.

KMail   The KDE project's KMail (`http://userbase.kde.org/KMail`) is well integrated into that desktop environment, but you can use it even in other desktop environments if you like.

`mutt`   This is one of several text-based email readers. Despite its text-mode interface, `mutt` is quite capable. You can read more at `http://www.mutt.org`.

Thunderbird   This program, based at `http://www.mozilla.org/thunderbird/`, is an email client that's closely associated with the Firefox Web browser.

 Certification
Objective

Email clients work in a similar way in any OS. Typically, you must configure them to know how to send and receive messages—whether to use the local computer's facilities or remote servers. Thereafter, you can read incoming messages and send outgoing messages.

Using Office Tools

Several office tool packages for Linux exist. These packages offer some combination of word processors, spreadsheets, presentation programs, graphics programs, databases, and sometimes other programs. Examples include:

GNOME Office   The applications in GNOME Office are developed independently of each other, but GNOME Office attempts to link them together into a coherent whole. Specific projects within GNOME Office are AbiWord (word processor), Evince (document viewer), Evolution (groupware and email client), Gnumeric (spreadsheet), Inkscape (vector graphics and presentation creation), and Ease (presentation). You can learn more at http://live.gnome.org/GnomeOffice.

KOffice   This office suite, based at http://www.koffice.org, is loosely associated with the KDE project, although you can use it even if you use another desktop environment. It includes KWrite (word processor), KCells (spreadsheet), Artwork (vector graphics), Showcase (presentation), and Kivio (flowcharting).

> A *fork* of a program is when a single project splits into two projects, typically because different groups of developers have diverging goals.

Certification Objective

LibreOffice   This office suite was created as a *fork* of the older OpenOffice.org suite (described shortly). It's becoming the most popular office suite in Linux. It provides six applications: Writer (word processor), Calc (spreadsheet), Impress (presentation), Base (database), Draw (vector graphics), and Math (equation editor). LibreOffice has a reputation for being a big and slow suite. The speed issue is not a major problem on modern hardware, but on older systems you may want to consider something else. You can read more at http://www.libreoffice.org.

Certification Objective

OpenOffice.org   Until early 2011, this office suite, based at http://www.openoffice.org, was the most prominent one for Linux. Its corporate sponsor, Oracle, stopped supporting commercial development of the project, which triggered the fork of the LibreOffice project.

Most of these programs support the OpenDocument Format (ODF), which is an open set of file formats that's slowly making inroads as a standard for word processing, spreadsheet, and other office files. Although ODF is intended to enable easy transfer of files across applications, application-specific assumptions often hinder such transfers, especially on complex documents.

Many other programs exist in this space, although many aren't part of office suites. Some are unusual. For instance, LyX (http://www.lyx.org) can take the place of a word processor, but it's rather unusual: It's built as a way to create and edit LaTeX documents, LaTeX being a document format that's popular in computer science, mathematics, and some other technical fields.

Using Multimedia Applications

Linux has an excellent reputation as a workhorse server platform, but until recently, its capacity as a multimedia OS has been lacking. This was largely because of a dearth of applications; however, Linux's multimedia application list has grown considerably in the last decade. Current offerings include the following:

Audacity This program, based at http://audacity.sourceforge.net, is an audio editor for Linux, similar to commercial products like Sound Forge for other platforms. You can use it to cut sections from an audio file, equalize volume, remove tape hiss or other noises, apply artificial audio effects, and more.

Certification Objective

Blender You can use this program to create complex 3-D images, including both stills and animations. You can learn more about Blender at http://www.blender.org.

Certification Objective

The GIMP The GNU Image Manipulation Program (GIMP; http://www.gimp.org) is a still image manipulation program similar in broad strokes to Adobe Photoshop. (The GTK+ toolkit, which is the basis of GNOME and many other programs, was originally created for the GIMP.)

Certification Objective

ImageMagick This is a suite of graphics programs, but with a twist: You typically use the ImageMagick programs from the command line. You can use it to convert file formats, add frames to images, resize images, and so on. You can learn more at http://www.imagemagick.org.

Certification Objective

HandBrake This program provides an easy way to convert between video formats, and particularly into formats that use the efficient H.264 encoding. You can learn more at http://handbrake.fr.

MythTV You can turn a regular PC into a digital video recorder (DVR) using this software, which is based at http://www.mythtv.org. MythTV uses a client-server model, enabling one recorder to service multiple players on TVs throughout your home.

A few motion pictures that used effects rendered via Linux include *Titanic*, the *Shrek* series, and *Avatar*.

Given this range of multimedia applications, you can use Linux for everything from cropping photos of your 2-year-old's birthday party to rendering the effects for major motion pictures. If you have very special needs, digging a bit may turn up something else—this list is just the start!

Using Linux for Cloud Computing

Cloud computing is the delivery of computer software as a service, typically over the Internet, rather than in the form of applications stored on the user's computer. In most cases, users access cloud computing resources via a Web browser. Thus, in theory Linux can function as a cloud computing client platform—just launch a Web browser on the cloud computing provider and away you go.

In practice, there can sometimes be complications. For instance, a cloud computing provider might require that you use a particular Web browser or have a specific browser plug-in installed. In some cases, it might be impossible to meet these requirements in Linux; however, if the provider supports a wide range of browsers as clients, you shouldn't have problems using cloud computing resources.

Examples of cloud computing include:

- ▶ Dropbox (http://www.dropbox.com), an online file storage and backup service

- ▶ Google Apps (http://www.google.com/apps)

- ▶ Microsoft Office Web Apps (http://office2010.microsoft.com/en-us/web-apps/)

- ▶ Web-based email, available from many providers

Using Mobile Applications

Although Android is a Linux-based OS, for the most part it runs entirely different applications than do desktop or server implementations of Linux. This is understandable—chances are you wouldn't want to try to write a long document, such as a book, with a cell phone, so many of the features in a big office program such as LibreOffice Write would go to waste on a mobile computing device.

Instead, mobile computing typically focuses on small programs known as *apps*. In the case of Android, you can download apps using an app called Market. (A Web-based version is available at http://market.android.com.) Apps typically provide quick and specialized computation, often employing features of the phone. For instance, an app can calculate the calories you've burned while riding a bicycle or retrieve a weather forecast for your area. Both these examples use your phone's global positioning system (GPS) features to identify the phone's (and your!) position.

Although most Linux applications for desktop and server computers are open source and available free of charge, Android apps are often non-free, albeit low in cost. Be sure to check the cost before you download an app!

Using Server Programs

Android apps are increasingly a source of malware. You can minimize your risk by downloading apps only from Google's own Market source.

Linux is a powerful OS for running server programs, so it should come as no surprise that you can find a wide variety of server programs for Linux. In the following pages I describe some common server protocols and the programs that use them. I also briefly describe the process of installing and launching servers and provide basic information on server security issues.

Identifying Common Server Protocols and Programs

Networks, including the Internet, function by means of network *protocols*, which are clearly defined descriptions of how two computers should exchange data to achieve some end, such as transferring email or delivering a file to be printed. Most protocols are described in one or more standards documents, known as Request for Comments (RFC) documents, each of which has a number. Typically, one RFC document defines the protocol, and over time additional RFC documents define extensions or modifications of the protocol as they become necessary.

Most network protocols involve transferring data over one or more *ports*, which are numbered resources on a computer. You can think of a port as being something like a telephone extension number—the main number (an Internet Protocol, or IP, address) identifies the computer as a whole and the port number identifies the protocol being used. A server program attaches itself to a port number and receives all incoming requests on that port.

Table 4.1 summarizes some common port numbers, the protocols with which they're associated, and the Linux programs that are often used in conjunction with these protocols. Note that many ports and protocols are associated with more than one program. This is because Linux provides choices for many protocols—you can choose which of several server programs to use for a given protocol, just as you can choose which of several word processors or Web browsers to use.

The `/etc/services` file links common port numbers to short names that are often used in other configuration files.

TABLE 4.1 Common port numbers and their purposes

Port number	Protocol	Common server program(s)	Explanation
20–21	FTP	oftpd, ProFTPD, Pure-FTPd, vsftpd	The File Transfer Protocol (FTP) is an old protocol for transferring files over a network. It supports both anonymous and password-mediated access. FTP is unusual in that it uses two ports.
22	SSH	OpenSSH	The Secure Shell (SSH) is an encrypted remote access tool. It also supports file transfers and encrypting other protocols.
23	Telnet	telnetd	This is an old unencrypted remote login protocol. It's seldom used today, although its client program, telnet, can be a useful network diagnostic tool.
25	SMTP	Exim, Postfix, qmail, sendmail	The Simple Mail Transfer Protocol (SMTP) is the main protocol for moving email on the Internet. The sender initiates SMTP transfers.
42	DNS	dnsmasq, named	The Domain Name Service (DNS) enables computers to look up an IP address by providing a hostname, or vice-versa. Without it, you'd need to refer to all computers by IP address rather than by name.
67	BOOTP, DHCP	dnsmasq, dhcpd	The Bootstrap Protocol (BOOTP) and its newer cousin, the Dynamic Host Configuration Protocol (DHCP), both enable a computer on a local network to help automatically configure other computers to use a network.

(Continues)

TABLE 4.1 *(Continued)*

Port number	Protocol	Common server program(s)	Explanation
80	HTTP	Apache	The Hypertext Transfer Protocol (HTTP) is the basis of the World Wide Web (WWW, or Web).
109–110	POP2 and POP3	Courier, Cyrus IMAP, Dovecot, UW IMAP	The Post Office Protocol (POP) has gone through several revisions, each with its own port. This protocol enables a recipient to initiate an email transfer, so it's often used as the last leg in email delivery, from a server to the recipient.
118	SQL	MySQL, PostgreSQL	The Structured Query Language (SQL) is a network-enabled database interface language. If you run an SQL server on your network, client computers can access and modify that database.
137–139	SMB/CIFS	Samba	Microsoft uses the Server Message Block (SMB)/Common Internet File System (CIFS) protocols for file and printer sharing, and Samba implements these protocols in Linux.
143, 200	IMAP	Courier, Cyrus IMAP, Dovecot, UW IMAP	The Internet Message Access Protocol (IMAP) is another recipient-initiated email transfer protocol, similar to POP. IMAP makes it easier for recipients to permanently store and manage email on the server computer, though.
389	LDAP	OpenLDAP	The Lightweight Directory Access Protocol (LDAP) is a network protocol for accessing directories, which in this context are a type of database. LDAP is often used to store network login information, among other things.

(Continues)

TABLE 4.1 *(Continued)*

Port number	Protocol	Common server program(s)	Explanation
443	HTTPS	Apache	This protocol is a secure (encrypted) variant of HTTP.
2049	NFS	NFS	The Network File System (NFS) is a protocol, and a server of the same name, for file sharing between Unix and Unix-like OSs.

Table 4.1 is incomplete; it only summarizes some of the more important protocols and the servers that deliver them. Numerous other protocols and servers exist, many of them for very specialized tasks.

Some protocols are most often used on local networks. For instance, DHCP by its nature is intended to help you manage your own local network by making it easier to configure client computers—just tell the computers to use DHCP and that's it. SMB/CIFS is also usually employed only locally, to enable users to more easily access each other's files and printers. Protocols like HTTP, on the other hand, are generally used on the Internet as a whole, although they can also be used on local networks.

Chapter 17, "Managing Network Connections," describes network configuration in greater detail.

SERVER PROGRAMS AND SERVER COMPUTERS

The term *server* can apply to an entire computer or to a single program running on that computer. When applied to a computer as a whole, the term identifies the purpose of the computer and the fact that it runs one or more server programs. Server computers typically provide services that are used by anywhere from a handful to millions of client computers—that is, the computers that use a server's services.

In the networking world, a server (computer or program) listens for a connection from a client (computer or program) and responds to data transfer requests. Server computers are often—but not always—more powerful than their clients.

When you read the word *server* (or *client*, for that matter), it may refer to either a computer or a program. The context usually makes it clear which meaning is intended, although sometimes this isn't the case—in fact, sometimes

(Continues)

> ## SERVER PROGRAMS AND SERVER COMPUTERS *(Continued)*
>
> the speaker or writer may not know! For instance, somebody might report "the Samba server isn't working." In such a case, you might need to figure out whether it's the Samba server program or something else on the server computer that's causing problems!
>
> Sometimes the client-server lines can get blurred. For instance, in office settings, it's common for many computers to function as file *servers* by running file server software such as Samba or NFS. Such a configuration enables Sam to make his files available to Jill, and for Jill to make her files available to Sam. In this situation, both computers function as both client and server, and run both types of software. In any given exchange, though, only one is the client and one the server.

Installing and Launching Servers

The topic of maintaining server programs is beyond the scope of this book, but you should be aware of the basics of this task. You can install servers in the same way you install other software, as described in Chapter 9.

Once the software is installed, you must launch a server. You do this differently than the way you launch a desktop application. Instead of clicking an icon or menu entry in a GUI, you typically launch a server by configuring the computer to run it automatically whenever it boots. Thereafter, the server program runs in the background, as a *daemon*—that is, as a process that runs unattended.

Most servers run via a startup script, which Linux runs automatically whenever it boots. You can also type the startup script name, usually followed by a keyword such as start or stop, to start or stop the server manually. Traditionally, Linux startup scripts have been stored in /etc/init.d or /etc/rc.d. This location, and the nature of startup scripts, has been changing with recent distributions, although most distributions retain compatibility scripts in these old locations.

Some servers run via a *super server*, such as inetd or xinetd. These server programs run constantly, keeping the servers they manage unloaded except when they're needed. This configuration can minimize the memory impact of running many seldom-used servers. The super server can also function as a security feature; like a doorman, it can keep out the riff-raff.

The word *daemon* derives from Greek mythology; daemons were helpful supernatural beings, just as Unix and Linux daemons are helpful programs.

Securing Servers

Whenever you run a server, you also run the risk of its being compromised and abused. Risks fall into several categories:

- ▶ Servers can contain bugs that enable outsiders to abuse the software to run programs locally.

- ▶ You can misconfigure a server, granting outsiders greater access to your system than you'd intended.

- ▶ Users with accounts and remote access via a server can abuse this trust. This risk is particularly great if combined with a server bug or misconfiguration.

- ▶ A server can be used as a stepping-stone to attack others, making it appear as if an attack originated from your computer.

- ▶ Even without breaking into a computer, an attacker can swamp a server with bogus data, thus shutting it down. This technique is called a *denial-of-service (DoS) attack*.

Server security is an extremely complex topic, and details vary from one server to another. For instance, if you run a server such as a remote login server, Samba, or a POP or IMAP email server, you probably want to pay careful attention to password security, since all of these servers rely on passwords. Passwords are unimportant to a DHCP or DNS server, though. Of course, even if a DHCP or DNS server program doesn't use passwords, other server programs running on the same computer might!

Broadly speaking, securing a server involves paying attention to each of the risk factors just outlined. Some specific steps you can take to secure your servers include the following:

- ▶ You should keep your server programs up-to-date by using your package management tools to upgrade servers whenever upgrades become available. You can also research specific servers to pick ones that have good security reputations.

- ▶ You should learn enough about server configuration to be sure you can configure your servers properly.

- ▶ You should remove unused accounts and audit necessary accounts to be sure they use strong passwords.

- ▶ You can use firewall configurations to restrict outsiders' access to server computers that are intended for internal use only. You can also use firewalls to minimize the risk of one of your computers being used to attack others.

Chapter 14, "Creating Users and Groups," describes how to create strong passwords.

Managing Programming Languages

Many users never need to deal with programming languages; however, basic knowledge of what they are and how they differ from one another is important for Linux users, for a variety of reasons. You might need to install languages for users on systems you manage, or use programming languages yourself to compile software from source code. You might also want or need to learn about programming, particularly if you find a need to modify your computer's configuration at a low level—many of the startup and other tasks are handled by scripts that you can modify yourself.

For these reasons, the rest of this chapter is devoted to presenting basic information on programming languages. I begin by describing the differences between compiled and interpreted languages, which are important to understand so that you can properly handle program files or choose which you want to use. I then provide brief descriptions of some common programming languages so that you can identify and use their source code files or choose which language you want to learn to use.

Choosing a Compiled vs. an Interpreted Language

At their core, computers understand binary codes—numbers that represent operations, such as adding two numbers or choosing which of two actions to take. People, however, are much better at handling words and symbols, such as + or if. Thus, most programming involves writing a program in a symbolic programming language and then translating that symbolic code into the numeric form that computers understand. Dozens, if not hundreds, of such *programming languages* exist, each with its own unique features.

Among high-level languages, two broad categories exist:

Compiled languages   Programmers convert (or *compile*) a program written in a compiled language from the original source code form into the machine code form when writing the program. The compilation process can take some time—typically a few seconds to several hours, depending on the size of the program and the speed of the computer. Compilation can also fail because of errors in the program. When the compilation succeeds, the resulting machine code executes quickly.

Interpreted languages   Programs written in interpreted languages are converted to machine code at the time they're run, by a program known as an *interpreter*. In fact, the conversion happens on a line-by-line basis. That is, the program is never completely converted to machine code; the interpreter figures out what each line does and then does that one thing. This means that interpreted programs run much more slowly than compiled programs. The advantage is that interpreted programs are easier to develop, since you don't need to deal with the compilation process. Interpreted programs are also easy to modify; just open the program file in a text editor and save it back. This feature makes interpreted languages useful for helping with system startup tasks that system administrators might want to change—administrators can make and test changes quickly.

PROGRAMMING IN ASSEMBLY LANGUAGE

In addition to compiled and interpreted languages, another option is *assembly language*. This is a language with a simple one-to-one correspondence between machine code numbers and the symbols the programmer uses. Assembly language is very low-level, which means that a skilled assembly language programmer can produce very compact and efficient programs. Assembly language is not very portable, though; it takes a lot of effort to convert a program written for, say, the *x86-64* CPU to run on a PowerPC processor. Writing assembly language programs is also harder than writing programs in most higher-level languages. For these reasons, assembly language programs have become rarer as computers have become more powerful; the speed and size advantages of assembly language just aren't very compelling for most purposes in the early 21st century.

In theory, most languages can be implemented in either compiled or interpreted form. In practice, though, most languages are most commonly used in just one form or the other.

Some languages don't fit neatly into either category. See the "Programming in Assembly Language" sidebar for one important exception. Some others fall into an in-between category, such as Java, which is compiled from source code into a platform-independent form that must be interpreted.

Identifying Common Programming Languages

Linux supports a wide range of programming languages, including the following:

Assembly   As noted earlier, this low-level language can produce very efficient programs but is difficult to write and is non-portable. In fact, referring to "assembly" as if it were one language is a bit misleading, since each architecture has its own assembly language.

C This language is arguably the most important compiled language for Linux, since most of the Linux kernel, as well as a huge number of Linux applications, are written in C. C can produce fairly efficient code, but it's also easy to write buggy programs in C because it lacks some error-checking features that are common in many other languages. C source code files typically have filenames that end in .c or .h—the .c files are the main source code files, whereas the .h files are *header* files, which contain short definitions of the functions in the .c files, for reference by other files in a program. A large program can consist of dozens, if not hundreds or thousands, of individual source code files. In Linux, C programs are generally compiled with the gcc program, which is part of the GNU Compiler Collection (GCC) package.

C++ This language is an extension to C that adds *object-oriented* features, meaning that greater emphasis is given to data structures and their interactions than to the procedures used to control the flow of the program. Many complex Linux programs, such as KDE and OpenOffice.org/LibreOffice, are written largely in C++. C++ source code files can have filenames that end in .cc, .cpp, .cxx, or .c++, with header files ending in .h, .hh, .hpp, .hxx, or .h++. In Linux, C++ is generally compiled with the g++ program, which is part of GCC.

Java Java was created by Sun Microsystems (now owned by Oracle) as a cross-platform language that's somewhere between being compiled and interpreted. It's become popular as a language for small applications delivered via Web sites, although some other programs are Java based as well. Java source code usually has a name that ends in .java or .class, whereas Java byte code files usually have names that end in .jar.

Perl This interpreted language is designed for easy manipulation of text, but it's a general-purpose language that can be used for many other tasks as well. Perl programs typically have filenames that end in .pl, .pm, or .t.

PHP The PHP: Hypertext Preprocessor (PHP; a recursive acronym) language was created for use on Web servers in order to generate dynamic content—that is, content that varies depending on the user, the time of day, or some other criterion. PHP is an interpreted language and it requires a PHP-aware Web server, such as Apache. Given such a server and appropriate configuration, a Web site can support user logins, shopping carts, different content based on users' locations, and so on. PHP files most often have names that end in .php, although several variants are common.

Python This interpreted language makes code readability a major goal. It supports (but does not require) object orientation. It's often used for scripting

Certification Objective

Although the Linux kernel is mostly written in C, parts of it are written in assembly language.

Certification Objective

Certification Objective

The Python programming language's name is a reference to the cult British TV show *Monty Python's Flying Circus*.

Certification Objective

purposes, but it can be used to write more complex programs, too. Python programs often use .py filename extensions, although several variants of this are common, too.

Certification Objective

►

Chapter 12, "Creating Scripts," covers the basics of creating or modifying Bash scripts.

Shell scripting   Most Linux text-mode shells—the programs that enable entirely keyboard-based use of the computer—provide their own interpreted languages. Of these, the Bourne Again Shell (Bash or bash) is the most common, so Bash scripting is quite common. Many of the files that control the Linux startup process are in fact Bash scripts. Such scripts frequently have no unique filename extension, although some use a .sh extension.

THE ESSENTIALS AND BEYOND

When you're just starting out with Linux, chances are you'll begin by using a desktop environment—the first set of programs you see when you log in. A desktop environment enables you to run more programs, including common productivity tools such as Web browsers, email clients, office utilities, and multimedia applications. If you're configuring a computer as a server, of course, you'll want to run server programs, but you'll do this by editing configuration files rather than launching them from a desktop environment. If you need to do programming, you should be aware of some common Linux programming languages, which enable you to write everything from trivial scripts to huge servers or productivity suites.

SUGGESTED EXERCISES

► Try at least two different desktop environments. Use each desktop environment for your normal computing tasks for a day or two so that you can decide which you prefer.

► Try at least two different Linux Web browsers. Use each to visit your favorite Web sites. Do you notice differences in speed or how the elements on the page are laid out? Which do you prefer?

REVIEW QUESTIONS

1. Which of the following are Linux desktop environments? (Select all that apply.)

    A. GTK+   **D.** Evolution

    B. GNOME   **E.** Xfce

    C. KDE

(Continues)

THE ESSENTIALS AND BEYOND (Continued)

2. If you want to enable one Linux computer to access files stored on another Linux computer's hard disk, which of the following network protocols is the best choice?

   A. SMTP   **D.** DNS

   B. NFS   **E.** DHCP

   C. PHP

3. In which of the following languages was most of the Linux kernel written?

   A. Bash shell script   **D.** C++

   B. Java   **E.** Perl

   C. C

4. True or false: OpenOffice.org and LibreOffice are very similar office suites.

5. True or false: Servers can be disrupted by malicious outsiders even if the computer that runs them is never broken into.

6. True or false: Python is generally implemented as an interpreted language.

7. Thunderbird is a(n) _____ program. (Specify the general category of the software.)

8. A Linux server that handles the SMB/CIFS protocol normally runs the _____ software.

9. A program written in a(n) _____ programming language is completely converted to binary form before being run.

Credits

Figure 1.11: From Hennesy and Patterson, *Computer Architecture: A Quantitative Approach, Third Edition*, © 2002, Morgan Kaufmann Publishers, Figure 5.3, p. 394. Reprinted with permission of the publisher.

Figure 5.13 adapted with permission from Sun Microsystems, Inc.

Figure 8.18: From *IBM Systems Journal*, Vol. 10, No. 3, © 1971, International Business Machines Corporation. Reprinted by permission of IBM Corporation.

Figure 10.9: From Leffler/McKusick/Karels/Quarterman, *The Design and Implementation of the 4.3BSD UNIX Operating System*, © 1989 by Addison-Wesley Publishing Co., Inc., Reading, Massachusetts. Figure 7.6, p. 196. Reprinted with permission of the publisher.

Figure 12.4: From *Pentium Processor User's Manual: Architecture and Programming Manual*, Volume 3, Copyright 1993. Reprinted by permission of Intel Corporation.

Sections of Chapter 6: From Silberschatz/Korth, *Database System Concepts, Third Edition*, Copyright 1997, McGraw-Hill, Inc., New York, New York. Section 13.5, p. 451-454, 14.1.1, p. 471-742, 14.1.3, p. 476-479, 14.2, p. 482-485, 15.2.1, p. 512-513, 15.4, p. 517-518, 15.4.3, p. 523-524, 18.7, p. 613-617, 18.8, p. 617-622. Reprinted with permission of the publisher.

725

Credits

The following photos were provided by third parties. All other images were provided by the authors and are copyright John Wiley & Sons, Inc.:

Figure 3-6 © Danita Delimont/Gallo Images/Getty Images

Figure 5-11 © Vicente Barcelo Varona/iStockphoto

Figure 5-12 © Lev Mel/iStockphoto

Figure 5-13 © Hans-Walter Untch/iStockphoto

294